THAT OLD

BLACK

MAGIC

THAT OLD

BLACK

MAGIC

ARTHUR

BLACK

Stoddart

First published in 1989 by
Stoddart Publishing Co. Limited
34 Lesmill Road
Toronto, Canada
M3B 2T6

CANADIAN CATALOGUING IN PUBLICATION DATA

Black, Arthur,
    That old Black magic

ISBN 0-7737-2353-6

I. Title.

PS8553.L318T5 1989   C817'.54   C89-094771-6
PR9199.3.B53T5 1989

Many of these sketches have been broadcast over the airwaves of the CBC or have appeared in the pages of various newspapers across the land. My thanks to the Corp., to *Ontario Living* and to those newspapers for permission to have them reappear in this book.   A.B.

Typesetting: Tony Gordon Ltd.

Printed in Canada

To Jess, Dan, and especially to Caitlin,
who holds it all together

Contents

PART 5   *Canada, Armageddon, and Kinky Sects*

PART 1

Gadgets, Gizmos, Fads, and Fanatics

No Sales
in the Sunset

I WAS JUST THINKING back to a couple of hours I spent in a tavern one afternoon about two decades ago, sipping a cold one as I watched U.S. President Richard Nixon on the fuzzy TV screen suspended over the bar. The fervent and life-long anti-Communist seemed to be tossing back a few cold ones himself. Only difference was that he was on the other side of the world — in China, where he'd gone to officially bestow recognition on the most populous nation on the planet. There was more than a little grumbling along the bar as patrons watched the most famous five o'clock shadow in history smiling and bobbing in a sea of attentive Chinese dignitaries. "Why'd he wanna go and reckanize China?" groused one of the clientele.

An ad salesman at the other end of the bar summed it up in seven words as he reached for the beer nuts.

"One billion toothbrushes," said the salesman, "and two billion armpits."

Ah, salesmen. Whether you love 'em or loathe 'em you can't help but admire their mercenary single-mindedness. Other observers might see the Chinese/American accord as a breakthrough for world peace and understanding, a chance to connect with an ancient and mysterious culture. Not my salesman. To him it was just one huge untapped market yet to discover the delights of oral hygiene and body odour control. A mother lode of potential sales commissions longer than the Great Wall itself.

I've always had a perverse fascination with the Art of Selling and I don't know why, because I'm utterly rotten at it. As an encyclopedia salesman, I lasted exactly one evening. In my callow

2

youth, I put in a few months as a newspaper advertising salesman. I'm reasonably certain I was the very worst representative they ever had. I just couldn't whip up the kamikaze upbeatness — the almost psychotic optimism good salesmen seem to radiate.

What put me in this reminiscent mood was a tiny item I saw in a news magazine about a rather unexpected American sales success recently. You'll never guess what the U.S. sold $20 million worth of to Japan.

Television tubes.

You read right. Japan, which has dominated the North American television market for at least the past decade, is now buying TV parts from a plant in San Diego.

Betcha a twenty-one-inch full-colour Panasonic there's a hotshot salesman behind that deal. Somebody like Joe Girard, maybe.

Joe Girard? He is possibly the most successful car salesman ever to don a fluorescent-green checked sports jacket. He used to work in Michigan — and *work* is the operative word. Girard won the Number One Car Salesman Award for eleven straight years, and we are not talking about selling cars by the fleet or on consignment. Joe Girard moved cars one at a time — "belly to belly," as he called it. He sold 174 cars one month. In his best year he flogged 1,425 of them. His lifetime total: 13,001 cars.

Joe Girard retired eight years ago — from the retail auto business, but not from selling. Nowadays he works the lecture circuit and plugs his book, *How to Sell Anything to Anybody*.

It's a bestseller, natch.

Which reminds me of my favourite salesman-as-hustler story. It concerns a young, aggressive fellow — let us call him Frankie Grice — who is eager to make his name as a Hollywood press agent (a salesman by another name). Our hero has what it takes — a brand-new office just off Sunset Boulevard. He has Art Nouveau bric-a-brac and designer furniture all over the place. He's got two telephones on a black onyx desk as wide as an aircraft carrier. On the floor he's got broadloom so deep that short people couldn't cross the room without a lifeboat. Frankie Grice has it all, except for one thing.

A client. Frankie Grice is brand-new to the game and he could dearly use a client. But, look! There's one now, coming through the door! Intuitively, Frankie grabs his phones, one in each hand.

3

"No!" barks Frankie into one receiver. "Absolutely not! Redford is all wrong for the part! I can live with Pacino or even Stallone, but if you go with Redford, I'll pull Streisand and Hoffman out immediately, understand?" Covering the phone with his palm, Frankie whispers to the visitor at the door, "Sorry . . . I've got Bob Altman on one line and Tokyo on the other. I'll be with you in a minute."

Into the Tokyo phone, Frankie growls, "Look, I toldja I wanna book the biggest stadium ya got in Japan, okay? Forty, fifty thousand seats minimum. I'm throwing a little party for my friends. Awright, see what you can come up with and get back to me today!"

Slamming down the phones, Frankie cranks up his thousand-megawatt smile and says to the visitor in front of the desk, "Sorry about the calls. Now what can Frankie Grice do for you?"

And the visitor says, "I just came to hook up your phones, Mr. Grice."

4

Armchair Paradise

NOT TO START in a panic or anything, but have you noticed how unreal things have been getting? I don't mean unreal as in Via Rail ads or political speeches — we're all accustomed to that. I mean unreal as in synthetic. Ersatz is everywhere. In sports, where players in plastic uniforms chase a plastic ball over plastic grass. You find unreality in fashion, you find it in architecture, you find it in your car, but more and more it seems to me, you find it at the dinner table. Food and drink are becoming less and less . . . well, real. My grandfather's not around anymore, and it's just as well. I wouldn't relish trying to explain to him why people in the late eighties actually line up to buy things like mock chicken, irradiated fish sticks, and vitamin-enriched bread.

And I know he'd really have trouble with Lite beer. Some brewers sold Lite beer back in my granddad's day, but they didn't brag about it. It was called watering down, and anybody foolish enough to get caught at it usually got a free ride out of town on the sharp side of a fence rail.

But I don't know why I keep bringing up my granddad and how puzzled he'd be if he were here. I am here and I'm not sure I can handle some of the new unrealities.

The smokeless cigarette, for instance. Tobacco retailers are now talking with a straight face about selling us smokeless cigarettes — fags that can be consumed in a crowded room without giving off any fumes. Mind you, they're still dangerous to the people smoking them — maybe even more dangerous, but the risk of dying hasn't deterred committed smokers so far. As a nonsmoker I have to applaud the idea of a smokeless cigarette, but I can't help wondering who's kidding whom.

In any case, I've got more important things to think about. Odorless garlic, for instance. The Sanko Chemical Corporation of Japan has brought into the world a bulb of garlic that you can eat without winding up smelling like a bounty hunter of vampires. Odorless garlic, eh? I see. Then what becomes of the point of eating garlic? Eating garlic that doesn't deliver the pungent punch of garlic makes about as much sense as . . . well, drinking watered-down beer.

But to appreciate the full flavour of the New Unreal, one would have to travel to Houston, Texas, there to visit the showroom of an artist/craftsman by the name of Adam St. John. Mr. St. John has designed and produced a limited edition of custom-crafted chairs. He calls his creation the Paradise Chair. It's for people who would love to get away but just can't find the time. The Paradise Chair is pretty comfy, all right, and it comes with its own swaying palm trees. Yours for only $4,000 U.S., providing you act now.

Somebody once said that thanks to our highway system it's now possible to travel right across the country without seeing any of it. Well, here we have another quantum leap for civilization. With the Paradise Chair you don't even have to leave your living room not to see the country.

Can't you imagine just sitting back in your Paradise Chair with maybe a lukewarm soyburger in one hand, a glass of Near Beer in the other, and a smokeless cigarette not smouldering away in the ashtray . . . and perhaps a little elevator music in the background?

Ah . . . all this and Disneyland, too.

Does Anybody Know What Time It Is?

I HAVE A brand-spanking-new wristwatch that I don't need, and I blame Ernest Hemingway for it. Let me tell you about the watch — I'll get to Ernie later. It is called (I have to squint to read the name) a Timex Quartz Triathlon. It claims to be water-resistant to a depth of fifty metres. It constantly informs me what day, month, and what year I am in. It has a button marked Mode. It has a button marked Light. It has a button marked Set. It has two other buttons marked Start/Stop and Lap/Reset respectively. Under that is a legend reading "8 Lap Memory," with a red arrow pointing to the Lap/Reset button.

Oh, yes . . . and the time. My new watch tells me what time it is, too.

I did not purchase my brand-new watch for any of the afore-mentioned features. I already have a perfectly functional big-hand, little-hand Timex that tells me the time. As for all that other informational data, well, waterproofing has never been a big priority with me. If I am ever discovered fifty metres beneath the surface of any body of water I will be experiencing problems of a greater magnitude than a soggy wristwatch. For the rest, I usually have a reasonably good idea what year it is, and more or less which month.

As for the date, I can't really afford to schlump around with the exact date riding casually on my wrist. That would rob me of fifty percent of my conversational opening gambits. The only two subjects I feel safe in broaching with strangers are "Cold enough for ya?" and "Say, what's the date today, anyway?"

No, the reason I prematurely pensioned off my perfectly sound, if somewhat old-fashioned, watch in favour of this Hi Tech, *Star Wars*-ish job is because the new one has a feature I'd never dreamed of in a wristwatch before — a teensy-weensy alarm. I read about it in an advertising flyer that came to my house. Down at the department store, I made the woman demonstrate it before I forked over my $39.95.

"Set it for 5:30 a.m.," I commanded. The lady did some sleight of hand, then fast-forwarded the digits until 5:30 came up. Sure enough — *bleep bleep bleep* — the most discreet and yet importunate little alarm you could ever hope to hear. "Don't bother with a bag, I'll wear it!" I shrilled. I ran all the way home. And why not? Didn't I have, right there on my left forearm, the answer to a problem that had bedevilled me all my adult life?

You see, a major tenet of my personal philosophy has long been that of Early Rising. I've always been a firm, even outspoken, exponent of the principle of getting up with the dawn. I believe that sluggards who wallow in the sack until ten or eleven of a morning are little better than human sloths, snoozing away the best and most productive hours of the day.

Must I enumerate the advantages? Early risers are rewarded with everything from the simple joy of witnessing the rosy fingers of the dawn palpate the neighbourhood awake to the more selfish pleasure of a couple of hours of pristine solitude uncompromised by whining children, jangling telephones, or tempting prime-time TV programs.

Plus, you get first crack at the bathroom.

But my love affair with daybreak springs from more romantic roots. It has to do with reading Hemingway as an impressionable stripling, and being enchanted with his boast that he had never missed seeing a sunrise in his life.

Imagine! Never missed a sunrise! That seemed to me an eminently worthy if somewhat Spartan goal to aim for. So as a teenager I solemnly vowed that I, too, would get up each day in time to see that great smouldering orb climb into the sky.

I've been trying to do it ever since.

My *heart* is in love with the premise. Each morning it pitty-pats up the back of my throat and whispers, *Come! Let's away to the window, throw open the casement and fling our arms wide to greet the burgeoning dawn!*

And right after that, my brain mutters, *Don't be a lunatic. Turn over and go to sleep.*

And I do. But that's the pattern — heart throws looping right cross, brain blocks same, throws devastating counterpunch, and the match is over. The rest of my body doesn't even get to vote.

I've tried the gimmicks most normal people use to trick themselves into wakefulness. Alarm clocks don't work. They're so loud and jarring that I wake up feeling as if I've been violated by an ambulance on distress call. Clock radios that bushwhack me with soft guitars and two-part harmony don't work either, because I'm a heavy sleeper and music just won't budge me. *Any* music. Give me a cup of hot cocoa and two chapters of *War and Peace* and I could sleep through a Twisted Sister concert.

I've even tried keeping pets in the bedroom on the theory that their primitive metabolisms would be more naturally attuned to early rising than mine. What a laugh. Cats are far too intelligent and snotty to play valet to any mere human. Besides, give a cat the choice between getting its paws all icky in the morning dew or snoozing on the eiderdown? No contest.

And dogs? Forget it. Oh, puppies are pretty good at rousing you out of bed — providing your idea of a reasonable wake-up call involves megadecibel yips in the earhole and slavering tongues that reek of last evening's Dr. Ballard's. The real problem is that adorable little puppies grow up to become large, regrettable dogs, and dogs are the original Uncle Toms of the Pet World.

You wants to sleep a l'il longer? Yowsuh, boss, go right ahaid. I'll jes be down here lyin' on de throw rug if'n you needs me.

Don't count on dogs to wake you up early in the morning.

For a brief period I enlisted the assistance of the only two early rising friends I had — one a chicken farmer, the other an inveterate prebreakfast jogger. I asked them each to give me a quick phone call before they started their respective morning rounds. My friends were less steadfast than I might have hoped. The chicken farmer hung up in disgust just because I hadn't managed to answer after a dozen or so rings. The jogger got all huffy because of the language that greeted her when I finally did find the receiver.

Professional wake-up services . . . autohypnosis . . . I'll spare you the litany — take my word for it, I have championed every known method of early morning awakening short of daylight-activated cattle prods, and nothing worked.

Until this watch. This, I said, leering, will do the trick. It can't miss! Not so loud as to induce coronary arrest, yet not so wimpy as to be ignorable. And I was right. The very next morning at precisely 5:30 my preprogrammed watch began to wail. I awoke, visually verified the miracle, and extended a triumphant index finger to press the Alarm/Off button.

There is no Alarm/Off button.

I stabbed Mode and Light and Set and Start/Stop and Lap/Reset and even in mounting desperation the buckle on the strap. The watch continued to *bleep.*

I took it off and shook it.

Bleep bleep bleep.

I rapped it smartly on the bedside table.

Bleep bleep bleep.

I caromed it off the open bedroom door several yards down the hall. It *bleeped* our faithful if easily confused hound into a frenzy of territorially defensive yapping.

And then . . . a miracle. In the midst of the chaos, a shimmering, crystalline instant of Zenlike epiphany burst upon me. *Hemingway,* I thought. Yes. Truly. He-of-the-Never-Missed-a-Sunrise-Boast. I said to myself, The man was seriously wounded during battle in Italy. The man went through two airplane crashes. The man brawled mightily and drank prodigiously and wrote reverentially of all-night pub crawls and near-fatal bouts of exotic illnesses.

And in a burst of clarity the truth came to me: *There is no way in hell that Ernest Hemingway never missed a sunrise!*

My life has changed greatly since my personal Moment of Truth. For one thing, I've gone back to my old-fashioned wristwatch. The new one is, as far as I know, still in the vegetable crisper section of the refrigerator, issuing muffled *bleeps* from under last summer's turnips.

I have also bundled up a fairly impressive collection of Hemingwayana — *The Sun Also Rises; To Have and Have Not; For*

Whom the Bell Tolls; Islands in the Stream; Death in the Afternoon.
All in hardcover; all for sale — cheap. First comer takes all.
But please . . . no phone calls before noon.
I need my beauty sleep.

Mouthy Mobiles

I LIKE TO THINK of myself as a reasonably modern, fairly open-minded man. I know my way around a vacuum cleaner. I have been spotted more than once at the kitchen sink, doing dishes. I have gone to a publisher's reception and met something wearing a black body stocking, a chartreuse Mohawk, reflector sunglasses, and jewels through its nose that tells me its name is Blueberry Greenpeace Krishna von Firstenburg. I did not tremble or hoot or whimper and run. I shook its hand like a civilized man of the world.

I have stood on the sidelines enthusiastically cheering the passing parades of black liberation, gay liberation, animal liberation, plant liberation, but at talking cars, I draw the line.

Yes. Talking cars. I rented one (unwittingly) at the airport in Montreal recently. Know what it said to me when I turned the key? A DOOR . . . IS A JAR!

A door . . . is a jar????

I stalled the car right there on the outramp of Dorval airport, utterly overwhelmed at the Zen ramifications of such a proposition. If a door is a jar, does it follow that a jar is a door? And if a door can be a jar, what's the metabolic potential for . . . a windshield? A gas cap? A catalytic converter?

If my rented car knew the answers to these and other cosmic questions I hurled at it, it wasn't telling. Perhaps it sensed that it had already blurted out more than it should have. I don't know. All I do know is, its lips — or whatever — were sealed for the rest of our time together.

Doesn't matter. I am in receipt of a press release from a Winni-

12

peg company that calls itself, sinisterly enough, Carshaw Inc. and shows that my rented Montreal car was but a monosyllabic harbinger of more garrulous gas eaters to come.

Carshaw Inc. has developed a microcomputer for cars — particularly company cars. When the devilish device is in place, an employee has only to turn the key in the ignition and he will immediately be *grilled* — by the car, mind — as to nature of the expedition, intended destination, estimated time of arrival and . . . reason for the trip. And once the car has been alerted to a human presence, it monitors mileage and maintenance — *the oil reservoir is down point five litres* — all of which can of course be transferred to a central cost control system back at your boss's head office.

There's a phrase that we used to use in the schoolyard to cover situations like this, and the phrase is: "No fair!" No fair because one of the very few perks available to salesmen and business people who spend boring hours on highways and in hotel rooms has been Creative Expense Account Rendering. Are we to throw hallowed tradition out the door in the name of godless silicon-chip efficiency?

Probably . . . but it's no fair.

Marshall McLuhan once said that mass transit — buses and trains — was doomed because North Americans would never surrender their cars. "It's the only place where a North American can be alone to think," he said.

McLuhan was a genius, but he didn't have to put up with bossy automobiles.

I'm going to stick with trains and buses. They're a little slower . . . a shade more inconvenient . . . but at least they don't talk back.

Say Geez!

WENT TO A WEDDING last weekend. Pretty normal wedding — a bride and a groom and a best man and a minister and tin cans tied to bumpers. Except for one thing. There was this guy at the wedding with one of those new videocameras — with the built-in mike and all? The guy was everywhere. You went to the punch bowl, the guy was there, videotaping your drinking hand. You lined up to console the bride, the cameraman was there, too, shooting away. Halfway through the spot dance, you'd glance up from the fragrant shoulder you were sniffing . . . and right into a glowing red light over a zoom lens.

It was a pain . . . but there's usually someone at every wedding who's a pain. Thing was, there was a party the day after the wedding at the bride's brother-in-law's place. Turned out the host of the party was the guy with the camera — the one who took all the pictures at the wedding.

Guess what we did at his house all that afternoon? Watched pictures of the wedding is what we did. We watched the crowd around the punch bowl; we watched the lineup to console the bride; we watched every dancer dancing every dance on the dance floor — the whole thing. We all went through that wedding *twice*. And Wedding Two, like most sequels, was not a major improvement on Wedding One.

Because the brother-in-law's video camera recorded *every*-thing. Including old Uncle Norris who, when he gets excited can . . . drool.

I can live with snapshots, even group photos, taken in moderation, but something about being videotaped forever gets to me.

I start smiling too much and clearing my throat and checking my tie and wondering about my fly and generally having about as good a time as I used to have at Sunday school a hundred years ago.

There's something else that's not quite right about the videocamera craze. I remember years ago I became obsessed with the idea of getting my daughter's first steps on film. I didn't have a videocamera — I'm not sure they were even around then — but I did have a pretty fair 35-millimetre reflex camera. And a flash unit. And plenty of film laid in for the occasion. And I was there with the lens cap off the day she made it from the arm of the chesterfield to a footstool in a semivertical position. And I went through the better part of two rolls of Kodak Plus X Pan recording the event for posterity.

Trouble is, I spent so much time checking the film advance and the exposure meter and the flash batteries and squinting through the viewfinder and the focusing ring that . . . I never actually got to *see* her take that first step.

Oh, I've got the snapshots in the photo album, of course, but . . . well, I just wish I'd had the presence of mind to rely on my personal videocamera. Full-colour resolution, no batteries, shock-resistant, reasonably rugged if somewhat battered carrying case.

You know . . . the personal videocamera that we all have.

On the tops of our necks.

Can't Lose If You Don't Buy a Ticket

I DON'T BUY lottery tickets — and it's not because I'm a prude. Some of my best friends, etc. It's not because I'm an unreconstructed Calvinist who believes you shouldn't get something for nothing, either. Anybody who's had cause to work alongside me knows that my adherence to any Work Ethic is directly related and inversely proportional to the proximity of a shady tree and/or a tall, cool one.

No, the truth is, I don't buy lottery tickets because I'm afraid someday I might actually win. Then I'd really be up the creek.

The problem with winning a lottery is the *suddenness* of it all. One day you're a working stiff shuffling along in the bus queue, the next day you're a capitalist pig plutocrat dealing in stock portfolios with one hand while you light twenty-dollar Havana coronas with the other. I couldn't take the pressure change. My eardrums would pop, or something.

Think about it before you lay out your money for the next 649. Are you really prepared to deal with all those relatives fawning all over you — the ones who, just last week, wouldn't have spit in your ear if your brain was on fire?

And what about the cons and scams you're going to have to contend with? The hustlers and rustlers that will be tracking you down, phoning you up, filling your mailbox, and waiting to flag you down at the end of your driveway to beg you to invest, donate, loan, or underwrite? The days of strolling down to an H. and R. Block office with a shoebox full of crumpled receipts under your arm are gone forever, bucko. From now on, you'll need your own personal, twenty-four-hour-a-day accountant and a lawyer — no, make that a whole firm of lawyers — just to protect your interests and keep your finances in order.

While you're at it, better hire a second firm of lawyers to keep an eye on the first one.

Speaking of getting flagged down, have you considered the very real possibility of being kidnapped and held for ransom now that you've won a lottery? Could happen. And not just to you but possibly your loved ones. Might as well start looking into electronic security systems, steel mesh fencing, and barbed wire. Your cocker spaniel's going to look mighty silly waddling out to sniff fire hydrants with his own personal Doberman in tow, but that's the price you have to pay for being rich.

You've barely crept over the threshold into the world of the well-heeled and already you've got headaches galore — and we haven't even mentioned the monster migraine of the piece: friends.

You don't have any friends anymore. Oh, you'll have old pals who'll swear the money doesn't make a lick of difference, but who's kidding whom? And even if *they* believe what they're saying, do *you?* From now on you will never know whether somebody likes you because of your cute nose or that even cuter bulge in your bank balance.

Not that I speak from experience or anything. I mean, I've never won a lottery — through not for lack of trying. Years ago, when it first became chic for governments to make money the same way cardsharps and racketeers do, I used to buy a lottery ticket for a draw that was held every Thursday night. After a few months of not winning I decided to increase my chances by buying a book of tickets every Thursday night.

I noticed two things: (a) I still didn't win; (b) Friday mornings had become my least favourite time of the week. I'd become grumpy, testy, and out of sorts. Sometimes the mood would slop right over Friday evening and ruin my weekend.

I finally analysed the problem. I was suffering from Greed Hangover. I'd spent much of the week fantasizing about what was going to happen when I won the Thursday night lottery. Come Friday morning I was still in debt, still nosing the same old grindstone. And I resented it.

I told my problem to a gambler I know. He's a guy who makes

his living, such as it is, off the ponies, football, hockey, and boxing. He laughed in my face. "You buy lottery tickets?" he sneered. "Biggest sucker bet in the world. Better you should bet the Canucks or the Leafs than lotteries. Statistical fact: ya got more chance o' bein' hit by lightning than ya have o' winnin' a lottery."

That did it for me — the lightning statistic. Haven't bought a lottery ticket since.

Right now, everybody in the office is going nuts about the big lottery coming up this week. They'll be sitting there on the night of the draw, dreaming big dreams, clutching their crumpled stubs in sweaty palms.

Not me. I plan to take a nice long walk while the draw takes place.

Mind you, if I get struck by lightning, I'm going to be really browned off.

Is That a Six-shooter That I See Before Me?

REMEMBER THE OLD TV Western "Have Gun Will Travel"? Did you know that the name for that program came from a Canadian? Yeah. CBC TV producer by the name of Fletcher Markle, as a matter of fact. I only bring it up because it represents possibly the last time Canadians were on the leading edge of handgun sensibility.

I don't know what it is with this country. Other nations are light-years ahead. Iran has the Revolutionary Guards, Israel has an Uzi in every pot. France, Germany, Britain — they all have elite strike forces armed to the eyeballs. And the U.S? Hah. Rambo. Dirty Harry. Bronson, Chuck Norris. Here in Canada? We have laws.

> Only members of registered target pistol clubs may possess handguns . . . Handguns in transit between an owner's domicile and the club shooting range must be disassembled and locked at all times. Failure to comply will result in arrest, seizure, and cancellation of handgun licence.

Wimpy, wimpy, wimpy.

You've heard about Florida? Do you have any appreciation how far ahead of us Florida is in the handgun libertarian field? According to their law, any and all Sunshine Staters are legally allowed to strap on a sidearm of their choice, without any danged permit, and wear it anywhere they please. Just like Matt Dillon or Wyatt Earp.

19

The new law has created a run on pistol ranges and gun-han-
dling courses. One gun range near Miami has put three thousand
people through its training course just in the past couple of
months! Nobody's quite sure if this is an upsurge of enthusiasm
for the new law or a knee-jerk reaction to the realization that from
now on Mr. Rogers just might be packing a .357 Magnum under
his cardigan, but hey . . . the National Rifle Association is hailing
the new law as a triumph of the Amurrican right to bear arms, and
I think they've hit the bull's-eye. Oh, sure, some nervous nellies
are nattering about the danger of armed citizenry roaming around,
but heck, it sure cleared the Sunday drivers off the L.A. freeways.
It's not as if we're talking about Belgians or Orkney Islanders or
Manitobans who don't know the business end from the butt end
of a gun. These are Americans. It's their constitutional right to be
prepared to blow one another away.

Or themselves, if they're so inclined. As in the case back in 1972
when a young Arizonian, for reasons perhaps best known to
himself, fired two quick blasts into a giant saguaro cactus in the
desert near Phoenix. The shots, which were right on, dislodged a
twenty-seven-foot section of the cactus, which fell on the man's
head, killing him on the spot.

Then there was the case of the American who, one night in 1982
peacefully reclining on his Sealy Posturepedic, spied a skulker
sneaking up at the bottom of his bed. The man, an Ohio bachelor
by circumstance but a Floridian pistol apostle by inclination,
snatched his Colt Python .38 from under the pillow and squeezed
off three quick shots in the darkness.

Shooting himself in the penis.

But, hey . . . you know the old saying. If you just lie back and
let life run all over you, you'll never get ahead. Nobody said the
right to bear arms was going to be a cakewalk. I'm sure the
Floridians will work it all out, once the smoke clears.

Won't be the same for Canadian tourists used to vacationing in
Miami or along the Gulf Coast. We'll be at a disadvantage because
we can't have gun when we travel.

Still . . . look on the bright side. Those tourists are going to save
a fortune in Coppertone.

Can't tan through a flak jacket, anyway.

Spare That Tire!

KEEP BOTH HANDS on the steering wheel there, Maude, I'm going to tell you about the latest automotive breakthrough and I wouldn't want you to lose control and smack into a lamp post. It's from the folks at Uniroyal. They're bringing out a revolutionary new concept in automobile tires — ones that absolutely cannot possibly go flat.

Which is not all that hard, because the new tire from Uniroyal has no air in it. Yessiree, they're calling it the "airless spare." It's made of polyurethane bonded to a stamped steel wheel disc. It weighs twenty percent less than a conventional compact spare and will take up thirty-five to forty percent less space in your trunk.

You realize what this means, don't you? Pretty soon new cars will be packing an even smaller spare tire than that ridiculous doughnut they come with nowadays.

Have you had the pleasure yet of driving on one of those "conventional compact tires," as they are so euphemistically called? It's quite a treat. Happened to me for the first time last spring. I was piloting a rent-a-car along the 401 when I heard the all-too-familiar *thwup thwup thwup* that tells you another steel-belted radial is on its way to the Good Year Permanent Parking Lot in the Sky. Great. Flat tire. I got out and opened the trunk, only to face what looked like a wheelbarrow tire lying in the bottom. "What's that?" I asked my more worldly passenger. She explained that it was the latest thing, a compact spare tire that, with a little luck and careful driving, should get me to the next gas station.

It did, but just barely. And I had a new experience to add to my Lifetime Thrill List: creeping along the 401 on a compact tire at thirty miles an hour while supersonic transport trucks honked and blared and swooshed by me, just inches from my side mirror.

And now it looks as if we're going from the compact tire — a dumb, small idea in its own right — to the "airless" compact tire — an idea that's even dumber and smaller.

Ah, well, let's face it. The whole concept of automobiles has been going downhill ever since they were called horseless carriages. I don't mean to come on like Methuselah, but I can remember when cars were cars, built with real steel and actual rubber — not a particle of polypropylene or a morsel of computerized mumbo-jumbo from bumper to bumper. Those cars had cloth-covered seats and leather-covered dashboards and doors that closed with a rich, satisfying *ka-rump!* when you shut them. Those cars had fenders that could actually take a whack or two without turning into accordion pleats the way modern ones do.

What *are* modern fenders made of, anyway — Reynolds Wrap?

The irony is, the cars I remember with such affection were dismissed by my father as just so much mobile tinware. I remember coming up the driveway in my first sports car, feeling fairly show-offish, skidding to a stop at my old man's feet.

"Whaddaya think?" I asked as I popped open the door. He tapped the front fender with his knuckles. The fender gave back a weak and effeminate *ping*.

"Try not to run into anything," he said.

Then he regaled me with tales of the cars of his youth — "Back when they really knew how to build a car" — especially the original Generic Car, the Tin Lizzie, a k a the Model T, which was built on Mr. Henry Ford's newfangled industrial invention: the assembly line. My dad owned a Model T, and he must have loved it because he was still talking about it half a century later. He told me that once during the war supplies of rationed gasoline dried up completely. He couldn't find any anywhere. "No problem, though — we just filled the tank with kerosene."

"Didn't that blow the engine out?" I asked.

"Naw," he said, "you couldn't hurt a Model T."

Ah, they must have really been something, those early cars. Vanished classics with names like Pierce Arrow, Stutz Bearcat, Stanley Steamer, and Phaeton. Some of them with rudders instead of steering wheels, with hand throttles and brakes on levers that you had to reach out on the running board to operate . . . .

And, come to think of it, some of them with one other feature I just remembered my old man telling me about.

Solid rubber tires.

Just like the brand-new ones from Uniroyal.

To Compute or Not to Compute — That Is the Input

Puh leeze haylp me, ah'm faaaaaaaallin'...

REMEMBER THAT nasal refrain? It's the title of an old country ditty sung by Ferlin Husky or Leroy Van Dyke or some such adenoidal crooner of the feathered-Stetson-and-beat-up-guitar persuasion. I've been humming it under my breath a fair bit lately, because, Lord help me, I'm a-fallin', too. Not in love, exactly. It's more like I'm being seduced.

By computers. I am going to buy a computer. I don't like the things and I certainly don't understand them, but just as sure as Santa's elves work time and a half at Christmas, I'm going to buy one soon.

Don't know why, really. I suppose it's partly because everybody I know in the newspaper business treats me like a shuffling Neanderthal for clinging stubbornly to my battered, unelectrified Olivetti. What's more, I am slowly coming around to appreciation of the idea that a floppy disc might be a more convenient way to file old columns and story ideas than the Duz detergent cardboard box I currently employ.

My boss is in favour, too. When I mentioned my intentions, the Editor You Love to Hate darn near slopped some of the bay rum after-shave out of the chipped coffee cup he carries around. "Good idea!" he burbled. "In fact, it's a great idea! Just be sure to insist on a model that can, you know, proofread your columns and correct your spelling and all."

I believe he's trying to tell me something.

At any rate, the signs of an impending purchase are unmistakable. I've been thumbing through computer catalogues a lot, trying to figure out my monitors from my printers from my coaxial duodenal modem cacciatores or whatever they're called. I button-hole computer owners and ask them for advice. Then I try to figure out what they told me.

There is just one tiny problem in all this: I don't *want* to buy my own computer right now — for several reasons. Number one, I can't afford it. My state of financial solvency would not sustain a layout of one or two grand just to bring another machine into my life. (As a matter of fact, I am not financially solvent enough to put stamps on my Christmas cards, but that's another story.)

Number two, I sense that it is the wrong time to buy a computer. No profound market analysis there — it's just that I *always* buy things at the wrong time. If I was to go out on a Wednesday and become the proud new owner of the best, most popular computer on the market — say, a Golgotha X/500 Deluxe with infinite megabyte capacity and extrasensory holographic disc drive — you could bet the mortgage money that by Thursday, company shares would have plummeted through the stock exchange base-ment, the chief executive officer of Golgotha would have taken up permanent residence in a Swiss Alps condo, and I would be the owner of the most expensive and complicated boat anchor in technological history.

I suffer, you see, from the reverse of King Midas's dread dis-ease — everything I touch instantly turns to dreck. Besides, the computer business is flakey enough on its own. Whole brand names rise up and crash back into the swamp of the marketplace overnight, disappearing without a trace. It would be just my luck to trudge on down to the local Comput-O-Rama, lay down my hard-earned credit card and come back home with the computer equivalent of the Edsel.

Those are just a few of the reasons I shouldn't be thinking of buying a computer right now — which in turn is why I keep the credit card I might use for the purpose wrapped in a yellowing scrap of newspaper. I've made a pact with myself to read that scrap of paper before I use the credit card. It's a story about a British computer installed a few years back by the Avon County Council. The computer was to assist in paying wages to Avon County staff, and it did . . . sort of. It raised one caretaker's wages from 75 pence to £75 per hour. On the other hand, it stoutly refused to pay anything at all to one cafeteria worker for four and a half months.

One janitor received the princely sum of £2,600 for one week's work. When he valiantly sent the cheque back, the computer instantly printed another one for the same amount and dashed it off to him by return mail. Before somebody finally managed to yank the plug on the beast, it was discovered that of 280 employees on the Avon County payroll, only eight had been paid the correct salary.

Pablo Picasso, who knew more than just which end of a paintbrush was up, once said, "Computers are useless. They can only give you answers."

Yup. And the answers they give you ain't necessarily correct, either.

Eat Rite —
Eat Lite!

A S I RECALL, it was in my local beer store that I first noticed the phenomenon. I was down there paying my respects to a few of my favourite Canadian families (Labatts . . . Molsons . . . the Carling-O'Keefes) when suddenly I noticed a few strangers in the lineup. One of them was called TriLite Beer. TriLite? I always thought that was one of those big fancy Erlenmeyer-flask-style bulbs that go in living room lamps. Besides, who'd buy a beverage concocted by a brewmaster who couldn't even spell *light* rite — I mean, right?

Well, I wouldn't, but millions would, apparently. The Lite plague spread through the beer brands like fleas through a dog-pound. Obviously Canadians were more than delighted to line up for the chance to buy watered-down ales and lagers. P. T. Barnum would have nodded approvingly.

But mere beer didn't begin to slake the thirst of the Lite invasion. It moved on to other alcoholic beverages. Lite wine began to appear on the shelves. And even (gad!) — something called Rye Coolers — diluted whiskey by any other name.

Tobacco was attacked next. In less time than it takes to blow a smoke ring, nicotine addicts were being offered a bewildering variety of Lite cigarettes.

I've never figured out if the All-New Lites were skinnier, shorter, or packed with damp granola, but somehow the fagfloggers managed to convince the gullible gasping public that smoking Lites would be a lot healthier for them.

Litemania developed a taste for solids, as well. It began to pop up on the supermarket shelves — particularly in the section for the calorie-conscious. A cursory cruise down that aisle turns up such gastronomic perversities as Lite Butter, Lite Mayonnaise, Lite Salad Dressing, and even, I swear — you can come shopping with me next Saturday if you don't believe me — even a prefrozen, ready-for-the-oven multicoloured Frisbee of dough labelled Lite Pizza.

The other day I overheard a radio station executive chatting about the new music format his station was adopting. They planned to play most of the hits of the past thirty years, he said — but not the raunchy stuff. No Jimi Hendrix or The Who, but plenty of the Carpenters and Babs Streisand.

And what was the name for this revolutionary new radio music format?

Why . . . Lite Gold, of course.

Good grief, I thought to myself. Where will Lite-ning strike next? Lite cars? Lite Movies? Lite beef?

Well . . . yes, actually. For some time now, beef producers have been taking their lumps from diet-conscious consumers. Vegetarians get the vapours just thinking about steaks and roasts, and even dietitians tell us we'd be better off substituting fish or fowl for all that red meat. People are worried about the high cholesterol in beef — not to mention all the hormones, stimulants, antibiotics, uppers, and downers that our farmers methodically pump into meat on the hoof.

But when Joe Public chooses chicken breasts over chuck steak, he is primarily making the same Pavlovian response he makes when he picks a Lite beer over Blatz Cream Porter. He knows (or thinks he knows) that anything designated Lite is less fattening than anything that isn't.

Ergo, Lite beef — an idea whose time was overdue. A Texas cartel of forward-looking cattlemen has introduced a whole new line of meat products. They call the new brand — wait for it — Key Lite. Key Lite beef is meat that has been genetically altered to lower the fat content. Each serving contains thirty-six percent fewer calories than the conventional variety. Naturally, the inventors claim that Key Lite retains all the flavour of ordinary beef. Equally naturally, Key Lite beef costs, as the saying goes, "a little more."

But, beef lovers, I've got a tip for you: save your money.

Are you worried about the fat content of that slab of beef on your plate? Here's what you do: pick up that sharp, pointy utensil on the right side of the dinner plate. We call that The Knife. Use The Knife to cut away all the white stuff attached to the meat. Feed the white stuff to your dog. Turn your attention to the nonwhite stuff. Hey, compadre — you've just made yourself some home-made Lite beef!

This calls for a celebration. Why don't you pour yourself half a glass of pilsener, take it over to the kitchen tap, and top it up?

Sure! Why not? Treat yourself to a glass of homemade Lite beer.

That's Not Fat —
Just Christmas
Calories

WATCHING DAYTIME TELEVISION is definitely not for everyone. Indeed, you could make a fairly good case for the proposition that watching daytime television is not for *anyone*. I'm pretty sure that prolonged TV exposure does for the human brain what prolonged exposure to Export Plain Ends can do for the human lungs. Still, watching TV in the daytime can be illuminating in totally unexpected ways. Yesterday, for instance, I caught a nutritionist chattering away on television about the latest health problem to beset North Americans. She called it "Holiday Fat."

Holiday Fat. What a perfect concept for the nineties!

The name describes the condition precisely. Holiday Fat is the excess suet that North Americans traditionally pack on their already overloaded carcasses by doggedly vacuuming up all the eggnog, fruitcake, and extra servings of turkey with all the trimmings that they can wrap their pudgy lips around during the week of orgiastic gorging that separates Christmas Day from New Year's Day. Caloric excess is not strictly limited to that seven-day period, of course. It slops over at both ends, with pre-Yuletide and post New Year's office parties and, neighbourhood get-togethers, not to mention rendezvous with perogy-laden visitors from the old hometown.

But then food isn't the only thing that disappears during the holiday season. We also abandon the find old maxims that we at least pay lip service to the rest of the year — maxims like "One second on the lips; forever on the hips" and "The best form of physical exercise is pushing your chair away from the dinner table." We forget such folk wisdom during the holiday season. Later for that fuddy-duddy stuff, we tell ourselves.

I should clear something up before I go any further. You are not listening to a holier-than-thou lecture from the Lean Machine here. I'm as big a glutton as any sinner at the groaning board. Granted, I have something in my wardrobe from my high school days that I can still slip into.

Trouble is, it's a kimono.

The problem with the concept of Holiday Fat is that it opens another ugly door — the gateway to a continental obsession. North Americans are not content with the condition of Holiday Fatness. It whips them into a Thinness Frenzy. Thus it is that for the ninety-seven percent of the year when we are not pigging out on holidays, we are in hot pursuit of the Enlightened State of Skinnyness.

It's true! We have Weight Watchers, Dancercize and Thursday Evening Keep-Fit Classes at the Y.

We have colour-coordinated sweatsuits, ninety-dollar jogging sneakers and hydra-headed Nautilus machines down at the corner gym.

We have Scarsdale, Beverly Hills, Hilton, Pritikin, Hollywood, and the Drinking Man's Diet.

And for what? What's the point? To be slim? Just a couple of generations ago the very stereotype of success and prosperity was a solid paunch stuffed into a vest with a gold chain stretched across it. Not anymore. Nowadays we recognize that look as pure coronary thrombosisville. We don't go for that. Instead we cultivate the emaciated look of a Gulag inmate.

We are becoming food-o-phobics. We spurn sugar in favour of some dubious laboratory concoction called Nutrasweet. We choose margarine over butter, desiccated wedges of cardboard called melba toast over good thick slabs of homemade bread. We drink Diet Coke and Diet Pepsi.

The irony is that we're turning antifood at a time when there's never been so much of the stuff around.

We've got so much food that our farmers can afford to dump tankloads of milk and truckloads of potatoes on the steps of City Hall or Parliament Hill to score political points.

We've got so much food that our politicians can afford to

stockpile tons of butter, rafts of cheese, and mountains of wheat to keep those prices up.

We've got so much food in this country that soup kitchens in Montreal and Toronto can actually operate on the food that city restaurants *throw into the garbage* every day.

Why we've got so much food in this country that a nationally respected nutritionist can get time on television to talk about the problem of Holiday Fat.

It's a weird phenomenon, all right.

I'm just thankful that I don't have to try to explain it to an Ethiopian.

Smoke Gets in
Your Eyes . . . and
Lungs . . . and . . .

IF THE FRENCH had any business sense at all they would copyright
the cliché *plus ça change, plus c'est la même chose.* That way
they would stand to make a few francs every time some lazy
scribbler like me used the expression to start a column. Don't
bother trying to pry Junior away from the television to translate —
the phrase means "the more things change, the more they stay the
same." It applies to a lot of situations in life — such as the tiny item
in my newspaper last week headlined "Smoking ban is recom-
mended." The story under the headline announced that my local
school board has approved a total smoking ban on all school
property, effective immediately.

Gee, that'll bring us right up to date with twenty-five years ago.

Back when I was a guppy in the fishbowl of academia, smoking
on the schoolgrounds was a heresy that ranked right up there with
robbing banks or shooting heroin in the halls.

Come to think of it, you might have been able to get away with
shooting heroin in my school halls. The staff probably would have
taken you for a rugged individualist on a self-vaccination program.
No smoking, though, pal — ever. I once saw a kid get sent to the
principal for having a pack of cigarettes *in his pocket.*

As for any wretch luckless enough to be nabbed with an actual
mouthful of smoke or an illegal Export "A" smouldering between
his fingers — instant expulsion. Student smoking wasn't frowned
on, it was stomped on with hobnailed boots. Not that such a
fascistic atmosphere deterred my fellow puffers and gaspers for
long — an addict is an addict is an addict. We smoked behind

telephone poles and clots of gossiping girls. We crouched down and lit up between cars in the parking lot. Before the bell rang in the morning you could see us in the nethermost reaches of the schoolyard, circled like musk oxen, furtively sneaking drags from cigarettes cupped in our palms. Some of us shamelessly cultivated the friendship of Olaf, the monosyllabic janitor, because rumour had it that if Olaf liked you, he'd let you tiptoe down to the boiler room for a clandestine smoke.

The biggest challenge was sneaking a smoke during PT, which is what we called gym class back in the Paleolithic era. It was a challenge because there are not that many places you can hide a cigarette and a book of matches in a pair of flimsy gym shorts, which is all we got to wear. What made PT puffing even more perilous was our instructor, Archie Bell — an ex-British commando-cum-raving-health-nut who liked to punctuate his character-building suggestions with a none-too-gentle cuff to the ear.

It is hard to imagine what Mr. Bell might have done had he collared one of us in the act of smoking while he was doing his evangelistic best to purify the temples of our bodies.

Hard to imagine and gruesome to contemplate.

But all our teachers were tough — so tough that the schoolyard smoking ban was extended far beyond the schoolyard itself. I remember an actual raid that the vice-principal and a couple of hand-picked flunkies from the history department conducted on a restaurant near the school. That restaurant was our equivalent of an opium den. The proprietor allowed us to sit in his booths and puff our brains out as long as we purchased a reasonable volume of Cokes, burgers, and chips with gravy.

It was a deliciously sinful way to spend our lunch hours — right up until the day the vice-principal burst through the restaurant door brandishing notepad and ballpoint, maniacally scribbling down the names of expellees-to-be.

Me? I'm a survivor. I hid under a table.

I tried to tell some 1980s-edition teenagers about the Great Restaurant Nicotine Raid, but they just gave me looks that suggested they thought I was smoking something a lot stronger than Virginia leaf. "You kiddin' us, Mr. Black? Heck, at our school the kids have special smoking rooms."

Well, not any longer they don't. After years of increasingly damning statistics, umpteen dozen irrefutable medical reports, and literally hundreds of thousands of lung cancer and heart disease deaths directly attributable to tobacco, the message is finally getting through.

The message is: Smoking Kills People. And any society that condones the practice in its educational institutions is guilty of something scandalously close to criminal negligence.

Twenty-five years ago our educators didn't have all the statistics and the evidence. All they had was The Rules.

It'll stunt your growth, they told us.

Well, they had that right.

Nothing like a tombstone over your head to severely stunt your growth.

Confessions of a
Baseball Hater

OKAY ... *hate* is a touch overstated. I don't precisely hate baseball, I just don't much care about it. But given the time of year and the fact that each working day I pass within a long fly ball's range of Toronto's SkyDome, such wimpy neutrality constitutes dangerous heresy bordering on treason. I'd be better off embracing the doctrines of Trotsky or the gospel according to Khaddafi.

I don't know where I went wrong. Cobb knows, I had an upbringing sufficiently pine tarred and resin impregnated to have produced a baseball fan every bit as fervent as the rabid souls I see around me. As a boy, I played moveups and Twenty-one, not to mention regulation soft, fast, and hardball. I still have my old First Baseman's trapper mouldering away somewhere up in the garage rafters. If we knew each other better I'd show you the scar on my left hip that I got from a cinder during a desperate slide into third about a quarter century ago. I've paid my baseball dues. So why is it I can't remember who won this year's Pennant Race? How come I couldn't care less about the World Series?

I used to care. I can recall childhood bouts of baseball-card collecting and World Series fever. I can even remember whole chunks of October afternoons in my grade 7 class.

You knew the World Series was on because suddenly Johnny Charlton was the only kid in class sporting a long-sleeved shirt. That's because Johnny Charlton was concealing a more-than-pocket-size radio under that shirt with an earphone wire running down the inside of his sleeve, Scotch-taped to his wrist. Johnny spent entire afternoons in a pose of studied boredom, leaning on one elbow, the heel of his hand hard against his earhole. When-ever Mr. Bartlett turned his back, Johnny would glance around furtively, then fiercely whisper something like, "Still three-two Yanks, top of the fifth."

This was the pretransistor era, you understand, when radios, not to mention teachers' attitudes, were a good deal heavier than they are today.

Oh, I was an avid enough baseball fan back then, but some-where between prepubescence and middle-aged spread, I let it go. Baseball got shuffled to the back of my Priorities Closet, supplanted by more urgent concerns such as Job Anxiety, Eroding Hairline, and the Mysteries of the Opposite Sex.

That change, of course, made me what I am today: a stranger in my own land. It seems as if everybody is baseball crazy but me. Some folks are colourblind or tone deaf or flat-footed. I happen to be Baseball Indifferent, and let me tell you, as afflictions go, it's lonely.

For many years it was no big deal. I live, after all, in the land of ice and snow. In my youth, the game of baseball was an exotic pastime like cultivating orchids or breeding tropical fish — a highly unnatural but acceptable indulgence. Then, an American invasion. First the Expos landed in Montreal, then the Blue Jays came to roost in Toronto. Nurtured on plastic grass, encouraged by the promise of protective domes, the All-American pastime, subspecies Northern Variation, flourished. Baseball experts bloomed like dandelions. Suddenly, dinner party and bar-rail chatter was all about Carter's knee and Carty's elbow. Day by day I found myself eating more and more solo chip dip as I communed with the rim of my wineglass.

It's only become worse with the passage of time. I type these very words furtively for, just a few desks away, fanned out around the water cooler, three colleagues — we are talking about grown men with kids and mortgages and their very own social insurance numbers, mind — are earnestly discussing last evening's baseball action. They actually *care* that the Red Sox nipped the Royals while the Cards crushed the Padres. The office air is abuzz with insiders' jargon and fan shorthand. I can make out references to phenomena that sound like ribbies and emveepees and ee-yar-ohs. My colleagues are animated, involved, having a swell time.

I feel like Kevin McCarthy in *Invasion of the Body Snatchers.*

You think I exaggerate? There's a guy in my department who hasn't done a lick of work since spring training! He's involved in something called Office Baseball. What happens is that he and his fellow fanatics make up their own teams, even leagues, out of existing, living, breathing, performing players. They follow the sports pages each day, keeping track of the real life statistics — home runs, hits, errors — and incorporate all this data into their mythical league. This particular guy spends about an hour and a half a day on the phone to other "team owners," discussing games that didn't really happen, standings that don't really exist and making player trades that will never actually occur.

Actually, I don't want to paint this chap too negatively. The fact is, he's been spending a lot less time on the phone with his fellow "owners" this past week, but only because he's been too busy planning the details of his spring vacation to — Cooperstown, is it? The baseball mecca/museum, anyway — there to gaze enraptured at Berra's bat, Kaline's cleats, Musial's mitt, and the preserved section of dugout bench where Babe Ruth once parked his ample backside.

I know, I know, I'm sneering and I really don't have any right. My condition is jealousy, not superiority. It would be simple to dismiss baseball fever as a disease of the mouth-snuffling, knuckle-dragging, beer-swilling bozos who too frequently mug for the TV cameras during otherwise civilized games. Simple and wrong. Baseball fever also takes in Vicki the receptionist and ninety-nine percent of the folks on the bus and the next three dozen people I will meet in elevators and supermarket lineups and cocktail parties and it even includes (sob!) my own dear mom.

Writers, too. Everyone from Mailer to Updike to our own Paul Quarrington and W. P. Kinsella regularly wax symphonic about the Zen overtones of the Brett swing and the sensory ambiance of the Comisky hot dog. Everybody seems to see something in baseball that I don't.

And yet . . . and yet . . .

I keep waiting for the Messiah. I see him as a ten-year-old kid, not unlike the one who put the finger on the naked emperor. In my fantasy the kid sits in the stands right along the first-base line. It's Casey-at-the-Bat time — bottom of the ninth, bases loaded, two out, score tied, a man on third, three and two the count. The batter goes into his crouch. The pitcher squints at first, then third, spits, winds up, kicks his leg, and . . .

Just before the ball leaves his hand, fans strung tight as banjo strings, holding their breath, forty thousand hearts in forty thousand throats trip-hammering as one, the kid says in a clear, piping falsetto that carries right across the stadium, "After all, it's only a game."

And everybody laughs.

That's one of my baseball fantasies. The other one involves watching a baseball game taking place in the Coliseum in Rome — possibly because baseball crowds remind me increasingly of the Roman mob. Is it too melodramatic to feel a certain uneasiness when you see most of a civilization turning orgasmic over a couple of squads of grown men playing a kids' game?

Yeah, probably. This is becoming way too solemn. I come neither to bury baseball nor to run it down unduly. I certainly don't come to praise it. That's been taken care of.

Let me conclude on an up beat. Here are two certifiably good things that the game of baseball has given us: Casey Stengel and Yogi Berra. Stengel and Berra both . . . *did things* to the English language. Stengel is the man who, as a septuagenarian, once sagely observed, "Most people my age are dead." He is also the man who, as manager of the then-fledgling and decidedly less-than-amazing New York Mets, took a long, baffled look at his ham-handed players and blurted, "Can't anybody here play this game?"

And Berra? Hoo, boy. Yogi's the man whose single-handed muggings of the mother tongue gave rise to such nuggets as "It ain't over till it's over."

On scouting: "You can observe a lot, watching."

On being five minutes late for a meeting: "I guess this is the earliest I've ever been late."

On a popular restaurant: "It's so crowded, nobody goes there anymore."

And for me, Yogi Berra is the man who summed up baseball in one pithy phrase. Berra once said, "If people don't wanna come out to the ballpark, nobody's gonna stop 'em."

Thank you, Yogi. I'm feeling better already.

It'll Never Replace the Ballpoint

IT PROBABLY DOESN'T SHOW, but the fact is, this column you're reading is being written — sorry, make that "processed" — on a home computer. A Tandy 1000 EX BIOS, if you want to get technical about it. Yes, amigos, the old Luddite has finally bowed before the juggernaut of modern technology, set his battered Olivetti manual up on the shelf, and gone with the phosphorescent flow.

Any difference? Well, it's quieter and there's less messy ribbon to change. My editor likes it better, too. He gets all the paragraphs in proper order now, without the familiar strikeovers, henscratches, wavy red arrows and cryptic directions like "Insert copy A from page four between paras two and three on page one." The machine even covers for my somewhat eclectic grasp on the English language. The program I use proofreads everything I write. Mind you, it's not foolproof. I could write, for instance, "My computer is simply two clever four words," and it'd be none the wiser. It doesn't differentiate between *two* and *too* or *four* and *for*.

But it's tough for me to get hot for technology. I am a Certified Clumsy Person, born at least two centuries after my time. I could have handled science in the age of wind-powered ships, horse-driven carriages, and kerosene-powered street lamps. In a world of lasers, silicon chips — hell, even electricity — I might as well be living on the second moon of Neptune.

But dammit, I'm being seduced by my computer. I've only had it a couple of months and already I know I'd never choose to go back to a typewriter. Just as anyone who's mastered the elementary hunt and peck of typing would be highly unlikely to revert to a goose-quill pen, so it is with me and my home computer. It is simply too fast, too sensible, too comfortable. My old Olivetti would feel impossibly clunky and antiquated now.

So how come I don't feel entirely at home with it? Is it that old sci-fi cliché about Sinister Computers Taking Over the World?

I don't think so. To use a computer — even a relatively home-spun one like mine — is to recognize the limitations of the genre. The difference between a computer and the human mind is the difference between a filing cabinet and a garden.

The brain drinks in life just as it comes — great ideas . . . itches behind the ear . . . the smell of steak broiling on a backyard barbecue three doors down . . . residual venom from that run-in with the parking lot attendant — takes all that in and somehow extracts from it our points of view, our attitudes, our beliefs, hates, loves. A computer on the other hand simply stores facts that we can summon up at the push of a button — providing we know which button to push. A book called *The Cult of Information* by Theodore Rooszak puts it much more succinctly: "Computer memory is no more like human memory than the teeth of a saw are like human teeth. [To suggest that] computer memory is superior because it remembers so much more . . . is precisely to misinterpret what experience is . . . "

Computers also have a huge Achilles' heel. It's access to infor-mation. The only way my computer can get information is for me to feed a disc into it (expensive and not always available), or for me to sit here laboriously transferring the knowledge from my source through my ham hands and into the memory bank.

You want Aunt Edna's letter on file? You have to type it in. You'd like a permanent copy of Milton's *Paradise Lost?* That *Playboy* interview with Woody Allen? Einstein's Theory of Relativity? Start pecking, bucko.

This fills me with the same sadness I felt when I realized that every silver-tongued oration Cicero delivered meant that some poor slob of a Nubian slave had to sit scratching feverishly on a wax tablet.

I'm no technological visionary, but I know that someday home computers will routinely feature a slot into which you can feed sheets, newspapers, books, and even voiced thoughts or obser-vations that will all go directly into the machine's memory bank.

41

In the meantime it's important to keep the whole concept of newfangled machinery in perspective. Never forget the story about NASA's search for an ultramodern state-of-the-art writing utensil that could be used by astronauts. The requirements were daunting. The new lithographic transcription system had to be capable of producing written characters in a vacuum, upside down if necessary, with a relatively limitless supply of fuel, ribbon, or whatever. Expense was no object — this was for the Space Race.

The word went out. Presumably geniuses around the world bent their considerable grey matter to the task — until NASA received a crusty, five-word telegram from a correspondent in Germany. The telegram read:

HAVE YOU TRIED A PENCIL?

Games People Play

L ET'S TALK A BIT about the games people play here. Not mind games, power games, head games or status games — I mean board games: chess and checkers, snakes and ladders, Scrabble, Monopoly, tiddlywinks, chrocinole, Clue and Trivial Pursuit.

We've been playing board games for a long time, you know. Chess, for instance, was knitting the brows of Persians back in 600 A.D. Speaking of which, here's a morsel for your next informal Trivial Pursuit bout: where does the chess term *checkmate* come from? Answer: from a Persian phrase *shah mat* — that's . . . *shah* (as in Shah of Iran?), and *mat* which means "the king is dead."

Board games go back further than that. The Roman emperor and certifiable filbert Nero was addicted to a gambling pastime very like backgammon, which he played for exceedingly high stakes.

And even Nero wasn't breaking new ground. Archaeologists have dug up less sophisticated gameboards and pieces that kept citizens of the ancient Mesopotamian city of Ur up past their bedtimes — and that was somewhere in the order of five thousand years ago, give or take a long weekend.

So much for ancient history, but what's *new* in the way of games people play?

Well, Divorce Cope is new. It's a board game aimed squarely at the children of divorced or separated parents. Psychologically laudable, I'm sure, but it's tough to imagine squeals of delight as the Christmas wrapping comes off. "Oh, Mommy, Mommy . . . a Divorce Game — for me?"

And for the other end of the human lifespan, a firm in Maryland

43

has come out with Eldertrivia . . . designed for oldsters who still love games but can't remember what's trump. Eldertrivia features a stack of cards called Memory Joggers — broad hints to get you over the hump of forgetfulness. My advice to any oldster who gets a game of Eldertrivia from a relative at Christmas: disinheritance on the spot.

There's another modern board game that's been around for a couple of Christmases now, without, I am happy to report, conspicuously capturing the imagination of the game-buying public. It is called Humanopoly. It is much like Monopoly, the game it derives from, except that pregnancy, not slum landlordism, is the aim of the game. Gone are the top hats and milk bottle tokens used to pursue Boardwalk and Park Place. In Humanopoly you push little plastic eggs and sperms from space to space and the winner is the first one to make it around the board and conceive.

No, it doesn't take a full nine months to play a round of Humanopoly. It just feels that way.

Ah, but the most definitively eighties board game I've come across is one I saw in the window of one of those Adults Only Novelty Shops (I was waiting for the bus, Mom). The game was called — are you ready? — Nuke: The Last Game on Earth.

Naw, didn't go in and ask if I could take a look at the rules.

I had the uncomfortable hunch that I'd open the box to find a picture of an Ancient Persian winking back at me over a caption that read: "*Shah mat*, sucker."

I'm in the Mood for Video

YOU KNOW WHAT I would like to do before I shuffle off this mortal coil? I would like to invent something. Nothing big — no nuclear particle fission transfuser or interstellar meteorological gravitometer or anything like that. I'd like to invent something more along the lines of . . . ohh . . . the paper clip, say. Or the zipper. Something small but meaningful. Something that someone someday somewhere in the world might look at, pause, hold up, and say to himself, "Gee, I don't know who invented this, but I'm sure glad they did."

Of course, it's not enough to have a good idea — you have to do something with it. There were at least three inventors in different parts of the world who had the idea of the telephone at roughly the same time, but Alexander Graham Bell was the only one who bothered to hoof it down to the patent office and make it official.

I know how the other two shmoes must have felt. I had a good idea a couple of years ago. I mentioned it on the radio as a joke . . . and that was it. My idea? Well, one day I came home for lunch, turned on the TV, and happened to hit the local cable station. Which, like most cable stations, doesn't have much money for original programming. My local cable station solved the problem cleverly. They filmed a fire. Just an ordinary fire in a fireplace . . . logs crackling, flames shooting up. Well, I sat down to watch it for a while and discovered that I kind of liked it. In fact, it didn't take me too long to realize that on most days my cable television fireplace was the best show on the box. No laugh tracks, no commercials, no machine gun and meathook violence, no dopey plot to follow. Just . . . logs burning in a fireplace.

More and more often I turned to the cable station first — and was disappointed if my fireplace had been replaced by some newscast or sports program.

Here's where the one brilliant idea of my life comes in. I have a VCR. So I lurked by my machine for a whole day, waiting for my fireplace to be televised. When it came on, I jabbed the Record button and taped the fire — about two hours' worth. It was wonderful. Now I had my own video fireplace whenever I wanted it. No ashes, no threat of fire, no messy logs, no need to fiddle with the thermostat. Just a beautiful fire, blazing in the corner, on my TV. I should've done the Alexander Graham Bell shuffle down to the patent office, but no . . . I went on the radio and bragged about it instead. My reward? A catalogue that came in the mail this week. A catalogue offering . . . Mood Videos. There is Video Aquarium, which offers an hour of undersea creatures dipping and darting around a coral reef.

There is Hawaii Experience described as a sixty-minute magic carpet ride overlaying natural surf sounds with Hawaiian music . . . and, of course, vistas of swaying palms, verdant valleys, and smouldering volcanoes. Lots of other Mood Videos, too — New England Bike Ride . . . Loon Country by Canoe . . . a Tropical Birds video . . . but oh, unkind cut — do you know what their lead-off video is? Actually you can choose any one of three . . . there is Video Fireplace . . . Fireplace TV or Fireside Moments. They all run sixty minutes, retail at anywhere from thirty to fifty dollars Canadian, and consist of the same thing. Fireplace logs snap, crackle and popping away on your TV.

So there it is . . . my idea . . . making someone else as rich as Croesus. Am I bitter at missing my one pass at fame and millionairehood? Naw, not really. Just remember the first time you hear your child call in from the den, "Dad, the fire's almost out . . . Can I rewind it?"

Just remember . . . I thought of it first.

Going Off
the Deep End

YOU SEE that weather out there? The summer is history and I'm glad. I'm glad because I have a swimming pool, and the coming of fall means I can forget that fact for six or seven months.

I'd never wanted a swimming pool. You'd come up to me a couple of years ago with a magic marker and a sheet of foolscap and said, "Art, quick — the ten things you want most in life . . . jot 'em down . . ." I dunno. I mighta written, *Peace on Earth,* a decent album from Dylan . . . a few red tomatoes . . . return to a size thirty-two waist . . . I can't "see my own swimming pool" rating any higher than twenty-five or thirty on the list.

But I got a pool. It came with the house I bought a couple of years go. It is kidney shaped and green. Various shades of green, depending on what's happening to it at any given time. When it's healthy, it's light green and you can see right down to the drain in the deep end. When it's not healthy it's *Creature from the Black Lagoon* green and you can't even tell which is the deep end.

Having your own pool is sort of like adopting a big stupid dog with a host of medical problems. Your life is never quite A-One again. What you try to do with a swimming pool is maintain it in a condition of perpetual unnaturalness. You see, in nature, pools feature lily pads, leopard frogs, tadpoles, slime, and mud. All of that is out in a personal pool.

What you're trying to do is keep a sort of a large chalice of inoffensive warmish liquid that your skittish Aunt Marion would be pleased to enter on a hot August day. That's a hard thing to do, what with June bugs and larvae and leaf mold and other messy forms of life roiling around looking for a place to light, gestate, and eventually overpopulate.

There is a way to keep a pool pristine and pure . . . and the way is called Chemicals. By the judicious application of algaeecides, bromides, chlorides, muriatic acid, oxalic acid, not to mention alum, ammonia, calcium hypocholorite, sodium bisulphate, sodium hypochlorite . . . Did I mention Cyanuric Acid, Phenol Red, or Volcanic Ash? Those too. Needless to say, a master's degree in chemistry helps.

Or you can do what I did — you can read your Homeowner Guide to Swimming Pools until you go cross-eyed, screech "The Hell with It!" run out to your pool, and nuke the sucker with supershock chlorine pucks. I stop lobbing them in when the pool starts to smoke. As a back-up test I drop a live Miller moth off the diving board. If it dissolves within fifteen seconds I figure the pool is ready for human use.

Unfortunately that's the easy part of keeping a pool. The hard part comes when other folks find out you've got one. You can be lolling around in your PJs on a Sunday morning and suddenly look up to discover a cousin you haven't seen for thirteen years standing at the end of the chaise longue. With his wife. And their seven children. Who are already in bathing suits. "Hope you don't mind," they'll say, "but it was so hot and the kids were so cranky and we were on our way home from church . . . Didn't see you at church . . ."

They will usually stay for supper, too.

But I don't know . . . sometimes I fall to grumbling and complaining about the trials of trying to maintain a swimming pool and some friend will call my bluff. They'll say, "Come on, Black . . . you tryna tell me that on a hot, muggy summer day when you've been humping around the city in the pollution and the humidity and you get home to your own pool full of cool water, you tryna tell us you don't like being able to go for a swim whenever you feel like it?"

My answer is "Swim? Who swims? I wouldn't swim in that pool. Neither would you if you could see what it does to a live Miller moth."

48

Smoking Can Be Dangerous to Your Health

Don't get stage fright, folks, but I believe we are living through what politicians like to call Historic Times. In years to come, when we're all ancient and doddering and decrepit, younguns yet unborn will toddle up to our rocking chairs, yank the Walkperson earphones from our wrinkled skulls and shout into our earholes:

"Tell us again, Grandpa! About the Olden Days when people set fire to little white tubes in their mouths and sucked hot smoke into their lungs."

Yessir, it's been about four centuries since Sir Walter Raleigh strolled down a gangplank onto British soil, puffing on a corncob, thus introducing the habit of smoking to the Old World. Ever since then, most of the world — New and Old — has been puffing and coughing and saving its spare change so that it could buy some fags to puff and cough some more.

It's been a long, expensive, painful and phlegm-filled trek, but I believe we are just about at the end of it. I believe that the smoking habit is on its last gasp.

In a way, it's a pity, because smoking is one of the few subjects I can speak on with authority. I've done a lot of it. Mind you, I wasn't always a smoker. For the first thirteen years of my life I indulged in second-hand smoke only (my old man was a puffer). For the next twenty-seven years I became an active participant and smoked like the Number Four Smelter at Stelco. For the past four years I have been clean — or as clean as you can be after you've spent a quarter of a century bathing your innards in sucked-in carcinogens.

There's been a lot of changes in smoking in my time. When I started you could buy a packet of five Winchesters for seven cents. Inhaling a Winchester was like breathing in napalm, but the price was right, and we schoolkids were convinced it made us look unbearably rugged. Smoking was so innocent back then! I can remember ads that featured movie stars and even doctors complete with white smocks and stethoscopes exhorting us to "get with it" by picking up a pack of Luckies or Export "A"s or Winstons.

Why, I'm so venerable I can remember when the Marlboro Man first rode over the horizon and onto our television screen back in the mid-fifties. The Marlboro Man — now there was a stroke of genius! Loping into our consciousness with his Stetson pulled low and his shoulders hunched, looking as if he were welded to the quarter horse he rode . . . all whipcord lean and hickory brown . . . You mean I can look as sexy as that guy just by smoking the right cigarette? Hey, bartender! I'll have a carton of whatever the cowpoke is smoking!

All lies. All illusion. And we nicotine addicts bought it, lock, stock, and Micronite filter.

Imagine what would happen if someone "discovered" the cigarette today. "Gentlemen, I have a glorious new product. It tastes like hell, gives you headaches, and makes your eyes water. It is more addictive than heroin and causes throat cancers, lung cancer, emphysema, and heart disease. It's expensive, messy, a potential fire hazard, and possibly fatal to innocent bystanders. Now what am I bid?"

Not only would cigarettes not be accepted, authorities would probably throw the discoverer in the slammer, along with the rest of the drug pushers.

But as I say, smokers are a dying breed, in more ways than one. They are finding themselves increasingly ostracized in buses, trains, and airplanes.

Businesses are instituting smoking bans, as are restaurants and theatres. It's getting harder and harder to find fellow nicotine junkies at parties or a sympathetic cabbie who lets you light up in the back seat. The message is as clear as it is insistent: the smoking habit is on the way out.

I predict that ashtrays will become as obsolete as spitoons in our lifetime. I'll go further. I predict that within a couple of decades at most, smoking will be little more than a historical curiosity — an obscure history question perhaps, in the 2010 edition of Trivial Pursuit. "What American President actually appeared in cigarette ads back in the mid-twentieth century?" Answer: Ronald Reagan, for Chesterfield cigarettes.

Speaking of trivial tobacco facts, here's one for you to file away: Whatever happened to David Millar, the actor who portrayed the original Marlboro Man?

Answer: He died in 1987.

Of emphysema.

A Hair-Raising Tale

THERE'S A SONG by Huey Lewis and the News called "I Want a New Drug." Well, Huey, have I got news for you. There *is* a new drug out there. It's called Rogaine. Not co-caine . . . Rogaine. "It's not as zippy as speed, as catatonic as junk, as mindblowing as acid or as unpredictable as booze. On the other hand, it's not too pricey, as street drugs go . . . and it's only mildly addictive. Twelve hundred bucks will set you up with a year's stash . . . and you'll never need more than two hits a day.

On the down side, Rogaine will not make you feel like a superman or a sage. All it will do . . . is grow hair on your head.

Maybe! And it's a gargantuan maybe at that. Last year in laboratory tests, a gaggle of male baldies smeared this Rogaine goop on their noggins, then retired to gaze at themselves in the bathroom mirror for a while. Four months later, thirty-three percent of them swore they could see some peach fuzz pushing through the arid wastes above their eyebrows. Another thirty-three said, nope . . . same old tundra. Couldn't see anything happening up there. (The study is suspiciously quiet about the remaining third of the glistery-domed guinea pigs — their eyelashes fell out, maybe?)

The other bad news about this Rogaine is that users really are wired to the stuff. You *must* slap some on twice a day. Miss a couple of applications and whatever wispy, hard-won filaments you've managed to sprout immediately croak, and once again your head looks like Lyell Island after a MacMillan Bloedel wet dream.

Well, I dunno . . . sounds like a longer shot than the 649 to me — not that that will stop lemminglike legions of shiny-pated male Canucks from lining up to lay their money down. There are some five million baldheaded Canadian men out there, most of whom, given the choice, would probably rather have hair to comb than extra face to wash each morning.

Actually . . . make that 4,999,999 baldheaded Canadian men out there. The other one's in here. I'm a career baldie, and I'm here to tell you that there are some real perks that come with nonhirsuteness. For one thing, your prebreakfast bathroom time is decimated. No shampoos, no Resdan, no Brylcreem . . . no whining hi-tech hair dryer. Just one swipe with the old washcloth and you're good for the whole day.

"Yeah," I hear you saying, "but what about, you know, the opposite sex?" Don't kid yourself. Any woman with an IQ greater than an empty Kleenex box does not select potential mates on the basis of the fecundity of their scalps. Baldophobia is an affliction almost exclusively found among males who have to weed their combs each morning.

Besides, guys like Yul Brynner and Telly Savalas have been out there doing ground-breaking PR for years. And how about those semibald sex objects — moulters like Jack Nicholson? Bruce Willis? Burt Reynolds and Sean Connery? Okay, Burt and Sean wear rugs from time to time, but they joke about it. They slap 'em on and whip 'em off like earmuffs. And why not? They know what's hair today can be gone tomorrow and it's no big deal.

Speaking of toupees . . . you heard what happened in Iowa? Like a lot of North American agricultural regions, Iowa is losing its young folks to the old How Ya Gonna Keep 'em Down on the Farm syndrome. But Leon Emmons knows how to fix that. Leon runs the Mr. Executive Hair Replacement Center in Des Moines, and he has promised a free hairpiece to any youngun who stays in Iowa for at least two years after college graduation. "We don't have jobs or nice beaches," says Mr. Emmons. "Maybe a full head of hair will keep them in Iowa."

Well, maybe . . . but if it works they're going to have to change the Welcome sign at the Des Moines airport. Right now it reads "Welcome to Iowa . . . a place to grow." They might want to consider something a little less misleading — tonier, too. Shakespearean, even. Such as, "Toupee or not toupee . . ."

Where Was I?

ALL RIGHT. I accept that I have this . . . disease . . . condition . . . affliction — whatever you want to call it. I can live with that. After all, I'm in good company. The great writer G. K. Chesterton suffered from it. So did Tennyson and Toscanini and Albert Einstein and just about every writer and/or academic I've ever met. Heck, there's even a whole subgenre of jokes about academics who have it.

You know . . . the Absent-minded Professor jokes.

Well, I didn't get the letters after my name, but I definitely got the adjectives in front. I'm absent-minded. I forget . . . a lot. And not just the little things like putting the cat out and whether I have anything at the cleaners and what oil I run in my car in the summer — I forget the big things, too. Things like dinner invitations. The name of the boss's wife. The location of Mutual Street. Telephone numbers? Everybody forgets telephone numbers. I forget *my* telephone number.

Here — honestly — is how one morning went for me two weeks ago: wake up half-hour late (forgot to set alarm), slam through usual predawn rituals of shave, shower, and rooting for matching socks while juggling mug of tepid Nescafé. Out of house and into car. Out of car and back to house for car keys. Back to car. Back to house while car warming up to make sure kettle turned off. Back to car to wrench keys out of ignition because house key on same key ring. Kettle is, of course, off. Back to car. On road at last, but only for two miles at which point execute desperate U-turn and return to house. Reason: cannot remember if I shut garage door. Had. Leave driveway once again in squeal of tires and sulphurous cloud of undeleted expletives that would have brought a blush to blue-black jowls of Richard Nixon himself. Decide to count blessings: at least there's not much traffic. Small detonation in nether reaches of consciousness — *why* not much traffic this morning? Check Timex digital on left wrist and divine answer. There is not much traffic this morning because it's Saturday morning. Most people don't go to work on Saturday mornings.

Including me.

Absent-mindedness — what a wonderfully evocative term. The mind is AWOL. Not in. Where does it go? You'd think if God was such a hot engineer, he might have turned us out with foreheads like illuminated dashboards that could light up during bouts of absent-mindedness. Just a short answering-machine-style message to avoid embarrassment and misunderstanding: "Hi! Arthur's mind's not in right now, but your call is important to him. Please try again later."

I wonder if we aren't all more forgetful these days. Bet we are. Look at the caveman — what did he have to remember? Come in out of the rain; keep your fingers out of the flames; if it's smaller than you, bash it over the head and eat it; if it's bigger than you, run like hell — that was pretty well it. Even in my grandfather's time there were not what you'd call serious overdrafts on the average memory bank. Back then a fella could get by just by remembering when to say gee! and when to say haw!; how to tell when the wheat was ripe and how long it took to drive thirty head of cattle from the barnyard to the abattoir. That and a couple of verses of "The Old Rugged Cross" would probably get you through. My grandfather did not have to bother his head remembering his social insurance number. Nor did my granddad have to remember a fifteen-digit driver's licence, eight numbers on an OHIP card, another eight for a personal chequing account, and the combination of the lock on a ten-speed.

Maybe that's why my mind seems to be more absent than usual. Maybe my mental floppy disc is full.

Which is another example of how modern life gives us more, not less, to remember. Before I could write this piece I had to remember to turn on my keyboard, turn on my monitor, then insert two floppy discs in my computer. I had to remember that one of them is called MS-DOS and the other is call MS-WORD VERSION

3.1. When I started out in the writing business twenty years ago, all I had to remember was the capital W on my Olivetti was broken and to change the ribbon every six months or so.

But it's not just computers, it's everything — parking, even. Have you seen the parking lot at Canada's Wonderland? It's bigger than most of the Benelux countries! I will never go to Canada's Wonderland because I know the gods are just daring me to park in that tract and then try to find my car at the end of the day.

I take it back. I may pay a visit, but I'll go by cab.

I have an abiding mistrust of parking lots, and so, I imagine, does James Hawk. Mr. Hawk is a prominent lawyer who practices in Portsmouth, Virginia. One evening Mr. Hawk skipped out of his office at close of day and down to his customary parking space, only to find it empty. His shiny new Cougar two-door was gone. Hawk called the police, then his insurance company. The police got right on the case while the insurance company hustled a rental car over for Hawk to use. The next day our lawyer arrived at work in his rental car, only to find that someone else had beaten him to his usual parking space. So he drove to a nearby city parking lot and pulled in.

Right beside his missing Cougar.

Which is when it all came back to Mr. Hawk — how two days ago, finding his favourite parking spot occupied, he had parked his own car in the municipal lot — right where it still, in fact, was.

Mind you, Annie McDonnell of Larchmont, New York, got an even stiffer jolt. She was fixing herself a late breakfast one morning when the doorbell rang. She opened the door to find her husband, Jim, standing there. "Hello, Anne," he said.

An unremarkable enough exchange — except for the fact that Mrs. McD. had not laid eyes on Mr. McD. for fifteen years — not since he'd suddenly disappeared after bumping his head in a fall. Jim McDonnell had spent the missing decade and a half working as a short-order cook and bartender in Philadelphia and answering to the name of Jim Peters. Finally something jogged his memory. Jim Peters of Philadelphia recalled that he was really Jim McDonnell of Larchmont. He caught the next train home.

Those stories both feature the three scariest things I know about absent-mindedness: it's easy; it's involuntary; and worst of all, the ramifications are impossible to foretell. Today, you might forget where you put your sunglasses; tomorrow, you could be grilling cheese dogs in Philadelphia.

There is, of course, one explanation of my affliction that I've avoided mentioning — the notion that perhaps there's nothing wrong with me at all. Or rather, nothing more than the normal wear and tear one would expect to find in a mileage-heavy machine that's been flicked on and off for forty-four years and expected to make sense of grocery lists, the east-west subway line, the Blue Jays' bullpen, the formula for finding the circumference of a circle . . . and where I left the car keys.

Maybe there's nothing wrong with my mind at all. Maybe I'm just getting . . . you know . . .

Old?

Well, if I am, I hope I learn to handle absent-mindedness with the aplomb of Alfred Edward Matthews. Mr. Matthews was a character actor who first appeared on stage in 1886. He was still going strong right up until his death in 1960.

Well, *strong* may be too precise a word. Mr. Matthews could still deliver a stirring performance, but once past his seventieth birthday he found himself blowing the odd line here and there.

Such as the time, deep in the sunset of his career, when he appeared in a West End play. His part required him to cross the stage and answer a crucial telephone call.

The phone rang. Mr. Matthews strode across stage, picked up the receiver . . .

And completely forgot who he was supposed to be talking to or what he was expected to say.

Alfred Edward Matthews may have suffered from absent-mindedness, but his talent for improvisation was well oiled. Holding out the telephone receiver to the only other actor on the stage, Matthews thundered imperiously:

"It's for you!"

Paint and Powder

THE SUBJECT OF PERFUME has been grabbing a headline or two of late. First there was the story that a brand-new and very expensive fragrance called Passion has been yanked from the shelves of several exclusive U.S. cosmetic boutiques by a federal court order. Seems that there is already a very expensive French perfume on those shelves called Passion, and the new bottle on the block was judged to be unfair competition. Tough news for the manufacturers of Passion the Sequel, who've spent something like $6 million on advertising and promotion of their brand.

Can you imagine spending $6 million just to promote perfume?

Then there was the news story that Tammy Faye Bakker is looking at a major career change. She'd like to move into something that would exploit her God-given talents . . . which appear to be shopping and makeup.

Tammy Faye called a press conference to say that she thought the cosmetics industry was "losing a big thing by not asking me to do commercials for their makeup. You know, I mean, I'm worldwide known for my makeup. You know, all the tons of stuff I'm supposed to put on mah face." Indeed we do, Tammy Faye — though I'm not sure the cosmetics industry wants to encourage the Tammy Faye Bakker Makeup Technique — unless of course I'm all wet and the next fashion craze turns out to be the "raccoon in drag" look.

At any rate it's comforting to see that something as seemingly trivial as makeup and perfume can still stir human passions on a variety of levels.

Hard to say when humankind first discovered that it could look and smell a lot better with a little chemical assistance, but archaeologists have proof that we've been rouging cheeks and painting lips and lining eyes and sopping on the scented oil for at least several thousand years. One of the first things discovered in Tutankamen's tomb when it was opened was a vanity shelf holding a half-dozen six-thousand-year-old jars of skin cream and lip colour and cheek buffer-upper — just in case King Tut needed to spiff himself up for the afterlife.

And it's still a multibillion-dollar industry today, with hundreds of chemists and researchers spending thousands of man hours — even whole careers in search of the Holy Grail — or Holy Aroma — the one scent that will make one half of the human race utterly irresistible to the other.

Aleister Crowley thought he'd found it back in the thirties. The occult author and Black Magician once announced that he had concocted the ultimate perfume . . . "the Perfume of Immortality," he called it. So why can't you buy the Perfume of Immortality? Because though it was attractive to women, it was also highly attractive to . . . horses. Male horses.

Even an expert in black magic like Crowley found it exceedingly difficult to conduct a successful man-woman tête-à-tête with an amorous stallion breathing down his neck.

Which kind of brings us back to Jimmy Bakker . . . and makes me wonder if maybe Tammy Faye might not be worth a whole lot more to the cosmetics industry than I gave her credit for.

Body Repairs

IF THERE IS such a thing as reincarnation, I would like to come back as a body repairman. Body repair is my idea of a truly noble, satisfying calling in life — and it's not just the money. No, it's the joy of taking someone else's rusty old hulk of a heap and, through knowledge and skill and hard work, resculpting and restoring that mess and making it shine like new!

All right, I lied — it's mostly the money. I fell to thinking about body repair as an alternative career right after an encounter with my local fin rejuvenator and rocker panel reconstructor in the grease palace just at the end of my street. The visit was inspired by the appearance of a few tiny but unsightly blemishes on the right rear fender of my own car. A minor infection, I told myself, best nipped at this, the inexpensive stage. "Four hundred bucks," said my body repairman, yawning and picking his teeth with a ratchet screwdriver.

Four hundred dollars! And all I would end up with would be a used car with a slightly less used right rear fender! I ask ya, where else can you make money like that?

Well, in body repair, as a matter of fact. I don't mean auto bodies, I mean real bodies — as in flabby, saggy, not-quite-over-the-hill-but-definitely-slouching-in-that-direction human bodies like yours and mine. I am talking face lifts and tummy tucks here.

It's big business — bigger even than auto repair. Consider: there is a doctor by the name of Lloyd Carlsen who works out of a clinic near Toronto who is considered to be one of the best cosmetic surgeons on the planet. For $1,500 he will smooth out your forehead. For $2,500 he will straighten your nose. A full face lift can be yours for as little as $4,500. Neck wattles, saggy chests, and saddlebag thighs? Well, they're all extra. Too expensive to be popular, you think? Listen: Dr. Lloyd Carlsen could probably employ another twenty Lloyd Carlsens around the clock. No doubt there is a financial ceiling to human vanity, but Dr. Carlsen's been far too busy in the operating room to speculate about it.

I don't suppose Dr. Carlsen has much time for mascots, either, but if he ever wanted one, I would nominate Phyllis Diller. At last count, the comedienne had gone through two face lifts, two nose jobs, a tummy tuck, a breast reduction, three teeth bondings, a forehead and undereye lift, an eyeliner tattoo, cheek implants, and a chemical peel.

Saddest thing I know is that after all that money and all that pain Phillis Diller came out looking like . . . Phyllis Diller.

But at least she didn't let the surgeons work on her sense of humour.

She was quoted in the paper the other day as saying, "I've done more for cosmetic surgery than Bayer has for aspirin. My doctor tells me I'm good for another twenty years."

The irony is, with her sense of humour, Phyllis Diller always was good for the next twenty years. She could have saved all that money.

Better still, she could have given it to me . . . so I could afford to get my rear fender repaired.

Yard Sales

I T'S HARD TO BELIEVE that they're sprouting already. Just a few short weeks ago all those front lawns were covered with snow and whipped with bone-chilling winds that nothing could survive. Now the snow is gone, the grass is green, and the beggars are towering over the lawns, even climbing up the sides of buildings and hydro poles.

Lower that can of 2-4-D, madam . . . stand easy with that Whipper Snipper, sir . . . I'm not talking about pokeweed, bindweed, chokeweed, or any of your common lawn and garden variety vegetative infestations.

I'm talking about yard sale signs.

A surer sign of spring than vireos on the verandah or potholes in the pavement is yard sales. An indication that hope springs eternal and a reminder that junk is forever.

That's what yard and garage sales are really about — junk. The fact that money changes hands at yard sales is almost immaterial. The Higher Purpose of the yard sale is to keep that junk circulating. It moves from my attic to your basement, from your basement to my garage, from my garage to your rec room.

I wonder why we like them so? Lord knows, most of us don't need any more baggage in our lives, but every Saturday and Sunday you'll see carsful of beady-eyed people, crawling down side streets and back alleys, eyes peeled for the cardboard signs or the telltale traffic jams that bespeak a yard sale in progress. I know families that have given up going to movies and baseball games in favour of yard sales. Each Friday evening they scour the want ads in the newspaper, plot their course as carefully as

Captain Cook in search of the Spice Islands, then spend their weekends blissfully prowling from one address to another.

Going to garage sales is only half of the experience, of course. The other half comes when — due primarily to the tons of thoroughly useless detritus you've picked up yourself at garage sales — the sickening realization dawns on you that you have to hold one yourself.

As a battle-scarred and shell-shocked veteran of two full-fledged yard sales, allow me to give any greenhorns in the audience a word of advice.

The word is *don't*.

Hold a garage sale, I mean.

Better to mail your junk to a Third World country, haul it to the dump, even dig a hole in the back yard and bury it — anything but hold a garage sale. You're not strong enough. Nobody is.

But I know you're going to ignore that advice. You have visions of dollar signs dancing behind your eyeballs. You think once you unload those two and a half lawn mowers, the torn trampoline that the kids won't play with, the patio umbrella that the squirrels got to, and all those stupid books that Harry's been collecting for years, you'll probably have enough money to take a little holiday together.

I can tell you that you're going to *need* a holiday — and not necessarily with your loved one, because you may not be speaking to each other after the garage sale — but don't plan on anything pricey. The average take from the average yard sale is $11.99 — and that's before you order in a pizza because you're too baffed to make dinner.

I really wish you'd reconsider. Hosting a full-fledged yard sale is not good for the heart. Oh, sure, it's kind of refreshing to participate in a little primary capitalism — no T4s to make out, no value-added tax to reckon, no Visa or MasterCard slips to juggle, just simple, straightforward dickering. You want this? I own it. How much you gonna pay?

That's the up side. The down side is that when you hold your yard sale you will witness human behaviour at its least attractive — naked greed. Total strangers will park in your driveway for the opportunity to make fun of your taste. "You're asking two dollars for *that?* I can get *five* of them for two dollars down the street!"

The other thing is dignity. For people who insist on holding yard sales, there is none. And let's face it, your mother didn't raise you to spend a Sunday afternoon popping blood vessels in your head as you try to blow up your kid's used wading pool (five bucks as is) to prove that it doesn't leak.

But there's a much more important reason not to have your yard sale. Look at it this way: holding a yard sale is going to punch a huge hole in your weekend. You have to man the cash box from dawn on Saturday until the last die-hard haggler shuffles off your trampled lawn on Sunday night.

You realize what that means, don't you?

Just think of all the yard sales you'll be missing.

PART 2
Saints and Sinners, Champs and Chumps

Famous Last Words

L IFE," as former U.S. President Jimmy Carter once observed,
"isn't fair." He was right. Life pulls a multitude of dirty tricks on
us all, but for me one of the most annoying of life's double crosses
is the fact that it doesn't guarantee each and every one of us the
chance to deliver a really swell Goodbye Speech.

You know what I mean. Famous last words. One final summa-
tion of all you've learned during your time on the planet. All the
things you'd like to say to your survivors to make them feel really
bad about having to slog ahead without you.

Oh, some folks get to deliver stirring exit speeches. Nathan
Hale's little gem "I only regret that I have but one life to lose for
my country" was pretty decent — but don't forget that he was
standing on a scaffold with a rope around his neck when he said
that. As Samuel Johnson once observed, "When a man knows he
is to be hanged in a fortnight, it concentrates his mind wonderfully."

The problem is that for the majority, the end comes suddenly —
a coronary bushwhack or a close encounter with the bumper of
a tractor trailer perhaps. Most of us don't get a couple of weeks of
pacing around in a jail cell, honing our rhetorical bon mots.

I also suspect that a lot of so-called Last Words have been
somewhat gussied up for public consumption. Sir Isaac Brock,
who died in the battle of Queenston Heights, was reported to have
cried, "Push on, brave men of York, push on!"

Well, maybe. But if I was lying in the gravel with a musket ball
in my brisket, I'm reasonably sure that my thoughts would not

issue forth in the form of poetic exhortations to a gaggle of colonial grunts.

Gwynne Nettler is a man who shares my pessimism about grandiloquent exits. He's professor emeritus with the University of Alberta, and he's written a paper called "The Quality of Crisis," in which he examines the things people *really* do and say when they're faced with life-threatening situations. His conclusion: most folks' final curtain calls are seldom as Cecil B. DeMillean as we'd like them to be.

He gives some examples. The bullfighter mortally gored by a bull remembers thinking, Now my whole afternoon is ruined.

The Second World War aviator going down in his crippled B-29 into the South Pacific mumbling, "Geez, how I hate asparagus."

The motorist, critically injured in a collision on a California highway, griping to a paramedic, "This would have to happen on my birthday."

Professor Nettler writes that he has closely analyzed some 211 separate crises with particular attention to the things people have done and said "at the great crossroad." He sums up his overall impression in four words: "Crisis trivializes and anaesthetizes."

There's some historical evidence to bear him out — Lord Byron, for instance. Now if anyone was going to write himself a grand finale you would think the famous and flamboyant poet would be the one to do it. His last words? Just one. "Goodbye."

Deathbed pronouncements can range from the depressing ("Oh, I am so bored with it all." — Winston Churchill) to the hilarious ("Either this wallpaper goes, or I do." — Oscar Wilde). They can be pathetic, as in Marie Antoinette's apology to her executioner for stepping on his foot: "Monsieur, I beg your pardon. I did not do it on purpose." They can be impossibly pedantic as in the final words of a famous French grammarian who announced, "I am about to, or, I am going to, die. Either expression is used."

But I think my favourite final words came from the mouth of an American Civil War casualty by the name of General Sedgewick, who, while observing far-off enemy snipers through a telescope scoffed, "Why, they couldn't hit an elephant at this dist —"

For all-round banality, though, it's hard to beat the last words of George Lincoln Rockwell. You remember George? He was the leader of the American Nazi Party until someone even wackier than he was gunned him down outside a Laundromat where George had gone, presumably to render his uniform Aryan white.

As he lay expiring on the sidewalk, Rockwell looked up, locked eyes with a fellow Laundromat user, and grumbled, "I forgot my bleach."

Felons Wanted — No Intelligence Necessary

In the war on crime, the bad guys are ahead.
Thomas Plate, Crime Pays! *1975*

WELL, PERHAPS Mr. Plate is right. Maybe the title of his book is accurate, too, more often than not. But not always. Sometimes crime not only does *not* pay, it makes a complete ass of the would-be criminal into the bargain. Ask the two amateur con artists who tried to put the arm on a little old lady in Mansfield, Ohio, recently. They were running the old bunko classic called "The Pigeon Drop." It works like this: a con goes up to some gullible-looking soul with a story about having found some money. The con says he needs help in finding the owner. If the mark helps out, the mark will get to keep some of the found money, but ahh . . . (slight twirl of mustachios here) . . . of course the mark won't mind putting up some of his or her own money as a sign of good faith. The so-called found money and the mark's cash are put into two envelopes. One goes to the con, the other to the mark. Actually the con has done a switcheroo and the mark's envelope is full of confetti. By the time the mark cottons on, you-know-who is long gone.

At least that's the way it's supposed to work. The two cons in Mansfield, Ohio, still have to do a little fine-tuning on their scam. Oh, they found an easy mark, all right. They even managed to convince her to withdraw $724 of her pension money and put it in an envelope. Then they did a fast shuffle, drove the old dear to her house, and took off, chortling under their breath.

Until they opened their envelope. They'd got them mixed up. Theirs was full of cut-up newspaper; the mark was sitting in her living room wondering why she had her $724 back . . . plus an extra $1,300 she'd never seen before. Mansfield police are looking for the two crooks.

But not too hard.

Then there's the story of the two grocery store robbers in Compton, California, who shoulda stood in bed. They made the heist easily enough, handcuffed a security guard to a sink, got back to the car with more than five and a half grand in store receipts.

That's when things began to go awry.

First they hit another car. Unfortunately, it was one of those cars with the revolving illuminated cherries on top. Belonged to the sheriff of Compton, in fact. Panic-stricken, the thieves squealed away, did a U-turn . . . and smashed into the sheriff's car again.

One of the thugs was knocked unconscious, the other escaped by running into a nearby house.

A house belonging to a police officer.

Authorities say that the two have been relieved from the rigours and stress of civilian life and put in a place where they can't harm themselves.

But America has no monopoly on luckless lawbreakers. We breed some uncommonly clumsy crooks right here in Canada. The shoplifter in Vancouver, for instance, who needs to clean up his act considerably. He tried to rip off a downtown liquor store by stuffing a bottle of vodka down his pants. He went to the cashier with a single bottle of beer. "Anything else?" asked the cashier. "Nope," said the thief, trying to look casual.

Which is tough to do when your fly is wide open and the neck of a twenty-sixer of vodka is hanging out.

A jewel thief in Dallas was a little more discreet but not much luckier. He walked into a jewellery store in Fort Worth recently and asked to look at some diamonds. While the clerk was distracted, the man grabbed a large stone and walked out the door. When an employee caught up to him, the man held out his hands and let himself be frisked. No diamond.

"Gee, fellas, guess you made a mistake, eh?"

Unfortunately, the jewel merchants had heard of swallowing.

Deep Throat was taken to a hospital where an X-ray confirmed that he had an uncommonly solid potato lodged in his tum-tum.

Fort Worth police have given the man a very potent laxative and are awaiting further developments.

Pardon Me, but Your Ego's Showing

People hate me because I am a multifaceted,
talented, wealthy, internationally famous genius.
— *Jerry Lewis*

A H, THERE IS NOTHING quite as magnificent as an entertainer's
ego in full flower — and nothing makes it blossom more
luxuriantly than the nagging suspicion that maybe, just maybe, the
adoring public might be growing disenchanted with the entertainer in question. Jerry Lewis is a perfect case in point. He's got
an ego the size of the Good Year blimp and about as much
sensitivity as there is lint in a cockroach's navel. A few years ago,
a Montreal newspaper reporter by the name of Lucinda Chodan
had less than kind words to say about one of Lewis's typically
brainless performances. Old Jer blithely explained the bad review
away with "You can't accept one individual's opinion, especially
if it's female, and you know — God willing, I hope for her sake
it's not the case — when they get their period it's really difficult
for them to function as normal human beings."

Spoken like a true multifaceted, talented, wealthy, internationally famous genius.

But Lewis isn't the only celluloid celebrity to be caught licking
his wounds in public lately; there's an absolute rash of thin skin
going around Tinseltown — and an utter plague of lawyers feeding off it.

You heard about the famous Joan Rivers phone call? Seems The
Mouth at Midnight decided that it would be a swell idea to phone
up Victoria Principal on the air and ask her all kinds of embarrassing questions while the studio audience — and millions of TV

watchers — listened in. The star of "Dallas" wasn't home, but La Rivers fixed her wagon, anyway, by giving out her unlisted phone number and urging everybody to give her a call.

The next day, Principal's attorneys called Rivers instead, and whacked the late-night comedienne with a $3 million lawsuit. The lawsuit claims that poor Victoria suffered "humiliation and anguish" as a result of receiving "numerous telephone calls from individuals she did not know."

Well, my heart is certainly hemorrhaging for the beleaguered soap opera star and I think three mil is little enough for such humiliation and anguish — especially if it means I can sue the next half-dozen folks who phone me with offers of vacuum cleaners, retirement property in Florida, and subscriptions to *Maclean's*.

Speaking of lawsuits, the famous Dr. Ruth has launched one of her own. Apparently the world's shortest sex therapist sustained a bruised ego as a result of a speech she failed to give.

It wasn't the speech, or even the audience — it was the excuse the speakers' agency gave for Dr. Ruth's no-show. The agency claimed that she was suffering from "emotional illness."

Dr. Ruth got quite emotional over that — so much so that she is suing the agency for slander — to the tune of a trifling $1.3 million.

But that is not the most delicious piece of egocentric litigation currently clogging the U.S. judicial system. That honour has to go to an action recently launched by "Miami Vice"-nik Philip Michael Thomas.

Thomas is the pouty fashion plate who portrays Detective Rico Tubbs — running, as Dorothy Parker once wrote of a Katharine Hepburn performance, "the whole gamut of the emotions from A to B."

He is suing the *National Enquirer* for a whopping $14 million. Why? Well, mostly because the Rag We All Love to Read at the Checkout Counter alleged that Philip Michael was "a mama's boy." The Thomas lawsuit actually blusters (would I make this up?) that Thomas had never been "a mama's boy" but was a high school athlete and a "masculine 'hunk.'"

Such supreme silliness will not surprise anyone who has followed Philip Michael Thomas's career. The man raises narcissism to an art form. If this guy and Jerry Lewis ever got together for lunch, they'd have to rent the SkyDome to ensure adequate headroom.

So much conceit and so little reason for it. Makes me wish Golda Meir were still around. She had a special talent for deflating bloated egos — such as that of the fawning government flunky who tried using fake humility to ingratiate himself with her.

After she'd endured a few tedious minutes of grovelling and bootlicking, Mrs. Meir took the wretch by the shoulders, fixed him with those marvelous deadpan eyes, and said, "Don't be humble; you're not that great."

Be Kind to Dumb Crooks

I'M A LITTLE CONCERNED about the image criminals are carving out for themselves these days. Television series such as "Miami Vice," "Police Story," and "Night Heat" depict overworked, underpaid policemen, shamuses, and other defenders of Law'n'order going up time and again against drug-money-rich, Uzi-bedecked thugs and gangsters — evil geniuses who seem to have a whole world of resources at their beck and call. Crooks are portrayed as Machiavellian masterminds of unlimited wealth who can unleash a whole fleet of sleazebag lawyers at the merest flutter of a parking ticket.

Same with movies — films such as *The Untouchables* show the forces of justice to be poor sad schlemiels hog-tied by red tape, inferior superiors, and bad tailors. Sure, the good guys in the movies and on TV usually win, but you get the feeling it's more by good luck than good management.

The casual observer (that's you and me) might get the impression that criminals are all devilishly clever and well-nigh invincible. The truth is somewhat less edifying. Fact is, statistics show that when it comes to klutzes, buffoons, and outright idiots, the World of Crime is, at the very least, an Equal Opportunity Employer. I won't bore you with a lot of charts and graphs — just three or four examples recently culled from the dailies.

Take the case of the bank robber in Miami who surrendered . . . to an envelope. The chap had just knocked over a branch of Barnett Bank and was sprinting out the door when he ran afoul of a customer by the name of Spurgeon Brown. Brown levelled a manila envelope — yes, a manila envelope — at the heister and snarled, "*Freeze!*" The crook did, dropping a switchblade and two bags containing more than two thousand dollars. Mr. Brown, with his envelope cocked and ready, picked up the money and the knife and marched his prisoner back to the bank to await the arrival of police, armed with more conventional weaponry.

Can't laugh at the crook, though . . . he probably suffered a nasty paper cut as a kid.

Besides, he wasn't as dumb as the burglar arrested in Pittsburgh last month. This guy was rifling an office when he came across a camera — one of those instant jobs that take your picture and develop it while you wait. Well, he got half of it right — he took a photograph of himself — but he didn't wait. Instead, he threw the still-developing print into the wastebasket, popped the camera into his gym bag, and took off.

And in case a personal mug shot wasn't sufficient for investigators, the burglar also left two books behind when he went out the fire escape. They were books he'd checked out of a local library that morning.

Poor guy. As soon as he finishes doing time for burglary he'll be slapped with a fine for those overdue books. It's not hard to see how people fall into a life of crime.

Then there's the case of the London man who broke down when authorities confronted him with a human skull unearthed in his backyard. The man crumbled and blabbed. Yes, it was the skull of his wife. He had strangled her twenty-three years ago in a fight over money. He was glad they had found her skull and ended his life of deception.

Well . . . actually they hadn't. The man had been so eager to confess that he hadn't given the finders of the skull time to explain that they were anthropologists, and the skull they'd dug up belonged to a Roman legionnaire who'd been tromping around that area about fifteen centuries earlier. The homeowner hastened to assure everyone that he'd, heh, heh, just been kidding about the murder, but police aren't laughing, they're digging. And the suspected murderer is awaiting Her Majesty's Pleasure in a London gaol.

What's that I hear you cry? All these second-rate felons are foreign? You want Canadian content? Fear not. When it comes to dumb crooks, Canada takes a back seat to no nation.

Ask the management and staff of the K Mart store in Whitby, Ontario. They recently had to deal with a young woman who swooned at the checkout desk and dropped to the floor. K Mart staff are competent and trained to deal with such emergencies. While one cashier felt for the woman's pulse, another, fearing that drugs (prescription or otherwise) might be involved, looked into the woman's eyes and asked firmly, "What did you take? What did you take?"

The swoonee's eyes cleared briefly and focussed on the K Mart official looming over her. Despondently, she whispered, "Two wristwatches . . . You want them back?"

The watches were returned. The woman was taken to hospital for observation. K Mart decided not to press charges.

Must have been Be Kind to Dumb Animals Week.

Meet Mike Mercredi

RECENTLY I DID an interesting thing. I hopped a westbound flight out of Lester B. Pearson airport, flew across a clutch of Great Lakes, a chunk of Precambrian shield, a good swatch of Prairie patchwork quilt, dropped out of the sky into the Saskatoon airport . . . and met Mike Mercredi.

Actually it wasn't quite that easy. Travelling almost never is. I was in Saskatoon because it has the nearest airport to Prince Albert National Park, a long drive due north. I was the guest speaker for a group called Misinipi Broadcasting. How was I to get from Saskatoon airport to the park? "Mike Mercredi will pick you up," said a cheerful voice on the phone. But how would I know Mike Mercredi? The cheerful voice broke into a chuckle. "Oh, you won't have any trouble recognizing Mike."

Fine. Thanks. Just what I need — a little game of needle-in-the-human-haystack. Saskatoon airport arrivals lounge turns out to be full of, as I feared, your average-looking, largely indistinguishable airport types . . . except for that . . . oh, my goodness, that must be Mike Mercredi.

The man is wearing a light Windbreaker, jeans, and cowboy boots. He would go about six foot three, from the peak of his shiny black hair to the tips of his equally shiny cowboy boots. He would weigh about 220 pounds, and if any of it is fat, it doesn't show. He carries himself fiercely erect, and he looks all in all like just about the last person whose toe you'd want to step on, except for one thing. His moustache. The man has a small beard and a moustache, the tips of which are waxed and standing off his upper lip at forty-five-degree angles. Somehow the handlebar moustache dissipates any menace in his carriage. "*Hi,*" he says. "I'm Mike Mercredi. This your bag?" And he tosses the suitcase I had been two-handing across the airport tiles lightly onto his shoulder and we're off to Prince Albert National Park.

It's a three-hour drive to our destination, and that's when I really get to meet Mike Mercredi. Turns out he comes by the military bearing and moustache honestly. Came out of Coppermine at the age of sixteen, scuffed around the streets of Edmonton for a while, went into a recruiting office, lied about his age, and signed up. Everybody thought Mike Mercredi was a career soldier. Everybody but Mike Mercredi. After twenty-three years in uniform, he got bored and quit. He was back on the street again, and just as well he had an army pension because Mike only had a grade 8 education when he got back into his civvies.

He decided to do something about that. At the age of forty-plus, he enrolled in university as a mature student. Twenty-two months later he graduated with a degree in business administration.

He told me a lot of good stories on that three-hour drive. About being stationed in Egypt. About canoeing down the Magnetawan with his preschool kids. About the jobs he's had since, all over Canada.

Now, his kids have all grown and spread across Canada, too. They try to encourage Mike to retire and move closer, but Mike just laughs. Too many people want to hire him for his talents. He knows that he'll be moving on one day, but it won't be to a retirement home. He and his wife love to travel and feel no need to settle down. "When I left home for the first time, I was twelve and I went to Winnipeg and I was scared," he says. "That night, I looked up in the sky and found the North Star. And I told myself, as long as I can see the North Star, I can find my way home."

That's the thing that's most striking about Mike Mercredi. He's the kind of guy who, no matter where you meet him — Egypt . . . Edmonton . . . canoeing down the Magnetawan or in the arrivals lounge of Saskatoon airport — you know right away that this guy knows the way home.

It's just as the woman on the phone said — you won't have any trouble recognizing Mike.

A Prince
of a Guy

YOU HAVE bad days, right? Everybody does — even fun-loving newspaper columnists. But I have a mantra that blows bad days right out of the water. Whenever I feel a bad day coming on, I stop whatever I'm doing, take a deep breath, and say, "It could be worse. I could be the Prince of Wales."

I know, I know. The guy makes a zillion pounds a minute. He gets to ride in tinted-glass limos, share a bathmat with Di, and who can remember the last time he picked up the cheque for a meal? I realize all that, but I still wouldn't trade places with him. Because for all the princely perks of his position, there is one sad fact to make that Royal's life pure hell on velvet: the British press is on his case and the newshounds won't leave him alone.

The British gutter press has to be read to be disbelieved. It makes scandal sheets on this side of the water look like Unitarian monthly bulletins. The U.K. tabs regularly print lurid lies and doctored photos that would have a Canadian editor thrown in the slammer. And they are not dainty about it. The editorial stance of rags like the London *Sun* and the *Daily Mirror* can display all the grace and subtlety of a British hooligan soccer fan after nine pints of bitter.

Like most cowards, the British tabloids relish soft, juicy targets. Who better than a young heir to the throne, prevented by his station from fighting back?

And so Prince Charles became one of their favourite sitting ducks. When he gave up shooting grouse in Scotland, they made fun of him for being a wimp. When he experimented with vegetarianism, the papers had a field day, intimating that he was not only off meat but off his nut, as well.

The guy can't win. When he's loving and deferential to his wife at public functions, the newspapers hoot that he's henpecked. Presumably if he slugged Diana on the steps of Buckingham Palace or dragged her around on a dog leash, he'd get better press.

The thing that seems to bug the British tabloids most about Prince Charles is a characteristic that you'd think they'd find attractive in a public figure — his thirst for adventure. Prince Charles has a penchant for visiting out-of-the-way places. This is a character flaw? Apparently to Charles's ink-stained critics it is. They found fault with him for taking a trip to the Kalahari desert, and even for a painting holiday in Italy.

They really had a feeding frenzy when someone at the palace leaked the news that Prince Charles had made a "secret visit" to a remote island off the coast of Scotland, where he spent three days planting potatoes, digging ditches, and herding sheep.

Sounds harmless enough, right? Not to guardians of normalcy such as the ever-vigilant London *Sun*. The next morning, its front page headline read, "A loon again, hermit Charles plants spuds on remote isle!"

Perhaps it was a slow news day.

It's my personal opinion that the hacks of Fleet Street have never forgiven Prince Charles for having a superior sense of humour. Back when he was just a pup, the prince confessed that he was an unabashed fan of "The Goon Show." "The Goon Show" was perhaps the most inspired half-hour of insanity ever to hit the BBC airwaves, served up by comedy geniuses Harry Secombe, Spike Milligan, and Peter Sellers. "The Goon Show" laid the foundation for subsequent comedy hits like "That Was the Week That Was," "Beyond the Fringe," and "Monty Python's Flying Circus." The Goons' humour was fast, cheeky, and very witty — not crude and obvious like the more popular British music hall variety. Perhaps the popular press took offense at a Royal who laughed at jokes they didn't understand. In any case, the tabloids set their sights on Charles, and they've been taking potshots ever since.

If it's any consolation to the prince, he's not the first Charles in history to suffer from a bad image. True, there was a Charles the Great and a Charles the Wise, but there was also a Charles the Foolish, Charles the Simple, Charles the Fat, and Charles the Bald. The royalty of Spain even threw in Carlos the Bewitched.

On the very good chance that the British press is once more giving Prince Charles a hard time today . . . and on the slightly more remote chance that his secretary slipped *That Old Black Magic* into the prince's morning mail, we offer one final royal anecdote. It comes, fittingly enough, from yet another blue-blooded Charles — King Carl XVI Gustav of Sweden. When told (at the age of seven) that he would one day become king, little Carl blurted, "I don't want the job. I want to be a taxi driver."

I have a feeling that the Prince of Wales could empathize with that.

Step Right Up, Folks!

It cannot be denied that in dealings with the public just a little touch of humbug is immensely effective . . .
— Canadian physician Sir William Osler

HUMBUG. Such a wonderful word. Pity it's not used much anymore. My dictionary defines *humbug* as "something intended to deceive; a hoax." The word has been around since the days of Dickens, but it was the nineteenth-century Yankee impresario P. T. Barnum who raised it to an art form.

Experts disagree about whether Barnum really said "There's a sucker born every minute," but nobody denies he made a lot of money out of fleecing the gullible. He founded a ragtag circus in 1871, modestly named it The Greatest Show on Earth, then sat back and waited for the money to roll in.

And it did. In the form of hard-earned nickels and dimes clutched tightly in the fists of naive Americans easily awed by bright lights, loud music, and wall-to-wall razzmatazz.

They came in droves. They came to see the Feejee Mermaid, advertised on a fifteen-foot-long billboard showing a gorgeous creature, half fish, half blond bombshell. Inside, customers beheld a taxidermist's bad dream consisting of a monkey's torso blanket-stitched to the tail end of a bluefin tuna. Altogether it was a foot and a half long.

They lined up to see George Washington's Nurse — a female dwarf hired by Barnum. He claimed she was 161 years old and had nursed the first American President. A newspaper reporter cried "Fraud!" and Barnum confessed immediately. He called a press conference to announce that the nurse was really a robot working with a ventriloquist. Was Barnum crazy? Like a fox. The people lined up to see the new circus sensation. Naturally they had to lay their money down again.

Barnum also showed a genius for traffic flow. In order to keep the customers moving briskly through the exhibits, Barnum printed up a fancy banner that read THIS WAY TO THE EGRESS!!!!! The crowds rushed forward, eager to see what they assumed was another display, only to find themselves outside, winking in the bright sunlight of the midway. Perhaps when they got home, the more scholarly among them took the trouble to look up *egress* and discover that it means *exit.*

If Barnum was the Crown Prince of Humbug, Joey Skaggs must be the Guerrilla Insurgent of the phenomenon. Mr. Skaggs is a present-day American entrepreneur and he, too, likes to perpetrate massive con games, but unlike old P.T., Skaggs doesn't victimize the public.

He goes after the media.

Many years ago, Skaggs developed an intense loathing for the way radio, TV, and newspapers trivialize and distort the news. But instead of writing letters to the editor, Skaggs decided to try another option: revenge. He started "planting" stories — absurd, impossible fairy tales — then he stood back to giggle as reporters scrambled all over one another to cover them. Skaggs pulled a lot of scams. He posed as an angry Romany demanding that the gypsy moth be renamed. In another, more prudish, guise, Skaggs campaigned to put diapers on the horses that pull carriages through Central Park. Still another Skaggs incarnation sent out news releases about a mythical robbery at an equally mythical celebrity sperm bank. He also posed as Dr. Joseph Bones, leader of a "Fat Squad," which could be rented by weak-willed porkies to make sure they stuck to their diets — with handcuffs, leg irons, and straitjackets when necessary. Did the worldly-wise and cynical New York press laugh him right onto the funny pages? Nope, they ate it up. Editors put him on the front pages of their newspapers and TV producers made him the lead item on the six o'clock news. They fell for it hook, line, and phony press release. Not a one of them ever said, "Hey, wait a minute, guys, this sounds fishy."

Which didn't surprise Joey Skaggs a bit. "Reporters are always more interested in a good story than they are in the truth," he says.

Well, that's a sentiment P. T. Barnum would share, even though he would no doubt lament the fact that Joey Skaggs makes no money from his hobby.

That's not a problem that plagues the New York Historical Society. The society staged an exhibit of "Barnumabilia" last year — a collection of letters, pamphlets, pictures, and displays from the colourful eighty-one-year career of the self-styled Prince of Humbug. It was a smash hit. New Yorkers couldn't get enough of old photos and posters showing such Barnum staples as Jo-Jo, the Dog-Faced Boy, General Tom Thumb, and Madame Clofullia, the Bearded Lady.

P. T. Barnum would have approved.

He might have had to bite his tongue to keep from snickering, but he would have approved.

Annie and Abby

SOMEDAY, FAR IN THE FUTURE, when anthropologists are sifting through the flotsam and jetsam of the late twentieth century, I hope they will pause to reflect on a phenomenon that's always been a bit of a head-scratcher for me. It had its origins on July 4, 1918. Twin sisters were born on that date in Sioux City, Iowa — Esther Friedman and Pauline Friedman, by name. Actually, their full names were Esther Pauline Friedman and Pauline Esther Friedman — folks didn't suffer from imaginative overload out there in Sioux City — but don't even take time to be confused by that, because both sisters changed their names soon after they hit their adult stride. Esther Pauline Friedman became Ann Landers and Pauline Esther Friedman became Abigail Van Buren, a k a Dear Abby.

You've gotta wonder what the odds are against twin sisters from the rural midwestern U.S. growing up to become the most popular sob sister columnists on the North American continent.

Truth to tell, *popular* doesn't quite cover it. Ann Landers claims more than seventy million readers in over a thousand newspapers coast to coast and gulf to tundra. I don't know the figures for sister Pauline — or maybe it's Esther — but I do know that any fair-size metropolitan daily that doesn't boast Ann Landers in its lineup usually has Dear Abby waiting in editorial ambush.

For all their popularity, the Friedman girls don't get a lot of respect. They're both routine fodder for stand-up comics. Folksinger John Prine wrote a wicked ditty about Abby; neither one rates a mention in *Encyclopedia Americana* or even the *People's*

86

Almanac — and the *Almanac* even devotes a couple of inches to Wavy Gravy.

It's too bad, because Ann and Abby have given us more than a few bon mots over the years.

Ann Landers on the Boob Tube: "Television has proved people will look at anything rather than each other."

Dear Abby on marriage: "In Biblical times, a man could have as many wives as he could afford. Just like today."

You want epigrams? The Friedmans deliver epigrams. Abby: "People who fight fire with fire usually end up with ashes."

Ann: "Time wounds all heels."

Ann's proved she's not just a pretty typist, she's also pretty spunky, one on one. Such as the time a pompous Southern senator accosted her at a cocktail party. "So yore Ann Landers," he drawled. "Say sumpin' funny." She looked at the senator coolly and replied: "So you're a politician . . . Tell me a lie."

They're getting on, you know, Ann and Abby — they're pushing seventy. I don't know what Abby's up to when she gets away from the typewriter, but her sister hits the rubber-chicken circuit pretty regularly. She breezed through Southern Ontario recently for a couple of speaking engagements. She says that after three decades of pondering people's problems, she's managed to boil the whole of human turmoil into a pithy, twenty-five-word credo: "The poor," she says, "want to be rich. The rich want to be happy. The single wish to be married, and the married wish to be dead."

She told a Toronto audience that she has also finally resolved the thorniest controversy to plague her entire advice-dispensing career — whether toilet paper should be put on the roll to hang down the wall, or to hang down the front. Ann Landers says she received *fifteen thousand* letters on that one subject. I don't know why but somehow that restores my faith in humanity.

What? Oh, it's down the front. You hang your toilet paper so that it rolls down the front.

Listen, if it's good enough for the finer bathrooms of Sioux City, Iowa, it's good enough for you.

I Dub This Dominion . . . Mesopelagia

L ET ME RUN some possible names past you. How do you feel about . . . Albertonia? Victoracia? Alexandrina? No? Then how about Albonia or Niagarentia? Nothing tickle your fancy there? Then what do you say to Transatlantia? Laurentia? Colonia? Or — and this may give it all away — Canadensia?

You guessed it. One tiny modification in the history of British North America and Any of the Above might have been the name of your country. Yep . . . if they'd passed around one more bottle of Scotch at that table during the Confederation conference, any one of those might be stamped on your passport today. They were all at one time or another seriously put forward as possible names for this country — and I haven't even mentioned the really weird candidates like Efisga, Tuponia, and Mesopelagia.

Names are fascinating — even more so when you realize how some of the more famous ones are firmly rooted in pure human confusion. The name we finally ended up with, for instance. One theory has it that we're all called Canadians because of a misunderstanding between Jacques Cartier and an Indian chief. Story goes that Cartier asked the chief what this place was called. The chief, thinking Cartier meant the Indian encampment on the shore, replied, "Kanata."

"Kanata" it is, Cartier decided, not realizing he'd just saddled a continent with the Huron/Iroquois word that means "a collection of huts."

Much the same story for the Yucatan peninsula, down in Mexico. A sixteenth-century Spanish captain asked the natives he found on shore what they called their country. "*Yuc a tan*," he heard one mutter. He thought it sounded like a pretty good name and wrote it down. It was actually Mayan dialect for "Anybody here know what this guy is talking about?"

Ah, well. As Humpty Dumpty said in *Through the Looking Glass*, "When I use a word, it means just what I choose it to mean — neither more nor less!"

John Desmond Lewis worked a variation on that theme. Mr. Lewis was a candidate in a British Parliamentary by-election in Liverpool recently, who decided to liven up an otherwise dull campaign by changing his name. So he did — to . . . Tarquin Fintimlinbinwhin bim lin Bus Stop-F Tang Olé Biscuit Barrel. Mr. Lewis never fully explained why he changed his name to that . . . and I guess it won't matter a great deal to posterity, because Tarquin Fintimlinbinwhin bim lin Bus Stop-F Tang Olé Biscuit Barrel lost the election. Though he did pull in 223 votes . . . which proves, I suppose, that eccentricity is alive and well and living in darkened ballot boxes in Liverpool.

In any case, John Desmond Lewis's name change for election purposes was not the most inspired in the annals of world politics. I believe that honour must go to Luther D. Knox of Louisiana.

I don't know much first-hand about Luther, but I wouldn't be surprised to learn that he's doing well in advertising. Or used cars. I know that he's a first-rate judge of voter disaffection.

In 1979, while a candidate for municipal office, Luther applied to have his name entered at the bottom of the election ballot.

His new name, that is. Luther had had it officially changed.

To . . . None of the Above. That's right — Luther D. Knox's new name was None of the Above. His election opponents protested and the Louisiana attorney general agreed with them, ruling that the state has a right to protect itself against candidates who were "fraudulent, confusing, and frivolous." Of course I don't have to tell you that the ruse didn't work — if it had, None of the Above would be governor of Louisiana today — if not President of the United States.

When you think of it, it's a good job Luther Knox's brainstorm didn't occur to our own Fathers of Confederation sitting around in Charlottetown 120-odd years ago. They might have gone for it. And it's traumatic enough travelling abroad without having to deal with questions like "Country of origin, sir?" "Ahh . . . None of the Above."

I think I'd rather be known as a Mesopelagian.

A Little Hurtin' Music

SOMEBODY ONCE ASKED Kurt Vonnegut, Jr., to predict the twentieth century's most enduring legacy to generations yet unborn. Vonnegut blinked those baggy beagle eyes he wears and thought for a while as he puffed on his umpteenth Pall Mall of the day . . . then he said, "Historians in the future, in my opinion, will congratulate us on very little, other than our clowning and our jazz."

Clowns and jazz. Why, shucks, I can think of a subcategory peculiar to the twentieth century that kind of transcends both achievements.

Country music. Specifically the titles of some country songs.

I can hear readers snapping books shut right across the nation. That's the problem with country music: people either take it dead seriously (usually people with names like Tammy Bodeen or Billy Joe Macafee) or they dismiss it as terminal cornpone stupidity. I suspect the truth lies somewhere in between.

Understand that we are not speaking here about country songs per se. Just the titles of those songs. People often get them mixed up. The *Book of Lists* once asked Johnny Cash to name his all-time ten favourite country songs, and he responded with some classics — "Wildwood Flower," "Cold, Cold Heart." Fine songs, I guess . . . but not especially magnificent titles. Nope, for *those* you have to go right to the back of the country corral.

That's where you'll find songs like, well, like "May the Bird of Paradise Fly Up Your Nose," for instance. That's the kind of title I mean.

When you study the genre you discover that such titles share some common characteristics. They tend to be longish and convoluted and inordinately fond of a hokey variation on the literary device called oxymoron. Or perhaps in this case just moron. Example: "I'm Playin' the Jukebox to Remember What I'm Drinkin' to Forget." That one's got it all. It's long, it's about heartbreak and booze, and it drops the *g*'s on the words *playin'* and *drinkin'*.

Religion frequently supplies a strong thematic subtext in the more memorable country titles. Such as the 1979 quasiclassic, "My Head Hurts, My Feet Stink and I Don't Love Jesus." And can any serious Biblical scholar ever forget "Drop Kick Me, Jesus (Through the Goalposts of Life)"? I think not.

Sexism, alas, is alive and well and wearing a Stetson with feathers at the front. Titles such as "If I Said You Had a Beautiful Body Would You Hold It Against Me?" And the all-time chauvinist porker, "I Never Bin to Bed with an Ugly Woman but I've Shore Woken Up with a Few." Feminists don't appear to be penning a lot of country song titles . . . though back in the mid-seventies Loretta Lynn was considered to have tromped on a few pointy-toed snakeskin cowboy boots with her hit, "Don't Come Home A-Drinkin' with Lovin' on Your Mind."

The beauty of dopey country song titles is that it's a participation sport. Anyone can play — and you don't even have to write a song to go with the title. Peter Gzowski, for example, back during the bittersweet years of hosting the nightly television show "90 Minutes Live," once came up with a potential song title that all TV hosts should have embossed on their makeup mirrors.

Gzowski's title ran: "When You Wake Up in the Mornin' and the Makeup on the Pillow Is Yore Own."

Now *that's* hurtin' music! I can't top that, so I'll just steal from another Canadian country classic written and sung by Nova Scotia's own Hank Snow, which is to say, "I'm Movin' On."

A Perfectly Good Explanation

SORRY I'M LATE, but I do have a decent excuse, for a change. You see, I was waiting for a call from the reference library. I wanted them to find me the best excuse ever used by anybody to get out of anything. They never called back and now it's too late, because that's what I wanted to talk about today — excuses. Oh, well, I have one or two that I've rustled up. I suppose I'll have to go with them.

First, let's visit the Halls of Justice. Judges get to hear some pretty good excuses from the poor arraigned wretches before them, trying to avoid fines or jail terms or worse.

Such as the fellow in a Louisville, Kentucky, court last year who pleaded not guilty to a charge of impaired driving with the excuse that he couldn't have been driving because he was legally blind. So who was driving, since police testified he was the only person in the car? That's easy. "My dog, Bud," said the man.

And you know what? He was telling the truth — sort of. Police determined that Bud had indeed been sitting in the passenger seat, dutifully barking each time a traffic light changed. The pair was nabbed only because the car was weaving down the road like a wobbly bowling ball. Keeping the car between the white line and the ditch was not Bud's department. A good excuse? Well, inventive, but not very effective. The court came down hard on the blind driver, but let Bud off with a warning.

When it comes to unusual excuses, there aren't too many that Robert Half hasn't heard. As an employment specialist, Mr. Half became fascinated by the breadth and variety of the "sorry I'm late for work" genre of excuses and began collecting them a few years

93

back. He's got so many that he's published them in a book. What sort of excuses? Well, excuses like "The reason I stayed off work was I thought Halloween was a holiday."

"The dog grabbed my toupee and hid it."

"My pig fell in the furnace."

"My parakeet spoke for the first time, so I waited for him to do it again so that I could tape-record it."

Indeed, when it comes to humans making excuses, Bud the Seeing-Eye co-pilot isn't the only animal that's been fingered as a patsy. There is, for instance, in Mr. Half's book, the story of the pet chicken that got frozen to the driveway during an ice storm. Its owner had to thaw it out and that's why he was late for work. Some chronic excuse makers even employ backup animals. Such as the man who said he was late for work because "My pet python was loose and I had trouble catching it."

Why, asked his boss, didn't he just let the snake roam around the apartment until he came home from work? "Because," said the man, "it might have eaten my parrot."

But I think schoolteachers get to handle some of the most bizarre excuses — excuses that show up in notes from parents or, dare we suggest it, from students pretending to be parents — explaining away a student's absenteeism.

"My son is under the doctor's care and should not take P.E. today. Please execute him."

And another unduly harsh note: "Please excuse Cynthia for being absent. She was sick so I took her to the doctor and had her shot."

"Fred was absent from school yesterday as he had an acre in his side."

Some excuses are positively existential. "Please excuse Johnny for being. It was his father's fault."

Others are, well, suggestive, to say the least. "Please excuse Tim for being absent on Tuesday. He had a cold and could not breed well."

My all-time favourite excuse? Well, I think it's one that appeared in Robert Half's *Book of Excuses*. It was used by a young chap to explain to his boss why he was late for work. He said that the anchor-shaped pendant that he wore on a chain around his neck got caught in his girlfriend's nose and he had to take her to the hospital.

You know, I would have risked the wrath of the Head Nurse for the chance to get just one glimpse of those two, sitting in front of the hospital admissions desk, filling out their hospitalization forms.

Two Cheers for Lawyers

J UST HEARD a new lawyer joke. What's brown and black and looks good on a lawyer? Answer: a doberman.

Boy, you know, I think if I was a lawyer, I'd sue. Somebody's always picking on them! Do you know that just about every culture has jokes, even proverbs, about lawyers? And none of them any too pleasant, either.

Rumanian proverb: The lawyers eat the kernel, the clients get the shell.

Danish proverb: Lawyers and painters can soon change white to black.

German proverb: A lawyer and a wagon wheel must be well greased.

Spanish proverb: Better to be a mouse in a cat's mouth than a man in a lawyer's hands.

Yiddish proverb: Two farmers each claimed to own a cow. While one pulled on its horns and the other pulled on its tail, the cow was milked by a lawyer.

Which is a variation of a joke that used to go around the Canadian schoolyards when I was a kid. "A lawyer," went the joke, "is the guy who, when you get into a fight with another guy, offers to hold your coats. Then when you and the other guy are slugging it out, the lawyer steals the coats."

What are we to call this plague of lawyer-baiting that clearly has worldwide roots — litigophobia? I don't know, but I do know that it's a feisty infestation — and that it's no Johnny-come-lately, either. People have been bad-mouthing lawyers in particular and the legal system in general for quite some time. The European republic of Andorra has a governmental decree that declares, "The appearance in our courts of these learned gentlemen of the law who can make black appear white and white appear black is forbidden." That decree was made law in Andorra in 1864. It's still on the books. In *Henry VI*, Shakespeare has a character give his recipe for the creation of Utopia: "First thing we do, let's kill all the lawyers!"

There is an ancient collection of knowledge called the *Wisdom of Anii* that contains this morsel of advice: "Go not in and out of court that thy name may not stink."

Now I ask you, what have lawyers, a group of folks whose only interests are truth, justice, and twenty-five percent of the settlement, done to deserve that kind of abuse?

I suspect it's not lawyers themselves as much as the system they represent. Someone once said, "Lawyers are just operators of the toll bridge across which anyone in search of justice must pass." Right. And folks who have been across that bridge tend to be a little more cynical and a good deal poorer when they get to the other side.

But in the interests of fair play, equal time, and possibly shaving a few dollars off the legal fee of my next libel defence, I'd like to close with a *good* news story about the law. It concerns a recent British Columbia court ruling in favour of one Mabel Forsythe of Smithers, B.C., who was arrested two years ago for shoplifting. It was a case of mistaken identity; nevertheless, Ms Forsythe had been publicly humiliated. She sued, and the court has ruled in her favour, declaring that she must receive restitution. But here's the kicker. The restitution in this case is going to be . . . a feast. The Gedumden Indian tribe, of which Ms Forsythe is a hereditary chief, has a ritual in which members regain lost face by throwing a huge feast for all clan members. Ms Forsythe intends to observe that custom . . . and the British Columbia County Court has decreed that the Mounties who arrested her and the owners of the store who falsely accused her of theft must pick up the tab for the festivities.

Isn't it comforting to be reminded that Madam Justice, usually blind, can occasionally get a pretty good squint out of her one good eye?

Does Anybody Care about the Farmer Anymore?

E ACH MORNING I wake up surrounded by a lush patchwork quilt of vibrant Southwestern Ontario farm country. I have a forest of pine seedlings on one side of my property, a dairy operation on the other, and my front window looks out over a field of corn more vast than many Muskoka lakes. A five-minute jaunt from my driveway takes me past acres of wheat, hay, barley, sunflowers, and crops I don't even know the names of. The local bestiary includes herds of dairy and beef cattle, flocks of chickens and turkeys, an apiary, two or three trout hatcheries and, unless my nose fails me when the wind is just wrong, a pig farm. My neighbours — many of them at any rate — are second-, third-, and even fourth-generation farmers.

That's where I live. On the other hand I earn my pay cheque toiling in the bowels of the biggest city in the country. Three days a week I drive to the station, board a Via Rail train, and make an hour-and-a-half trip to downtown Toronto.

As odysseys go, mine's not too far behind Dorothy's in *The Wizard of Oz*. I journey from cardinals and blue jays squabbling over sunflower seeds on my verandah to secretaries and punk rockers jostling for seats on the subway. My morning safari begins amid corn silos, quaint old red brick farmhouses, and rickety chicken coops; it ends up in a yammering stew of skyscrapers, multilane expressways, and thickets of high-rise apartment buildings — "people coops," by any other name.

I am trying not to make a value judgement about this. I need and savour both environments. One of the things I like best about my seesaw lifestyle is that it gives me a chance to keep tabs on attitudes in both camps, urban and rural.

It seems to me that farm people by and large can't quite get their minds around the concept that anyone would actually choose to live in the city. They don't hate city people or snicker about them or anything. They just wonder what went wrong to make them turn out that way.

But it's the attitude of city folks towards farmers that really scares me.

They don't seem to have one — an attitude, I mean. Near as I can make out, city people just don't think about farm people much at all.

Well, why should they? Food in the city is cheap and plentiful. It comes to the corner store or supermarket all squeaky clean, graded, and neatly wrapped. Fresh picked or flash frozen. Sliced, diced, and ready for the table. Just heat 'n' serve.

It is difficult, I admit, to hold a Big Mac or a vanilla milkshake in your hand and try to make any kind of connection with a beef feedlot operation outside Schomberg or the owner of a hundred head of Holsteins near Woodstock, but we should try a little harder, because our farmers are in deep, deep trouble.

You don't have to look far to find the evidence. The auctions page of any Saturday edition of the *Kitchener-Waterloo Record* will do. The *Record* is a daily newspaper that serves a goodly swatch of prime Southwestern Ontario farm country. Each Saturday it prints a full page of farm auctions that are coming up. The page I'm looking at lists a dozen such sales happening within the next week. Heaps of bargains — everything from a china toilet seat to a Cockshutt 1255 Diesel tractor; from an antique press-back child's high chair with tray to entire herds of Charolais and Guernseys. And farms, of course. Plenty of good acreage up for grabs. Terms: cash or cheque with proper ID on sale day.

A full page. Just think what it means when a single farmer decides he's had enough and dials the auction house number he's been carrying around for weeks in his wallet. Never mind the crops that will never get planted, the livestock that will never get raised. Think about the faces around the kitchen table some evening when, right after grace he clears his throat and announces huskily, eyes on his plate, "We can't make it. We have to sell the farm." That's what too many of those farm auction ads mean — the end of a whole way of life for a piece of land and the people who worked it.

Why are so many farmers throwing in the towel? Name your poison. Poor markets, restrictive government agencies, asphyxiating interest rates, impossible prices for new farm equipment, the lure of steady well-paid work in factories and towns, not to mention the perennial reefs and shoals of agriculture — frosts, blight, scours, mastitis, hail, drought, floods . . .

The question is not why so many farmers quit but how so many have managed to hang on. The survivors are paying the price for their obstinacy. Authorities note marked increases in marital fights, nervous breakdowns, and child abuse. The Canadian Mental Health Association says that nearly ninety percent of farm families now complain of such stress-related ailments as migraine headaches and ulcers.

Suicides are up, too. In Alberta the rate of self-inflicted deaths among provincial farmers has tripled since 1981.

Some farmers must feel like expiring from sheer disbelief at the way they're portrayed — or ignored — in the media. They read about a University of Manitoba geographer who says the wheat fields of Saskatchewan should be returned to grass — that bison should be allowed to roam once again. Does the geographer know that farmers are the backbone of Saskatchewan — that agriculture is the very foundation of the whole province? Does he acknowledge that those grain farmers who for decades have worked eighteen-hour days to put bread in the bellies of a goodly portion of the humans on this planet might experience some difficulty reincarnating as buffalo shepherds? The article doesn't mention it.

Farmers can read about the dramatic new hormone discovery at Cornell University. It's called somatropin. Experts claim it is going to increase milk production by as much as twenty-five percent per cow. Have the Cornell researchers done any studies on the effects this will have on a dairy industry already plagued by overproduction? The article doesn't say.

Farmers don't have to read the news columns of their newspapers. They can check the real estate sections and find out about all the brand-new subdivisions going up. They may not get to the top of the CN Tower very often, but farmers know that if they did so on a clear day they could see more than half of the best farmland in all of Canada without a pair of binoculars — providing they hurry. Toronto gobbles up three thousand more acres of that prime land every year.

Farmers can read the bad news in billboards too, like the ones on the outskirts of Brantford last summer that read PRIME LAND DIRT CHEAP!

Farmland, of course.

Recently the Toronto *Globe and Mail* ran an article about farming that contained this paragraph, "Farmers have become such a drain on the public purse that academics, bureaucrats, and politicians are beginning to wonder how long the country can afford to support them. And they are beginning to ask "Should Canada get out of farming?"

Now if you were a farmer, wouldn't a statement like that make you want to just step down from your tractor, hand the ignition keys to the nearest academic, bureaucrat, or politician, and walk off into the sunset?

My weekly three-day waltz with the city ends on Friday evening, and one of my small Saturday morning pleasures by way of rural reentry entails poking around the local farmers' market. That's where I buy my weekly supply of orange-yolked, obscenely delicious free-range eggs from a Mennonite farmer. Last week I told him my only farmer joke — the one about the farmer who wins the lottery. In the joke a reporter says, "Mr. Jones, what are you going to do with your million-dollar prize money?" The farmer ponders for a moment and replies, "Waaall, I reckon I'll just keep farmin' till it's all gone."

My Mennonite farmer friend chuckled dutifully and then shook his head. "That's the 1980s version," he said. "In the 1990s version, the reporter asks what he's going to do with the million dollars and the farmer says, 'Waaall, I reckon I'll just pay a couple of bills.'

"Then the reporter says, 'But what about the rest?'

"And the farmer says, 'Oh, the rest will just have to wait, I guess.'"

Nutty Names

I DON'T KNOW if it's true, but I've been told that certain Indian tribes refrain from naming their children at birth. They prefer to have the kids around for a while, until they can settle on a moniker that actually suits the child. Makes perfect sense to me — I think that most of us treat the naming of children entirely too frivolously. Most, but not all. In many Catholic countries, parents are required by law to name their children after saints. Argentina's even tougher. There, all names have to be approved by a civil registrar, and if they don't like the name you've chosen, then you'd better find another one or face jail. Arthur, for instance, would not be acceptable. Arturo might be okay, but not Arthur. Wolfgang would be verboten, as would Brent or Jessica or Gwen — too un-Hispanic. Argentinians are allowed to name a boy Sol after the sun, but they can't name a daughter Luna after the moon. The registry has decided that Luna is just not Argentine enough.

Some national name policies are deadly serious; some swerve right into the ludicrous. In postrevolutionary Russia, Melor was a popular name. M-E-L-O-R, standing for Marx-Engels-Lenin-October-Revolution.

There were also reports of glum-looking children growing up with names like Tractor and Electrification. Which reminds me of the recent reports over Radio Havana that the Cuban government has decided to lighten up a bit in the name department. There is a brand-new law in Cuba that bans "names that could create problems for children when they grow up because they could feel shame or inconvenience." What sort of shameful, inconvenient names? Well, names such as those mentioned by the announcer of twin Cuban girls he knows, girls who answer to the names of Biela and Propela. In English, that translates as Connecting Rod and Propellor. One can appreciate that a schoolgirl registered as Connecting Rod Anderson or a debutante coming out under the name of Propellor Gottlieb is going to run into more than a modest amount of friction.

Not that we here in North America have grounds for smirking. Few places on the planet can compete with us when it comes to weird names. John Traine, who has written a book on the subject, called *Most Remarkable Names*, goes so far as to postulate that America's *only* truly indigenous art is that of the free-form nutty name. Mr. Traine has powerful ammunition to back his case . . . such as Oldmouse Waltz, Eucalyptus Yoho and the magnificent Humperdinck Fangboner. Those are the registered and thoroughly verified names of three living, breathing, cheque-signing Americans. Oldmouse Waltz lives in New Orleans. Eucalyptus Yoho is an oil dealer in Portsmouth, Maine. Humperdinck Fangboner is a timber merchant in Sandusky, Ohio.

Not that Americans get all the points for weird names. There is that Argentine couple who tried to get their favourite name past the aforementioned civil registrar in Buenos Aires. What was the name they wished to call their child? asked the registrar director. "Hey Hoo," they replied. The official consulted his book of unusual but acceptable names. Nope, no Hey Hoo there.

Well, said the couple hastily, Hey Hoo is quite a religious name. It refers to a visitation of the Virgin Mary to Paraguay. The officials consulted with religious authorities. Another blank. Plus a growing suspicion. The parents were grilled as to their real fascination with the name Hey Hoo. Turned out they were avid Beatles fans. Hey Hoo was as close as they could come to the title of their favourite Beatles song, which in Spanish would go "Hey Hude . . . doan mak eet bad . . ."

Pity they weren't fans of American music. They could have named their son Jose after the U.S. national anthem — as in "Jose, can you see . . ."

Chairman of
the Bored

I F BY CHANCE you should one day have the great misfortune to
be browsing by the chip dip and look up to see Dr. Ashley Clarke
bearing down on you, here are a couple of things you could do.

You could pass yourself off as a recently arrived Tamil gas-
meter reader by speaking in tongues and pretending to look for
a gauge.

You could fake cardiac arrest, sudden spinal paralysis, or some
other attention-riveting physical affliction.

You could swiftly light your serviette and toss it in the direction
of the punch bowl on the off chance that it's alcoholic and
inflammable.

You better do something, though, because if that is Dr. Ashley
Clarke bearing — make that boring — down on you, then you're
in big trouble.

Not that the man is without honour. He did receive the Golden
Pillow Award back in 1974. It was in recognition of one of his
lectures, voted most boring of the year. Title: "Mechanical Formal-
ism of Emulsion in an Infinite Viscous Medium."

Sounds like a snore for sure, but what really copped the coveted
Golden Pillow for Dr. Clarke was the closing statement of his
lecture, delivered after two hours of bum-numbing drone from
the doctor. It read, "This only applies in an infinite viscous medium, so in practice it doesn't work."

Now that is boredom breathtaking in its bathos.

Of course, doctors and professors have a sort of licence to be
somewhat boring. It's much less acceptable in other lines of work.
Play writing, for instance. I suppose if Edward Falconer were with

us he could testify to that, but he's not. Mr. Falconer is dead. He died a few years after his play did at Covent Garden on November 19, 1866. The play was called *Oonagh . . . or Lovers of Lismonah.* A double title for a valiant attempt to merge two long, exceedingly tedious Victorian novels into one vibrant stage presentation. Regrettably, the result was a doubly long, stupendously tedious play.

The curtain went up at 7:30 sharp. By 11:00 p.m. the last eyelid in the audience had closed. By midnight only the author's relatives and one or two desperate bag ladies were still in their seats. As the hour hand on the clock staggered towards the three, the stage hands — the stage hands! — held a meeting, took a vote, and lowered the curtain, not to mention the boom, on Falconer's *Oonagh . . . or Lovers of Lismonah.*

Mind you, it's the old "no omelettes without smashed eggs" syndrome. Boring works of art have created wonderful reviews that made up in brevity and wit what their subjects lacked in both departments. Alexander Woolcott went to see a Broadway production entitled *Wham!* He turned in a one-word review: "Ouch!" Back around the turn of the century a play opened at the Duchess Theatre in London with the hopeful title *A Good Time.* Next day the London *Times* carried a two-character review. Under the headline "A Good Time," the review read, in its entirety, "No."

Not my all-time favourite rapier run-through, though . . . that honour goes to the New York critic who had to sit through a play adaptation of a Christopher Isherwood novel. The play was called *I Am a Camera.* The critic's two-word review: "No Leica."

Taking Leisure Seriously

EVERYBODY IS FAMILIAR with the saga of the Ant and the Grasshopper, right? Fairly classic morality fable designed to ease kids into the old Work Ethic harness. Good-for-nothing Grasshopper parties the summer away while stolid, antennae-to-the-grindstone Ant just keeps toiling on, filling the larder with whatever it is well-stocked ant larders are full of. Come first frost, there's the Ant all set to weather the winter in comfort. And there's the Grasshopper hung over, strung out, wondering who turned the thermostat down. Moral: drudgery is good; leisure is suspect at best and probably immoral.

Sounds dopey, but I bought that as a kid. We all did. Didn't have much of a choice. Work is good; play is sinful — that was the prevailing notion back then.

Which makes it all the harder for old codgers like me to warm up to the new work/play ethic — kind of the reverse of the old one. Leisure is where it's at now. Indeed, leisure is so where it's at that it's become a problem. And it figures that if leisure ever did become a problem it would first become a problem in California. Most everything that eventually swamps North America is spawned in California. Windsurfing started there. So did stonewashed Levi's . . . and I think maybe Farrah Fawcett, too.

And now there is Bruce F. Morehouse. Mr. Morehouse is president, general manager, and founding father of an enterprise called The Leisure Company. Know what he does for a living? He tells people . . . how to spend their spare time.

Not just tells them . . . *guides* them. A leisure-stressed client seeking relief first antes up forty bucks to The Leisure Company.

Then he or she is lumbered with a six-part, 240-question Leisure questionnaire. The client fills that out and the results are fed into a computer that masticates the data and eventually spits out a half-dozen spare-time activities most likely to be suitable to the client in question. Still uncomfortable, leisure-wise? No problem. Bruce F. Morehouse or one of his friendly helpful staff will be more than happy to sit down and personally counsel you — talk you through racquetball or square dancing or petit point or whatever your personal leisure dilemma happens to be. "Sometimes," says Bruce F. Morehouse, "we use this time for attitude changing." In a businesslike way, you understand. The tab for personal hands-on leisure counselling will set you back an additional seventy-five bucks an hour.

And what does Bruce F. Morehouse do for leisure activity? Oh, pretty conventional stuff. He plays a couple of rounds of golf once or twice a week, goes for a bike ride, or plays Trivial Pursuit with his wife.

But to keep the really big muscle groups toned up I would imagine he relies on those daily deposit runs to the bank.

Hair Today and Con Tomorrow

YOU KNOW WHAT Richard Nixon's main problem has been all along? Lousy timing. A guy with better timing would've made sure his little band of merry burglars waited until *after* the Watergate security guard made his rounds.

Better timing and Nixon might have been able to overdub a few whistled bars of "Hail to the Chief" to fill in that famous eighteen-minute gap on the White House tapes.

Better timing and Nixon could've made his first bid for the Oval Office in 1992 instead of 1960. Because what sank Nixon in the famous TV debates more than a quarter of a century ago would put him over the top by a landslide today. You know why Nixon got whupped by JFK in the debates, don't you? Five o'clock shadow. Here's Kennedy all scrubbed and spiffy and Ivy League-ish. And there's Dick, looking as if he just slithered in from an all-night snooker tournament.

Lousy timing again. In 1960, a man who looked badly in need of a shave was out. Nowadays that look is *in, in, in.*

Look around. At the movies you've got Sylvester Stallone monosyllable-izing his way through *Rambo II* and *Rocky IV.* On the ice you've got Paul Coffey, on the courts you've got Bjorn Borg, and on the Boob Tube you've got "Miami Vice"-nik Don Johnson — and what do they all have in common? Chins that are gritty enough to refinish furniture with, that's what. The nether reaches of their mugs all look like corn fields, postharvest.

The un-Shicked cheek is suddenly chic.

We're not talking beards here, you understand. Just beginnings of beards. Two, three days' growth, tops. Stubble.

Why would a guy choose to look as if he just rode into town in an open boxcar? Well, supposedly because it looks rebellious and virile. Some of the latest adherents to the fad have been carolling and trilling about their "liberation" from the daily shaving ritual.

Aha . . . but this is where Irony raises its unique rotary-action head. Tempus tends to fugit. Five o'clock shadow becomes eleventh-hour fungal infection. Three days' growth may be sexy stubble. Six days' growth looks like Yasser Arafat.

Thus is born a whole new etiquette for the nurturing and maintenance of the grizzle-jowled look.

The owner of a *très, très* New York hair salon advocates electric clippers to keep those chins just blue and nubbly enough. And Patrice Serrani, grooming editor of *Gentlemen's Quarterly* — yes, *GQ* now offers tips on achieving the derelict look — recommends shaving in downward strokes, *with* rather than against the beard . . . the better to achieve a nonclose shave and thus the look of which we speak. This doesn't sound like liberation from a daily ritual to me. It sounds like a bigger pain than a cold water shave with a linoleum knife.

Nope, I figure if you really want to get away from that morning bloodletting ceremony, then let it all hang out. Grow yourself a full beard. By not shaving at all you'll gain five minutes a day (that's a full two weeks over the next ten years) — plus, you get insulation for the winter, camouflage for zits, and something to do with your hairbrush if, like me, the barren lands begin just north of your eyebrows.

Not Dick Nixon, though. I don't figure there's much point in Dick's growing a beard this late in the game. I think he should go with his strength. Call up the producer of "Miami Vice" and ask if he and his famous muzzle can do a guest appearance on the show.

Wouldn't have to be a major part. Nixon could play a member of the kitchen staff, say, in some sleazy Florida burger joint that's really a drug front.

It'll be great! Crocket and Tubbs could burst through the swinging kitchen doors . . . there's Dick in a chef's hat, hunched over the stove. Crocket levels his cannon . . . Dick raises his arms in that famous double-V sign, looks straight into the camera and says:

"I am not a cook."

Open Wide and Say Bah!

OKAY, OKAY, I admit I'm a little crankier than usual. I'm sorry I burned rubber out my driveway and snarled at the security guard in the CBC parking lot. But there's a reason.

I've got to go to the dentist this afternoon.

Why does it never get better? I've been deking and dodging dentists for the best part of four decades, even though I know that there are *lots* of things in the world worse than a dental appointment. Acute appendicitis is worse. A divorce lawyer is worse. And yet I would rather be seasick than go to the dentist this afternoon. I would rather rewrite my grade 13 physics exam. I would rather be lashed spread-eagled and cupless to a hockey net facing a Fetisov/Makarov two on one — I would prefer to do most anything rather than lower my quaking corpus into that leatherette-and-chrome torture chamber this afternoon.

Bad enough that it's always been bad — I think it's getting worse. It's getting worse because the dentists are losing patience with the patients. Dentists are getting as cranky as I feel this morning!

You heard about Michael Mendelson? He's a dentist in Long Island and he's fed up with the dentist jokes. All because of a monologue Johnny Carson did on "The Tonight Show."

All Carson said was that a recent study had reported that American dentists were going out of business. Then Carson added, "Imagine dentists going out of business. I haven't been so happy about a group disbanding since the Gestapo."

Michael Mendelson, D.D.S., didn't laugh. He sued instead, demanding $5 million U.S.

Plus an apology.

Carson did not pay the five million. Perhaps he's putting it aside for a rainy alimony suit, but he did deliver an on-air apology to Michael Mendelson . . . but out of the side of his mouth, as it were.

Dentistry, Carson related with a smirk, has indeed an honourable tradition, stretching all the way back to the Spanish Inquisition. And dentists work hard, said Carson. Why, they only take three holidays a year: Thanksgiving, Christmas, and the Marquis de Sade's birthday. Besides, said Carson, going to the dentist is really, when you get right down to it, kinda fun.

"What better way to spend an afternoon," asked Carson, "than reclining in a dentist's chair listening to a six-thousand RPM high-speed drill, smelling your tooth enamel burn as clouds of smoke billow out of your mouth?"

Yeah, well, thanks for that, Johnny. I don't know how Michael Mendelson took your apology, but it sure makes me feel good about my appointment this afternoon.

I'll go . . . I'll go. Because there is, when all the snickering dies down, one thing worse than going to the dentist: a toothache that won't go away at two-thirty in the morning. As the poet Irving Layton once wrote, "When I realized that a toothache caused me more agony than all the wretchedness and misery of Africa and Asia, I resolved to give up worrying my head about man's destiny and to see my dentist more often."

Right, Irving. Thanks for the inspirational one-liners, Johnny. I'm putting on my stiff upper lip now. And Michael Mendelson, D.D.S., if you read this . . .

I mean that tongue-in-cheek, eh?

The Wolf Was Railroaded

I'VE FIGURED OUT why I scribble for newspapers rather than bilking widows and orphans out of their life savings — I'm not smart enough to be a lawyer.

One of the sophisticated legal concepts I've never been able to wrap my rough, untutored mind around is the not-guilty-by-reason-of concept.

Let us say a guy is arrested and charged with murder. A corpse has been found with its head bashed in. Accused was discovered with brain-splattered ball peen hammer in hand. Accused has written thirty poems, half a novel, and an exclusive article for the *Toronto Sun* on how much he hates the deceased. Seven nuns, two airline pilots, a couple of NHL referees, and a Supreme Court bailiff swear they witnessed the accused bludgeon the victim into the hereafter.

So what happens when the case comes to court?

Something that looks like an overfed otter in a $600 three-piece stands up and intones, "Milud, my client pleads not guilty by reason of insanity."

My problem is with the word *guilty*. I figure if I cream somebody with a hammer, then I am guilty of creaming that person with a hammer, no matter what my mental state might have been at the time of the creaming.

Our system of jurisprudence sees it differently, and I've never been able to understand why. But that's okay — I've never understood f-stops, metric conversion, or slam dancing, either.

In any case, I'm not the only one who's in the dark about our legal system. Here's an "amended fable" that I received in the mail last week:

Once upon a time, there lived a little girl called Little Red Riding Hood. One day her mother asked her to take a basket of fruit to her grandmother. A wolf, lurking in the bushes, overheard the conversation and decided to take a shortcut to the grandmother's house. The wolf disposed of the grandmother, then dressed in her nightgown and jumped into bed to await the little girl. Little Red Riding Hood arrived but soon became suspicious. The wolf tried to grab her, but she escaped and ran screaming from the cottage. A woodcutter working nearby heard her cries, rushed to the rescue, and killed the wolf with his axe. All the townspeople proclaimed the woodcutter a hero.

But at the inquest, the following emerged:

1. The wolf had never been advised of his rights.
2. The Wildlife Federation determined that the wolf was a subspecies, might be endangered, and hence should have been accorded more consideration.
3. The woodcutter had made no warning swings before striking the fatal blow.
4. The Animal Lovers Association submitted that killing a wolf with an axe (as seal pups with clubs) was cruel and unusual punishment, and that the woodcutter should have adopted a more humane method of dispatching the wolf.
5. The Citizens' Liberties Association stressed the point that though the act of eating Grandma may have been in bad taste, the wolf was only "doing his thing" and thus did not deserve the death penalty.
6. A schoolfriend of Red Riding Hood testified that she was "a bit of a tease," and a neighbour of Grandma's gave evidence that Grandma had "had occasional male visitors" and may have behaved in a seductive manner.
7. The Forest Bar Association contended that the killing of the grandmother should be considered self-defence, inas-

much as it could be reasonably assumed that Grandma had resisted and might, given the opportunity, have killed the wolf.

On the basis of these considerations, it was decided that there would have been no valid charges against the wolf. Moreover, the woodcutter was indicted for assault with a deadly weapon, with more serious charges under consideration. Several nights later, his cottage was burned to the ground by a person or persons unknown. One year from the date of "The Incident at Grandma's," her cottage was made into a shrine for the wolf that had bled and died there. All the village officials spoke at the dedication, but it was Red Riding Hood who gave the most touching tribute. She said that while she had been selfishly grateful for the woodcutter's intervention, she realized in retrospect that she had overreacted. As Red Riding Hood knelt and placed a wreath in honour of the brave wolf, there wasn't a dry eye in the forest.

As I said, that "amended fable" arrived in my letter box last week. The best thing about it is the letterhead on the note that came with it. The letterhead reads: "Morris Cherneskey, Q.C., Barrister and Solicitor."

A lawyer laughing at his profession. It's almost enough to renew one's faith in the species.

Privies of
Privilege

THERE IS ONE TINY TREMOR — a mini-*tsunami*, if you will — eddying out of the Jimmy Tammy Bakker Sex Drug Brainwash Scandal Swindle — that no one has paid much attention to yet. I'm talking about the spotlight that the whole affair has fixed on state-of-the-art bathroom fixtures. Much has been made of the fact that the Bakker biffy features gold-plated plumbing. Well, I'm with Jim and Tammy on this one. Big deal, I say. That's nothing.

Bigger people than the Bakkers have devoted time and money to their personal privies. Former U.S. President William Howard Taft, for one bigger person. Why, the first thing President Taft did on moving into the White House in 1909 was to have the Presidential tub ripped out and his personally customized porcelain wallow installed. Actually that was the *second* thing Taft did. His preceding move was to jump into the original White House tub and wedge his 350-pound body so thoroughly that White House pages had to be summoned to winkle the Presidential carcass free.

President Taft was not the first to try to turn the Saturday night scrub into a quality experience. Way back in the nineteenth century some forward thinker in France brought out *La Naiade*, a newspaper specifically designed for perusal when the suds were dancing over the reader's sternum.

Unlike newspapers even today, *La Naiade* did not decompose to pulpy flotsam at the first kiss of bathwater. That's because *La Naiade* was printed on . . . rubber. Brilliant, *n'est-ce pas?* Apparently not. *La Naiade* ran for only a short while before it . . . sank.

But rubber dailies, President-size tubs, gold-plated hot and cold taps . . . all that pales beside bathroom splendours that are available in the market place right now for the ablutionally discerning. Take Environment Masterbath, the flagship product from Kohler Company, bathroom designers for the world. Environment Masterbath is a completely enclosed unit that delivers sunshine (by sunlamp), rain (via myriad out-of-sight shower heads), wet heat (for steambath fanciers), and dry heat (for sauna lovers). Did I forget the six-jet whirlpool? The inlaid teak panelling? The pop-up stereo panel with recessed speakers? *And* the gold-plated faucets? Heh, heh . . . Environment Masterbath makes the Jim and Tammy Watercloset look like a Petro-Canada pitstop — and it's a steal at only $40,000 U.S.

Which, truth to tell, makes it far too intimidating for my modest requirements. When it comes to lavatorial perks I'm kinda rough and ready. Very much like Billy Wilder.

Once when the American film director was heading for France to supervise the opening of his production *Some Like It Hot*, Wilder's wife, who had just returned from Europe, asked him to send back some Charvet ties plus that quintessentially French bathroom fixture, a bidet.

The crusty Wilder grunted assent and sailed for Paris. A week or so later his wife received a telegram from Paris. It read: "CHARVET TIES ON WAY STOP IMPOSSIBLE TO OBTAIN BIDET STOP SUGGEST HANDSTAND IN SHOWER STOP."

PART 3

Some of My Best Friends Are Furred, Finned, or Feathered (And I Don't Mean Madonna)

Our Symbol —
The Rat

I BELIEVE I have discovered the very headwaters whence springeth Canada's renowned reputation for meekness and compliance beneath and below the norm. It's our national mascot, the beaver. If Canada wants to play hardball with the big guys, then the buck-toothed rodent with the bug eyes has got to go.

That revelation struck me while browsing through a book entitled *The Bestiary: A Book of Beasts, Being a Translation from the Latin Bestiary of the Twelfth Century.* That's where I came across the following:

> This is an animal called the *Beaver*, none more gentle, and his testicles make a capital medicine. For this reason . . . when he notices that he is being pursued by the hunter, he removes his own testicles with a bite, and casts them before the sportsman, and thus escapes by flight. What is more, if he should again happen to be chased by a second hunter, he lifts himself up and shows his members to him, and the latter, when he perceives the testicles to be missing, leaves the Beaver alone . . . The creature is called a Beaver (Castor) because of the castration.

It is difficult to guess just which nonprescription chemicals the twelfth-century reporter who recorded those observations might have been ingesting. Beavers, of course, do no such thing. They couldn't if they wanted to, as their testicles are internal. And yet the name — Castor — and the image — wimpy — endure.

Well, doesn't the foregoing sound like a fair metaphorical reprise for the faltering diffidence our country displays on the international stage? Bush denounces, Thatcher chastizes, other nations preen and strut and posture . . . and here comes Bucky the Honest Broker, hiking up his guard hairs, exclaiming in a shrill falsetto, "See? No threat here! We're harmless! Don't mind us, folks, we're just here to check the waterworks!"

It's ironic that Canadians, who have been fighting the stereotype of being hewers of wood and drawers of water, should select as their symbol the original hewer of wood and, well, dammer of water. America has the majestic eagle, the Soviet Union the mighty bear. Great Britain gives equal time to ferocious lions and stubborn bulldogs; Frenchmen line up behind a comely and capable-looking Amazon called Liberty . . .

We chose a rat.

A healthy rat, I grant you. A clean-living, outdoorsy, industrious, and unusually clean rat — but a rat for all that.

And not a terribly bright one, either. Before the rapaciousness of the European fur traders decimated their numbers, beavers were so plentiful and docile that Indians knocked them off with sticks. After three centuries of hot pursuit, the beaver is only marginally more prudent, still easy prey for pelt hunters with a single-shot .22 or the most rudimentary of traps.

Back in the 1700s a North American Indian with a finely honed sense of drollery remarked to a Jesuit priest, "The beaver does everything perfectly well; it makes kettles, hatchets, swords, knives, bread; and in short it makes everything."

In short, the Indian was absolutely right; Europeans paid well for the beaver. In the long term, it was quite a different story. The traders brought dazzling luxuries and captivating trinkets the likes of which the Indians had never known. Mind you, they'd never known smallpox, typhus, venereal disease, alcoholism, or lust for money, either. They got those, too.

Perhaps the most sinister stowaway that sneaked from the *canots du nord* into the Indian encampments was an abstract one: total dependence on a single, fragile industry. In the early years of the nineteenth century an Indian chief saw it all coming and laid it out for explorer David Thompson:

"We are now killing the beaver without any labor," he said. "We are now rich, but shall soon be poor, for when the Beaver are destroyed we have nothing to depend on to purchase what we want for our families. Strangers now overrun our country with their iron traps, and we, and they will soon be poor."

That was about the size of it. In the early 1800s the fur trade collapsed as precipitously as it had begun. The furs were suddenly too far inland and too sparse to chase. Relations were dodgy among the superpowers of the day — England, France, and those belligerent Yankee upstarts to the south. And anyway, Europe didn't seem all that interested in beaver hats anymore. Some enterprising haberdasher had come up with a technique of lacquering silk and turning it into headgear that was lighter, cheaper, and almost instantly *à la mode*.

Many fortunes were made during the fur trade — none of them by the Indians who were the very spine of it. In the waning years of the enterprise, a Saulteaux chief by the name of Peguis looked around and lamented:

"Before you whites came to trouble the ground, our rivers were full of fish and woods of deer. Our creeks abounded with beavers and our plains were covered with buffaloes. But now we are brought to poverty. Our beaver are gone forever . . ."

Well, not quite, Peguis. It certainly looked as if things would wind up that way as the beaver waddled to the edge of extinction. But we all overlooked that one activity the beaver practices even more diligently than dam building. It's a phenomenon to which human eyes are not privy, going on, as it does, behind the impermeable walls of the beaver lodge. The mechanics of the operation are the beavers' secret; all we know is that, whatever the beavers do in there, it results in an awful lot of little beavers. The animal is so prolific that despite continued trapping, encroaching suburbs, intruding highways, shrinking wetlands, air pollution, water degradation, acid rain, the question of Palestinian autonomy — despite all the Bad Things that seem to mitigate against all that is good and true these days — the beaver is flourishing.

Better than that — what used to be our endangered species of indigenous dam builders has become . . . well, just a damned nuisance, actually. In Saskatchewan the beavers are creating such agricultural havoc that the provincial government recently launched a Nuisance Beaver Program to prune the rodents' furry ranks.

Government sanction to kill the National Symbol? Isn't that . . . un-Canadian, sorta?

Don't ask me — ask Argentina. Preferably on a clean, well-lit street among plenty of reliable witnesses.

Argentinians know all about our national emblem. Back in 1946 the Canadian government gave that country twenty-five pairs of the critters as a gesture of international goodwill. I don't know the Spanish for "Go forth and multiply," but the beavers must have figured it out pretty quickly. When their travelling cages were opened they took one look around, saw a land full of gnawable timber, dam-able rivers, and Glory be, not a natural predator in sight . . . and they went to work. And play. In the next forty years Canada's furry foreign aid chalked up an Argentine rap sheet that included everything from chewing down the country's softwood forests to flooding valuable sheep pastures to disrupting the spawning patterns of trout.

The beavers also obviously did a lot of cuddling on those nippy Argentine nights. Authorities there would dearly love to gather up Canada's gift and pop it in the mail in a plain brown carton marked Return to Sender. Trouble is, the original twenty-five beavers have swollen to an estimated *25,000*.

Beavers. I know (only casually) a pair that live in a pond about five minutes walk from my back door. Every once in a while when the world gets too much with me, I wander over there and sit on a log to watch them doing their yardwork. They ignore me, just as they ignore the busy highway nearby, the kids noisily hunting frogs, and the Air Canada 747 from Winnipeg that drones overhead each afternoon about 3:30.

My beavers couldn't care less. They just go on shuttling across their custom-made pond, catering to the Unseen Foreman as they have for centuries — millennia perhaps. Living. Thriving. Not terrorizing or subjugating or proselytizing or taunting or threatening or humiliating or patronizing their neighbours. Just doing what they do as well as they can do it.

Not a bad lifestyle . . . for a rat.

Not a bad example for a country, either.

Boys and Dogs

A boy can learn a lot from a dog: obedience,
loyalty, and the importance of turning around
three times before lying down.
                                    — *Robert Benchley*

W ITHOUT BECOMING overly sober-sided on the subject, I'd like
to point out that a boy can learn a whole lot more than that
from dogs. I speak if not as an authority then at least as a veteran
who has at one time or another pampered and paper trained,
coaxed and cursed, romped with and stumbled over five or six
in-house mutts. Some of them were better than others, but I
remember even the most forgettable of them with infinitely greater
clarity than, say, anybody in my grade 10 class.

The first dog in my life was Willy, short for Wilhelmina. As with
most dogs, Willy came to me in a casual and unpremeditated way.
She was a white-and-black vaguely fox-terrierish pup that waddled out of the folds of my sister's raincoat and onto our kitchen
linoleum one evening when I was still a preschooler. Willy had
been kidnapped. My sister had rescued her from a revolving
restaurant stool. Her drunken owner kept trying to set Willy on
the stool and Willy, not surprisingly, kept falling off. After the third
swan dive, my sister pounced. She scooped up the pup, tongue-
lashed the drunk, and swept out the door and down the street
before he had time to hiccup.

Willy was a squat and stumpy pooch that grew to become . . .
well, squatter and stumpier, actually. There wasn't much that was
remarkable about Willy, aside from her predilection for walking
on three legs as opposed to four. Whenever she got going at a
pretty good clip, Willy would just tuck a rear leg — sometimes the
left, sometimes the right — up close to her belly and chug along

on the other three. She wasn't favouring an injury and she didn't limp. In fact, you wouldn't even know about the reserve limb unless you actually counted the paws that were hitting the ground. Willy on three legs could stay ahead of the four-legged competition, even when she was in heat.

Except once. Some anonymous canine Lothario had his way with Willy on at least one occasion. The result was a litter of six puppies, one of which died at birth, four of which went to other homes, and the last of which stayed home with Momma. And me. My older sisters were moving on to more mature pastimes — notably boys. Consequently the pup was pretty well exclusively mine. I chose him mostly because of the sooty patch of hair that surrounded his right eye. I dubbed him Shiner, of course. I was eight or nine years old, and the name struck me as the very acme of wit.

For many years we did all the things that kids and dogs growing up together do — things involving rabbits and sticks and tennis balls and mock battles on the grass. I still remember the terrible day Shiner reappeared after a three-day absence.

He staggered stiff-legged across the lawn. He was hideously emaciated and his eyes were full of pain and focussed off somewhere that I couldn't see. I kept stroking his head and offering him water that he couldn't drink until he died later that evening. Distemper.

There were community dogs, too — ones that I didn't own but spent more time with than their owners did. I remember a German shepherd named Rocky. He was the Cary Grant of dogdom — the kind of dog that gives German shepherds a good name. Rocky was bright and alert. His nose was wet and his ears stood up and he had those big chestnut-coloured eyes you could practically curl up in. He also had a butler complex. Rocky would approach visitors at the end of the driveway and escort them up to the front door by gently taking their wrist in his massive maw. A bone china teacup would have been safe in that mouth, but first-time visitors, looking down at one hundred-odd pounds of magnificently conditioned police dog, weren't always aware of that. I still remember baby-sitting for Rocky's folks one night and opening the front door to find Rocky on the porch with a strange man in tow. The man was sweating heavily. He was also on his knees. "Dog!" he managed to gasp out, and then, "Arm!" Over a calming pot of tea, he explained that he was a real estate agent and had been checking house numbers from the end of the driveway when he'd suddenly experienced a . . . constricting sensation between his right forearm and his briefcase. It was only Rocky, trying to be helpful.

The real estate agent panicked and started to trot towards the porch light. Rocky deduced that his guest wanted to go faster, so he picked up the pace. Trot became canter, canter became gallop. It's a cruel thought, but I have often wished I'd been able to videotape the last few yards of that incredible journey. I can visualize the real estate agent, fedora gone, overcoat flaring out behind him, briefcase bouncing through the gravel as he lurched along in a kind of desperate running half crouch, his arm clamped in the mouth of a huge dog that thought this was a wonderful game.

Rocky had a kennel colleague named Mike, also a German shepherd, but as different from Rocky as a rink rat is from Wayne Gretzky. Mike always reminded me of one of those B-movie characters played by Sal Mineo — tough kid from the slums who scrabbles through life with a chip on his shoulder and Don't Tread on Me tattooed on his forearm. Mike was one of those there-but-for-the-grace-of-God dogs. Where Rocky's coat was smooth and lustrous, Mike's was dull and kind of kinky along the spine. Rocky had eyes that made you want to sit down and tell him your troubles. Mike's eyes were furtive and shifty. Mike was the kind of dog that you instinctively walked around in a wide semicircle, with your hands in your pockets. I liked Mike, but I didn't entirely trust him.

There were other dogs in my life. I remember a dippy Dalmatian named Duchess who had one blue eye and one brown eye and not a lot of grey matter behind either of them. There was a pseudo-Labrador named Chris that I inherited in midlife (hers). Chris was mortally terrified of anything that could conceivably be mistaken for a rifle. This included yardsticks, fishing rods, garden rakes, snow shovels, French bread — anything that was long and thin and carried by humans. One look and Chris would hurl herself under the verandah where she would stay, whimpering for hours. I always regretted that I couldn't find a Freudian vet for Chris.

124

Ah, but then there was Angus.

I found him in a Cabbagetown pet store in the spring of 1973, just hours away from a one-way trip to the Humane Society. Instead he got to ride out of the store in my coat pocket. What came into my life as an animated dustball grew to become a full-fledged sheep dog. We called him Angus because of his obvious lineage, a certain Celtic canniness in his expression plus the fact that I purchased him for a bottle of Cutty Sark. We spent the first two years of his life together in Southern Ontario and the next decade in Thunder Bay.

Magical wouldn't be too strong a word to describe Angus. Total strangers would smile at the sight of him and come up to pat him on the head. It was reciprocal. Angus had uncritical tolerance for the entire human race. He loved everybody on sight. He was totally untrainable, but it didn't matter because aside from shedding a few bales of hair each spring, he never did anything objectionable.

Unless you happened to believe strongly in obedience and dog tricks. Angus did not deign to chase balls or fetch sticks. If commanded to Sit Up or Beg or Heel or Roll Over, he would look at you with large molten chocolate eyes that seemed to say, "Surely you don't mean me?" Then he would discreetly look away, pretending your descent into bad taste never happened.

I never figured out what Angus thought cats and rabbits and wild birds were — oddly built children, I suspect. All I know is, he might sniff them or nudge them with his nose or even put his head down between his front paws with his bum in the air, tail swishing like a feathery metronome, but he would never chase them. Bad form.

As for guard dog duties, Angus only barked at family members. To strangers, he was Mother Teresa. I have the eyewitness account of a next door neighbour who swears she saw Angus licking the hands and faces of a gang of late-night thieves trying to steal a tent from my backyard.

Angus was a flop as a hunting dog and a failure as a watchdog. He was also, paws down, the finest four-footed friend I ever had. Last summer as we prepared to move from Thunder Bay back to Southern Ontario, I worried about how a twelve-year-old dog would handle the arduous two-day car trip.

It turned out not to be a problem. Angus died in his favourite armchair on the front porch two days before the moving vans came.

E. B. White, the great American essayist, once wrote, "I can still see my first dog in all the moods and situations that memory has filed him away in. For six years he met me at the same place after school and convoyed me home — a service he thought up himself. A boy doesn't forget that sort of association."

Indeed he doesn't — no matter how old the boy might be. We have a new house now and a new dog to go with it. His name is Rufus, and the pet store he came from insists he's an Australian shepherd. He doesn't look much like an Australian shepherd. He looks like a cross between a border collie and a dingo, but that's all right. He has a good spirit and boundless energy and a pair of absurd ears that seem to rotate independently like radar dishes. He is still a chuckle-headed puppy who digs in flowerbeds, gnaws on table legs, gets swatted routinely by the family cat for his impertinence, and carries off anything he can fit in his mouth. But he's growing up. This week his voice is changing from puppy whimpers to a surprisingly deep-chested bay, the sound of which frightens him more than whatever it is he imagines he sees or hears out there. Rufus has bonded, as well. He looks to the adults of the household to feed him and let him in and out and make sure the water bowl is topped up, but his heart incontestably belongs to a young male resident by the name of Danny.

A boy and his dog. It's a corny, overworked theme, but it happens. It's happening right now, as I type this. I can see Rufus on the lawn, looking towards the front gate. His right ear is cocked, the left sits crumpled at half mast. From the way his head lists eastward I know that he's listening for the growl of the school bus as it rounds the last bend before our place. In a moment he'll start emitting little yips and his tail will thump and he'll *boing* down the lawn like a springbok to greet his master.

A boy and his dog. If Dan's life unfolds like most boys' lives, Rufus will be only the first of several canine chums.

But in countless small and immeasurable ways, he'll always be the best.

Dairy Diary

CANADIANS ARE BY AND LARGE a cheerful lot. We cheer hockey teams, the return of summer, and "Front Page Challenge." So I'm wondering . . . isn't it time we devoted a least two and a half cheers to the cow?

I mean your ordinary, run-of-the-mill, pasture-variety Ayrshire, Holstein-Friesian, Jersey, Guernsey, Shorthorn, Brown Swiss dairy cow. Just think for a moment what we owe to this, umm, lady. Milk, of course. And cream and butter and cheese and all the dairy products. And also — oh, unkind cut — steaks and roasts and various dishes of meat. Oh, I know that milkers are milkers and beef cattle are beef cattle, but where do you think beef cattle come from? From beef *cows*. We also take the hide from her back, the hairs from her tail, the glue from her hooves, and a host of pharmaceutical byproducts it would take the rest of this piece to list. Oh, yes, and lest we forget, the cow gives us one more precious gift on her brief wander through this pasture of tears. Little cows. To start the cycle all over again.

But cows don't get the respect they deserve. They're considered stupid and docile. Stupid? The Moscow Circus has trained a team of cows to play a creditable game of soccer. Docile? Next time we're alone, remind me to show you the two parallel divots in the flesh above my right knee. Picked those up in an alley at the Ontario Public Stockyards. From the left rear hoof of a "docile" Holstein cow.

Cows used to get more respect. In Anglo-Saxon times the penalty for insulting the king's bard was six cows and eight pence. In 1740, a cow was tried and hanged in Paris for sorcery. (Jumping over the moon, perhaps?) Doesn't matter. The point is, the French respected the cow enough to think it capable of sorcery.

But such respect is long gone. In fact, these days we're more inclined to contempt than respect. I just read an environmental report that heaps a little more abuse on their poor horned heads. Now the cow's getting blamed for a methane buildup in the atmosphere. Seems that despite its four stomachs, the cow only digests about half of what it eats. As for the rest, well . . . cows get gas. Methane gas. It comes out in bovine burps. Scientists have determined (I don't even want to think how) that your average cow burps about three-quarters of a pound of methane gas a day. They also estimate that the billion — that's *b* as in "co-bossy" billion — plus cows on the planet put about 325,000 tons of methane into the atmosphere every day. The scientists fear that all that methane is contributing to an overall global temperature increase . . . which accentuates the Greenhouse Effect, and poor old Elsie, minding her business, chewing her cud, outstanding in her field, every once in a while firing off a discreet belch, is getting blamed for it all.

There is one bright spot in the whole story. A fellow in the farming community of Breslau, Ontario, an ex-dairyman, as a matter of fact, by the name of Thomas Hagey, has come to the cow's defence. Thomas is in the magazine publishing business. A few years ago he gave the world a swine-oriented monthly called *Playboar.* No, I'm not making this up. And now Mr. Hagey has decided that what's swill for the sow can be fodder for the cow. He's brought out a new magazine dedicated exclusively to our boon bovine companion.

Name of the magazine? *Cowsmopolitan,* of course.

Hey! Could be worse. He might have called it *Mooclean's.* Or *Breeder's Digest.* Or *East Village Udder.*

Old Prickly

Among the porcupines, rape is unknown.

A Canadian writer by the name of Greg Clark made that observation at least half a century ago. It marks one of the very few times anyone's bothered to even notice the humble porky, much less enshrine him in print.

Not the only time, though. Thumb through your copy of *Hamlet* until you find the part where the melancholy Dane gets chatted up by the ghost:

> *I could a tale unfold whose lightest word*
> *Would harrow up thy soul, freeze thy young blood,*
> *Make thy two eyes, like stars, start from their spheres,*
> *Thy knotted and combined locks to part*
> *And each particular hair to stand on end,*
> *Like quills upon the fretful porpentine.*

Porpentine. How typical of the porcupine's Sad Sack run of luck that in his one shot at literary immortality, Shakespeare spells his name wrong.

I always felt sorry for porcupines. They are the gentlest of creatures and, it must be said, one of the dumbest. Nature gave them neither brain nor brawn nor fang nor claw. Their eyesight is pathetic, their speed a joke. All they have to defend themselves against predators are quills, needle sharp and barbed.

Approximately 36,000 per porcupine.

It must work out pretty well because there are plenty of porcupines around. I'm told that the smarter coyotes, fishers and wolverines have learned to flip porcupines over, exposing the soft underbelly, but most of the animals that try messing with porcupines aren't that creative. The last three dogs I've owned, for instance. They all wound up with quills in their paws and their snouts — and a decided aversion to bothering porcupines ever again.

Quills serve the porcupine pretty well against his natural enemies, but they are not infallible. Each time I drive to the city I pass two, three, sometimes half a dozen prickly grey-black mounds on the pavement. Porcupines that couldn't shuffle across the road fast enough to avoid being kayoed by cars or trucks.

Against a speeding Dunlop radial, quills aren't worth a damn.

Funny animal, the porcupine. An old Finnish bushworker I knew up in Thunder Bay used to call them "the greenhorn's friend." He explained that porcupines had kept many a lost hunter or prospector from starving to death. He said that even a greenhorn with a broken leg could probably knock a porcupine out of a tree, kill it with a stick, and get some meat in his belly.

Well, the porcupine may be the greenhorn's friend but he's not exactly buddy-buddy with a lot of camp and cottage owners I know. That's because of the porkies' addiction to anything salty.

And I mean anything. If a human hand has touched it, that's like chip dip for the porcupine. They'll gnaw their way through shovel handles, paddles, canoe gunwhales, outhouse doors — you name it, the porcupine will take a chunk out of it. He's got the tools for the job: four chisellike incisors backed up by a set of sixteen ridged cheek teeth that can grind down just about anything the incisors bite off.

For all the damage a porcupine can do, you seldom hear people cursing them the way they curse wolves and rats and groundhogs. I wonder why that is? Maybe it's because we all feel a little bit sorry for the porcupine. He is so awkward, so clumsy, so slow, and so flat-out dim-witted.

Perhaps he reminds us of the closet nerd that lives in all of us.

The poor hapless porcupine even makes a hash of romance. Peacocks and ruffed grouse strut and perform dances for their mating rituals. Moose trumpet. Deer and mountain goats have skull-bashing gladitorial contests. Even humans lay on candlelight, wine, and a little Debussy on the stereo.

What does the porcupine do?

Well, part of the mating ritual of the porcupine involves the male drenching his would-be life mate with urine.

Is this to make her, in some perversely porcupine way, more attractive to him? No. Biologists figure the point of the golden shower is to deter any other possible suitors.

Figures.

Let me leave you with the only porcupine riddle I know. It's not magnificent as riddles go, but hey, we're talking porcupines here, remember?

Question: How do porcupines make love?

Answer: Verrrrrrrrry carefully.

A Kind Word for Sturnis Vulgaris

IT'S PROBABLY MY IMAGINATION, but every morning when I go for a walk — every single morning! — it seems as if more of them have moved in overnight. Every morning I look around and say to myself, "There goes the neighbourhood." Sure enough . . . they've taken up residence across the street . . . they've moved in next door. They've even taken over the vacant lot a few doors down.

I don't have anything against foreigners, but I've done research on these immigrants, and I'm not the only one who considers them suspicious. John Mackenzie in his book called them, "thoroughly unpleasant . . . dark, and ugly." And in his guide, John Dennis dismisses them as "cantankerous bullies . . . one of the most quarrelsome and aggressive members of an Old World family."

Before the phone rings off the hook with calls from custodians of the Canadian Charter of Rights and Freedoms, I should explain that Mr. Mackenzie's book is called *The Complete Outdoorsman's Guide to Birds of Canada and Eastern North America*; Mr. Dennis's book is entitled *A Complete Guide to Bird Feeding . . .* and the unsavoury character under discussion here is *Sturnis vulgaris . . .* a k a the common starling.

You all know that chap I speak of . . . he's black and spotted, with iridescent green and purple overtones. He has a variety of songs, a multiplicity of hangouts, and is considered by most human beings to be an all-round pain in the neck. Starlings travel in large rowdy gangs that can strip an orchard, raddle a garden, or speckle a patio in less time than it takes to say Alfred Hitchcock.

Starlings are not appreciated. Even bird lovers go out of their way to suggest devious methods to foil and discourage the starling. Farmers invent means of harassing them and town councils dream up ways of diverting them to other municipalities. The starling doesn't have a human friend in the world. What a sad fate for a bird with the very loftiest of origins. Did you know that we in North America can thank Shakespeare for the starling? Indirectly, anyway. Eugene Scheillfin is the man who really deserves our appreciation. Back in the last century, Scheillfin (a lover of birds and the Bard) took it on himself to bring to this continent every bird mentioned anywhere in the works of Shakespeare. Oh, joy untrammelled! This meant peacocks and skylarks . . . finches and thrushes. It also meant noting Hotspur in *Henry IV* Part I, act 1, scene 3, saying: "I'll have a starling shall be taught to speak . . ." In 1890, Eugene Scheillfin set loose a dozen starlings in New York's Central Park. By 1914, the first starlings had reached Niagara Falls. By 1945 they were carpet-bombing strollers in British Columbia and already they numbered in the hundreds of millions across the land.

By the middle of the century, the starling had replaced the buzzard as the bird it was all right to hate. Well, I may make some enemies with my next statement, but I kind of admire the starling. Oh, I know he's messy, I know he's hell on berry crops and a squatter at nesting sites and an absolute gate crasher at bird feeders, but the starling is also tough, and smart — too clever, in fact, for his own good. You know, if there weren't millions of them they would be prized for their beauty and their strangely haunting songs. I still remember getting up one very frigid sunny Thunder Bay winter morning — thirty, thirty-five below — and peering out my frost-rimed bathroom window to see the smoke rise from the chimney on the house next door . . . and ringed round the very rim of the chimney like four old duffle-coated vagabonds . . . a quartet of starlings, grumbling and shifting from foot to foot. I wouldn't think of going out on a morning like that . . . and here these four were, naked, on a roof. Tough.

I'll tell you one other good thing I know about starlings. Guess where Mozart got the melody for the Andante of his Piano Concerto K.453? From a tune whistled by his pet starling, that's where.

Now I don't know much about classical music . . . or birds, come to that. But I do have a standing rule. What's good enough for Wolfgang Amadeus is good enough for me.

A Living Fossil

G OT A ZOOLOGICAL RIDDLE for you: What kind of critter is both stupefyingly ugly and breathtakingly beautiful, swims with fins yet walks with legs, died out ninety million years ago and yet cavorted for underwater cameras just recently?

The answer is the coelacanth. A large-scaled, big-eyed lizardlike fish whose heyday was prehistory. Fossil remains reveal the coelacanth looked like an early working model for a fish. Which it sort of was. It had a broomlike tail and many fins that grew out of stumpy appendages that looked like — and functioned as — rudimentary legs. And that's what made the coelacanth, for all its undeniable homeliness, breathtakingly beautiful to zoologists. The coelacanth was the missing link between sea creatures and land creatures. It could both swim and, thanks to its strange fins, walk. The only problem is that the coelacanth is extinct. Disappeared twenty-five million years before the dinosaurs left. Every zoologist knew that. Said so right in the books. And that's the way it was until Professor John L. B. Smith, a famous South African ichthyologist, opened his mail one sunny morning in 1938. In his mail was a letter from a colleague. It contained a drawing of a strange creature that had been hauled up in the nets of a fishing trawler off the coast of Africa. Could the professor identify it? He could, though he had trouble believing his eyes. It was a drawing of a coelacanth.

The fish had long since been gutted and cut up, but its discovery launched Professor Smith on a lifelong quest: to find another coelacanth, one that scientists could examine and dissect. He haunted the fishing ports of East Africa, canvassing taverns and

134

other sailor hangouts, handing out leaflets offering a £100 reward for the body of a coelacanth, warning them that if they caught one not to clean it or cut it in any way but to get it to cold storage as soon as possible.

Fourteen years later, a fisherman walked into a market in Madagascar and asked if anyone wanted to buy the ugly monster he'd found snarled in his nets. Someone dug up a yellowing leaflet that had been hanging around. Professor Smith was contacted. In his excitement he commandeered a government aircraft to get him to the place the fish was being kept in ice and sawdust. They pulled back the cover and Professor Smith looked down. "I am not ashamed to say I wept," recalled the Professor. "It was a coelacanth."

Indeed it was — it was also the most important zoological find of the century. Well, that was in 1952.

Remember how for years runners were trying to break the four-minute mile . . . then when Roger Bannister did it, suddenly everyone was running subfour-minute miles? The same thing seems to happen in Nature. Professor Smith waited for fourteen years to see his first coelacanth, then suddenly they were being hauled in all over the place. Today many world-class museums have their own stuffed and mounted coelacanths — including the Royal Ontario Museum in Toronto.

And there are live ones still down there. In the fall of 1987, a team of West German scientists in a miniature submarine saw some off the Comoros Islands. The sub crew was treated to an underwater coelacanth ballet. A half-dozen of the prehistoric creatures did headstands on the ocean floor, swished by the cameras swimming belly up — even swam backwards, as if they hadn't heard that "The Ed Sullivan Show" was off the air.

I don't know why the coelacanth troop decided to launch into a vaudeville routine at forty fathoms, but I hope it inspired some affection among the scientists. We have enough dead coelacanths around. Let's leave the live ones alone. Especially now that they've shown us that they can put on a pretty good song-and-dance show. And that they're more than just pretty faces.

Here, Gunnar!
Nice Goose!

I JUST HAD a revolutionary thought. It came to me as I sat here watching Rufus, the family dog, doing what Rufus does best. He is doing it right now, unfazed by the clicking, humming computer being jockeyed by his ham-fingered and occasionally cursing Lord and Master (that's me) — right overhead.

To the untrained eye, Rufus might appear to be asleep, splayed as he is across the floor. His eyes are shut, his tongue lolls limply on the broadloom. Every once in a while one paw will quiver as if its owner was involved in some dream chase. Rufus's impersonation of a sleeping dog is absolutely uncanny. One could almost swear one heard the faint whistle of a snore as he maintains the pose for hours on end.

It is, of course, exactly what Rufus hopes to lull potential intruders into believing — that he is asleep. Lesser breeds such as Dobermans and German shepherds may bark and snarl and lunge at the ends of their chains, but Australian shepherds — for that's what Rufus is — operate on an infinitely subtler tactical level. One can almost discern the von Clausewitzian stratagems unfolding behind that shaggy brow. *Lure the enemy inside your perimeter,* it whispers, *the better to envelop him in a pincer movement.*

Well, that's one interpretation. There is also the possibility that Rufus is a bone-lazy lout of terminal uselessness just like every other dog I've ever owned.

After several months of observing Rufus in action (?), I have reluctantly concluded that the latter assessment, though brutal, is probably correct. Rufus is my very own in-house Welfare Bum.

Which brings me — at last! — around to the revolutionary

thought I mentioned at the top of the page. Namely that what Rufus needs is a good goose.

At ease, Vicar . . . I refer to *Branta canadensis maximus,* those gorgeous long-necked creatures that wing across our skies each spring and fall in huge, flapping communal arrowheads. I'm talking about the good old Canada goose. That's what Rufus needs to start earning his keep. Why? Because geese happen to make terrific watchd—, um, watchgeese, that's why. Europeans have been using flocks of geese for years to do night patrol at vineyards, golf courses, even military installations. Geese are ferociously territorial, alert to the slightest sound or movement, and fearless. When a goose starts cussing out an intruder, he can outdecibel any mechanical burglar alarm. They're tough, too. I've yet to meet a dog that's a match for an angry goose defending its nest. Quite aside from the fearsome hiss and their jackhammer beaks, geese can use their wings to deliver volleys of lefts, rights, and combinations that Mike Tyson could use in his business. Unwary birdwatchers and greedy poachers have had arms and even legs broken by those wings.

As for improving Rufus's performance by taking a wild goose under my wing — that's not as far-fetched as it sounds. It happened to the Nagy family recently. Scott Nagy runs a farm outside Carthage, Ontario. One evening Scott was on his porch, reading the paper while his German shepherd, King, snoozed contentedly by his boots. Suddenly a full-grown Canada goose came in like a B-29, landing right on the front lawn.

Mr. Nagy looked at the goose. King looked at Mr. Nagy. The goose honked and waddled over to King. He showed absolutely no fear of man or dog — in fact, he displayed out-and-out affection for poor bewildered King. This dog had no previous history of wimpdom, but in no time he was smitten, too.

"He (King) would never let my wife or kids near him while he's eating, but that thing (the goose) was eating out of the same dish as he was," Nagy said.

The Nagys dubbed the newcomer Gunnar, and stood by watching as the goose/dog romance bloomed. "Gunnar followed King everywhere he went," says Nagy. One time the goose followed the dog right into the Nagy house, where Gunnar did an impromptu fan dance, stretching his massive wings out to their full width, right between the TV set and the Barcalounger.

Gunnar and King even worked up an interspecies musical routine of sorts. King would gambol up to Gunnar with a ball in his mouth, drop it at Gunnar's webbed feet, and bark. Thereupon Gunnar would launch into an earsplitting aria of honks and squawks. As near as the Nagys could tell, Gunnar and King were having a heckuva good time.

All love stories, alas, wind down eventually. There came a morning when King awoke in his doghouse to find that his feathered pal no longer snuggled beside him. Gunnar had flown the coop, as it were.

"He's gone back to be with his own kind," says Scott Nagy philosophically. Perhaps, but Gunnar left a couple of legacies behind on the Nagy farm — a broken-hearted German shepherd, for one thing. In addition, a brand-new resolution for Scott Nagy. He's hanging up his twelve-gauge pump-action for good. He says he could never hunt another goose. Not after Gunnar.

All I know is, somewhere out there, wheeling around the sky, there's a Canada goose that can probably whip a fairly useless canine into shape in a matter of hours.

If any of my neighbours are reading along right now, consider this an apology in advance. Don't panic if some morning you catch me leaning out my bedroom window howling like an Arab muezzin, "Gunnar! Nice Goose! Down here, Gunnar! C'mon, boy!"

Don't call the cops. It's just Rufus's Lord and Master on another wild-goose chase.

The One That Got Away

I THOUGHT I'd talk a bit about fish stories. Now, I've never really caught the fishing bug. Not really. Oh, I can be seduced. Give me a warm sunny day, a nice stretch of lazy river, a casting rod that isn't too complex, and a couple of Canadian Tire lures that I don't care if I ever see again and I'll try my luck for an hour or two. Which is about how long it usually takes me to remember that fishing is essentially a very boring pastime. But that's okay. I know that people who do enjoy fishing have simply reached a higher plane of patience and understanding than I, and I respect them for it.

Anyone who can deal with fishing-reel backlashes, underwater snags, triple gang hooks, and petulant outboards, all in a tippy boat with a slow leak — anybody who can handle all that without at least fantasizing about nuking the entire Canadian watershed has my vote for Dalai Lama.

All of which is not to say I don't enjoy fishing byproducts. I do. My favourite fishing byproduct is the Fish Story. Here is my all-time favourite fish story.

Two brothers out fishing in a rented boat run into a school of silver bass. They are pulling them in faster than they can get their lines into the water. Rowing back to the marina that night, one brother says, "That was fantastic! If only we could find that same spot tomorrow!"

"Already thought of that," says Brother Two. "Look, I carved an X on the side of the boat right where we were casting."

Brother One looks at Brother Two in disgust. "You simpleton!"

he sneers. "And what happens if they don't give us the same boat tomorrow?"

Most fishing stories don't have a laugh in them, they have a cry of anguish instead. I'm referring to the One That Got Away school of fish stories.

But there was a weird one in the news last week that did not get away. About a Russian fisherman who called to his dog, sniffing around on the other bank of the river. Dog starts swimming across; suddenly, gulp — dog's gone. Heartbroken fisherman hauls in his net in which he discovers a huge pike . . . a pike with a puppy's tail dangling out of the corner of his mouth. Man cuts open the fish and out steps a highly indignant dog that commences to yap at the late fish that had bushwhacked him. You with me so far? This is not a joke. This story came over Radio Moscow. The radio report then went on to say that the pike, which was three feet long, weighed 145 pounds.

At which point I have to say . . . whoa.

Something that is three feet long and weighs 145 pounds is not a pike. Pike are long and skinny. They call them snakes in Northern Ontario. A three-foot pike would weigh, I would guess, somewhere around twenty pounds for a hefty one. I don't know what it is the Russian fisherman netted — an abandoned vodka still . . . perhaps a minivan . . . but it was not a pike.

Which brings me to my second-favourite fishing tale. It's about an avid fisherman named Samuel Clemens. One day the author of *Tom Sawyer* was returning on a train from a fishing trip on which he had somewhat exceeded the daily limit. Clemens was boasting about all the fish he had caught to a fellow passenger who didn't seem to be favourably impressed. "By the way, who are you, sir?" Clemens asked airily.

"I'm the state game warden," said the stranger. "And who might you be?"

"Me?" said Clemens in a strangled voice. "Why, I'm the biggest damn liar on the continent."

I guess if the game warden was keeping track, he'd have put that in his One That Got Away file.

Porkers

THEY CALLED HIM BIG BILL, and he certainly was that. He'd have stood more than nine feet off the ground — if he'd been able to stand, which he wasn't. Big Bill was so fat that even when he was on all fours his belly dragged on the ground. He tipped the scales at a gargantuan 2,552 pounds.

His massive weight came from a lifetime spent pigging out and sowing around. Big Bill, you see, was a Poland-China hog who wallowed around the Jackson, Tennessee, area back in the 1930s. According to the *Guinness Book of Records*, Big Bill is the heaviest hog ever recorded.

Impressive as he undoubtedly was, it's a safe bet that Big Bill's bulk didn't do anything for the image of pigdom in general. Was there ever an animal so maligned? Next to the cockroach, the pig has received just about the worst press of the entire animal kingdom — and most of it undeserved, at that.

As a fellow who's done some time on the nonprickly end of a manure fork, I can testify that comparatively horses are more unpredictable, cattle are messier, and just about everything in the barnyard is a whole lot dumber than the average pig.

The smelliest? Well, you go clean out an old henhouse or a goat shed. We'll resume this discussion after you regain consciousness.

It's possible that the pig's number-one enemy is language. The English tongue is awash with references to greedy pigs and dirty pigs, road hogs and filthy swine who live in pigsties. We like to point out prissily that you can't make a silk purse from a sow's ear, that it is foolhardy to purchase a pig in a poke and pointless to throw pearls before swine. We speak disapprovingly of people who eat, wallow, lie, grunt like a you-know-what. If we're crossed by a cop, he's a pig. If we don't like an actor, he's a ham. As for the fat little new kid in class, you know that before the week's out it won't matter what his real name is. He is doomed to be known forever after as Porky.

Poor old pigs.

They even get their lumps in folk mythology. I mean, we all know that pigs like to eat garbage, roll around in slime, and are so dumb that they cut their own fat throats when they're forced to swim, right?

Bunk, bunk, and bunk.

In his *Dictionary of Misinformation*, author Tom Burnham says the belief that pigs cut their own throats with their forehooves when they swim "is absolute nonsense. They can swim perfectly well." A pig, he admits, does like to wallow in mud on a hot day, but only because the pig lacks sweat glands and mud is a good way to lower the temperature of his skin.

What about the common belief that pigs love to eat garbage? Mr. Burnham points out something that should have been obvious: "In captivity . . . they eat what they are fed . . . [but] of all domestic animals, the pig's preferred diet is closest to that of human beings."

Perhaps the biggest misconception humans hold concerning the pig is in the IQ department. Contrary to popular belief, they are not dumb. Professor Edward O. Wilson, curator of entomology at Harvard University, ranks the pig among the ten most intelligent animals on the planet, just behind the dolphin and the elephant — well ahead of Fido and Minnie the mynah bird.

And anyway, we have the example of Louise.

Louise is what the Germans call a *schnueffelwildschwein* — "tracker pig" is about as close as we can get in English. Her job was to help German police by sniffing out illicit drugs. And she was very good at it. Much better than German shepherds or Dobermans or bloodhounds or human officers with mechanical sniffing machines. But there was a problem. It stemmed from Louise's *pigness*. Some timid German bureaucrat decided that a drug-sniffing pig was bad for the police image. Accordingly, Louise was stripped of her badge, demoted to civilian, and sentenced to the German equivalent of Canada Packers.

Then a wonderful thing happened. Louise's sad story was leaked to the public, and instantly the police department was swamped with calls from outraged German citizens. Louise's plight was even taken up in the State Assembly by the opposition Green Party.

And there's a happy ending. Louise not only had her death sentence lifted, but she was also reinstated to her former position with the police and dispatched for duty in another, more pig-supportive, precinct.

Ah, it almost gives you hope that the human race might be on the verge of granting the lowly pig the respect it deserves.

You think that's possible? You think a species that still believes snakes are slimy and eagles snatch unattended babies and packs of evil wolves are skulking just beyond the campfire waiting to dismember unwary travellers — you think the human race is ready to reassess the humble hog? To clasp the porker to its bosom?

In a pig's eye.

"Harvesting" Canadas

THERE ARE A LOT of ways to come back to the world each morning. Some of us "come to" with the bray of an alarm clock, the whining of a dog that wants out, or the tried but true ice-cold foot in the middle of the back. But every once in a while I get a singular treat by way of a wake-up call. It starts way off on the edge of unconsciousness and gradually flaps in until it's right overhead.

Geese. Big Canadas. Whole skeins of them. About two or three times a week they fly past my house at dawn. It's a funny sound that geese make in flight . . . far from melodious like the oriole or piercing like the blue jay. Geese always remind me of something between a suburban coffee klatch and a holiday weekend traffic jam. It's not a pretty sound, but it is pleasant somehow . . . and it does grab your attention. What I find sobering is the realization that they've been honking and flying in those ragtag V formations for thousands and thousands of years over the heads of pioneers and voyageurs, Cree and Ojibway, back to the mists of prehistory — and probably on flight paths right above this selfsame hill where my house stands.

There were a lot fewer of them when I was a kid. Back then a flock of geese going over was cause to drop everything and rush out to the backyard for a peek.

There's no shortage of Canada geese in Southern Ontario now. In fact, some folks claim they've become a nuisance. A nuisance that needs to be dealt with. Which is why the Ministry of Natural Resources is in the midst of planning a shotgun solution right now.

They are talking of holding "controlled hunts" in several parks and recreation areas around the Guelph area, where I live, to thin out the goose population and encourage some of the idle birds to reconsider the virtues of migration, instead of setting up permanent residence as some of them have.

"There is a limit," says a ministry spokesman, "to how much crop damage and defecation on beaches, lakes, golf courses, and parks can occur before the public says that's too much and something has to be done."

Well, I suppose there's some truth to that, but I get a little nervous when I hear of a government bureaucracy advocating capital punishment as a solution for littering. And so, apparently, does Vern Thomas. He's a professor of zoology at the University of Guelph, and he calls the idea of a shotgun hunt of geese in the parks "buckaroo biology." Claims it's dumb and it won't work, either. Professor Thomas also thinks the damage caused by geese has been overstated and overrated. He says, and I quote, "For the most part, the geese are doing the farmer a favour by eating grain or corn that would grow wild after being left behind by machine harvesting."

Well, I'm neither a biologist nor a farmer, so I don't know much about that. But I do know that there's something dangerously final about shooting anything you've got too many of. I remember that back in the 1960s people talked about the Canada goose as a species threatened with extinction. Are they so robust now that we can unleash hunters on them, scarcely a quarter century later?

If the idea goes ahead, I hope in the interests of plain speaking that they will use some word other than *hunt*. The geese that inhabit our parks and recreation areas are not that wild. Some of them will eat out of your hand. There are a lot of words to describe what will happen if the ministry proposal gets approved, but *hunting* and *sportsmanlike* will not be among them.

Aside from the inconvenience of my having to buy a new alarm clock, I think the whole idea of a hunt is monstrously unfair to a fellow earthly tenant. After all, if a little shootout is all that's required for crowd control, how come we haven't tried that on our own undeniably overpopulous species?

The other thing that worries me is the memory of what happened the last time we used guns to "manage" huge hordes of birds. Well, not memory, actually . . . written accounts. The last passenger pigeon died in the Cincinnati Zoo in 1914.

Whatever Happened to Peter Cottontail?

YOU DON'T HEAR about rabbits much anymore. Which is a shame, because rabbits used to be very big. Heck, I can remember when Bugs Bunny had his very own television series.

Maybe they've withdrawn because we've been so rotten to them. What's the worst a rabbit can do — decapitate one or two tulips? Leave a little buckshot on the front lawn? And for this we turn him into ladies' coats and good-luck key chains. Never mind guinea pigs, scapegoats, and sacrificial lambs, who gets fingered for the Wasserman tests? We not only "off" the rabbit, we rub his nose in it: favourite cliché for declaring pregnancy: "Honey, guess what? The rabbit died!" This is a joyous announcement? Ask the rabbit. We show them no respect. Our name for those dinky little indoor antennas you see on motel TV sets? Rabbit ears. What do we call the dirty, illegal blow to the back of the neck that bad-guy wrestlers like King Kong Bundy and Abdul the Butcher use on good-guy wrestlers like Hulk Hogan and Corporal Kirschner? The rabbit punch.

We dismiss nerds and nebbishes as "weak and rabbity looking." We melt a glob of cheddar on a slice of toast and call it "Welsh rabbit." We don't even get the names straight. We talk about snowshoe rabbits and Belgian hares — it should be snowshoe hares and Belgian rabbits. It's easy to tell the difference. A rabbit is born bald; a hare isn't. So the hare . . . has hair.

You'd think we could at least get *that* right.

Oh, yeah, and there's that libellous implied insanity rap we've

147

been trying to stick them with. They even have their own month, right? Mad as a March Hare?

Wasn't just *Alice in Wonderland* that spread that slander. Charles Darwin put it around, too. He claimed that male hares went nuts every March, thumping each other out in an endless series of Duelling Bunny showdowns, all for the paw of some comely doe. Well, not true. Experts have discovered that hares do fight all right, but almost never in the month of March . . . and it's never two guy hares. It's males versus females.

Kind of a Me-Bugs-You-Flopsy macho scenario, you figure? Naw, more Me-Flopsy-You-History. The females win virtually every fight. Nothing personal. It's just Flopsy's rabbity way of saying "Not tonight, Bugs, I have a headache."

But the crowning insult about the mad March hare rap is that it's all a misquote. Away back in the Middle Ages, the Dutch philosopher Erasmus referred to someone being "as mad as a marsh hare." *Marsh*, not March. The whole March hare myth is the result of a medieval misprint.

So what's so psycho about a marsh hare you ask? Don't ask me, ask Jimmy Carter. Back during the final, feckless days of the Carter adminstration, the soon-to-be civilian Carter took a couple of days off for a canoe trip in the wilds of Georgia swamp country.

A few days later a small story appeared about Carter's canoe being attacked by . . . a swimming rabbit. Came right at the canoe, he said. Took a chunk right out of his paddle, he said.

Well, it wasn't an incident of the scale of, say, the Iran helicopter fiasco or the Carter budget deficit, but it was kind of symbolic of Jimmy Carter's whole unravelling string of luck. It figured that he would eventually be attacked by a rabbit. And a swamp rabbit, at that. Which is probably what they call marsh hares in Georgia.

Not that Jimmy Carter's successor turned out to be a whole lot luckier, in the end. He had bigger problems with Iran than Jimmy Carter ever had. And he ran up a budget deficit bigger than any President's worst nightmare.

As for the current resident in the Oval Office rabbit hole, I don't know for sure that he carries one on his key chain, but if George Bush does have a rabbit's foot, I'll bet by now it's . . . pretty well . . . hairless.

Our Feathered Janitors

WENT ON A CANOE TRIP last weekend down a long and mean-dering coffee-coloured river through all kinds of land-scapes, including a huge wilderness swamp.

I think canoe trips are a bit like childbirth — better remembered than lived through. There's a lot of pain, frustration, and sheer, shoulder-sagging, knee-buckling work on your average canoe trip. Those are the kind of petty details that tend to be glossed over, rosied up, or even forgotten in time.

But this trip is still fresh in my mind. I can still taste the instant coffee with the pine needles and fire ash in it. I can still remember digging in the paddles to cross a windswept lake and realizing that if all three of us in the canoe stroked as powerfully as we could in perfect unison, we might, just might, be able to stop the canoe from going backwards.

Most of all, I remember a particular portage deep in the belly of the aforementioned wilderness swamp. It was, like all classic portages, Not Featured on the Map.

The portage snaked for about three-quarters of a mile through scratchy bracken and treacherous deadfalls, all served up on an icing of slippery, oozing, thick grey gumbo that apparently thrived on a diet of rubber boots, moccasins, and sneakers, but was not averse to sucking on a plain bare ankle if one came its way.

Did I mention the mosquitoes? There were mosquitoes. Refu-gees from some insect version of the Scarsdale Diet, I would judge.

Everybody, I suppose, has a most memorable moment from a canoe trip. Mine came halfway along that portage, up to my barked shins in muck, laden down like an army mule with pack-

149

sacks, tents, and paddles, feeling for all the world like a stricken American aircraft carrier in a bad war movie and suddenly understanding why they called those Second World War dive bombers "mosquitoes" . . . wondering if, short of a lightning strike, things could get too much worse, then looking up and seeing a large — a very large — black bird gliding, wings outstretched, high overhead.

"What's that — a hawk?" I gasped to the young naturalist who was with us.

"Nope," he said. "Vulture."

And I thought to myself, no, no . . . not vultures. It's too *pat*. I'm willing to be on the flight deck in an old American war movie, but I refuse to play Humphrey Bogart on the desert in *Treasure of the Sierra Madre.*

But our young naturalist was right, it was a vulture — a turkey vulture, more interested in dead rabbits or groundhogs than the thrashings and flailings of fourteen struggling two-legged portagers far below.

It's funny the way movie stereotypes stay with you. All those old cowboy movies taught me that vultures are evil, malevolent creatures just waiting to pick off wounded or weakened pilgrims on their way to the promised land. Truth is, vultures are more like janitors in charge of carrion. They take care of dead bodies. Aren't you glad they do, so we don't have to? The other truth is, if anyone's a predator in the vulture-human equation it's the other way around. *We've* just about finished *them* off. Two years ago the last wild California Condor — the most magnificent bird, never mind vulture, ever to grace North American skies — was captured by U.S. Fish and Wildlife Experts. They have twenty now in captivity, which they hope will breed offspring for release into the wild. Problem is, wild condors need space. Hundreds and hundreds of square miles each. And there's not enough "wild" left in California for the condor.

All of which has me rethinking the experience I had with the condor's cousin, the turkey vulture I saw watching me watching him over that swamp last weekend.

Makes me think that maybe *he* felt like Humphrey Bogart in *Treasure of the Sierra Madre.*

150

Toad Alert

There are a lot of wonderful stories told about Winston Churchill, but one of my favourites involves Churchill's pet dog, a poodle named Rufus. One evening at Chequers, Sir Winston, holding Rufus on his ample lap, was watching the film *Oliver Twist*. At the point where Bill Sykes prepares to drown his dog to throw the police off his trail, Churchill covered Rufus's eyes with his hand saying, "Don't look now, dear. I'll tell you about it afterwards."

I think what I like most about that story is what it says about the British. They are animal lovers . . . with a vengeance. Consider . . . this very evening on roadsides all over England, countless human volunteers will begin to gather as the sun goes down. These people will be armed with flashlights, butterfly nets, and buckets. They will spend the next few hours playing Good Samaritan to . . . Are you ready?

Toads.

You read right. We are talking about the latest manifestation of Britain's love affair with the animal kingdom — the toad patrols. It has to do with road traffic, you see. You don't have to live in England to know that vehicles and toads don't exactly coexist. Any toad that has the temerity to try to cross a highway faces a very high risk of streamlining its silhouette severely. In most countries this is treated as a regrettable but undeniable fact of life. Not in Britain. In Britain they organize toad patrols.

There are two hundred of these patrols. They have their own national advertising campaign, the slogan of which is Help a Toad Across a Road. They even have official Department of Transportation road signs that command: "Slow down. Toads' migratory crossing for next one and a half miles."

Toads aren't the only animal to enjoy the protective custody and eternal vigilance of the British Bulldog — bats do very well in the U.K., too. Ask Mark Edmondson. Mr. Edmondson is a housebuilder in Yorkshire. Last fall he routinely sprayed the rafters of a cottage to kill an infestation of woodworms. Two months later he found himself in front of a judge to answer for the inadvertent assassination of fifty former tenants of the cottage attic. Bats. "I didn't know there were bats up there," said Edmondson.

"Were there no bat droppings on the aforementioned rafters?" intoned the judge.

"There were droppings," said Edmondson, "but they weren't signed." Edmondson then confessed to a lamentable inability to distinguish bat droppings from rat droppings.

"Perhaps a fine will sharpen your perception next time," said the judge. Five hundred pounds. Case closed. Mark Edmondson says from now on he'll inspect every attic on his hand and knees.

I guess it would be easy enough to laugh at the sometimes neurotic bond so many two-legged Britons seem to have for their four-legged, furred, and/or feathered co-islanders . . . until you remember that less than a century ago, bull baiting and bear baiting were common spectacles in the British Isles. So were cock fights. And don't forget this is the nation that gave the world the barbarism known as the fox hunt. Something that Oscar Wilde dismissed as the unspeakable in pursuit of the uneatable. No, as ludicrous as the idea of bat legislation or trans-highway toadlifts might seem, I think they represent a step forward.

A small step for man . . . a giant hop for toadkind.

Freeze-Drying — The Ultimate Senate Reform

THE AMERICAN HUMOURIST James Thurber wrote a lot of funny stuff about the dogs in his life, but he never did get used to the concept of dog . . . lovers. As he once said, "I've always thought of a dog lover as a dog that was in love with another dog."

Now you see, Roger Saatzer would never make that mistake. Roger knows that while a dog might be fond of or lust after another dog (or dogette), to get true, soaring, majestic higher-than-a-mountain Love, you have to throw a human being into the equation.

Roger Saatzer banks on it. He's president of Preserv-a-Pet Inc. of Niswa, Minnesota. Preserv-a-Pet does just what it says: you send 'em your pet and they preserve it for you. Matter of fact, they can fix it so that Fido is around long after *you're* gone. Only difference is, Fido won't be perhaps quite as yappy or demanding or affectionate as you remember him. That's because Preserv-a-Pet preserves your pet the same way Nescafé and Maxwell House keep your instant coffee fresh.

That's right. Fido will be freeze-dried.

Sounds a touch ghoulish, I realize, but just think about it a moment.

You know full well that sooner or later Fido is going to shuffle off to the Golden Fire Hydrant up yonder. And how are you going to remember him? By bronzing his water dish? By declaring that chewed-up leg on the coffee table a Heritage Site? With a few yellowing snapshots in the family album? Cheesy. How much better to have Fido freeze-dried in his favourite pose . . . snoozing by the hearth, say . . . or maybe sitting up, ears perked, mouth open, waiting for you to drop the Milk Bone. Forever.

Roger Saatzer says freeze-drying is the next best thing to being . . . well, alive. It's quick and easy, too. Customers just ship their defunct, furry companions to Preserv-a-Pet, along with one or two photos to show how the animal looked in life, and modern science does the rest. The process takes all the water out of the body without changing the size or shape. No shrinkage, no odour . . . no sweat!

What about other kinds of pets? Hey, you name it, they'll freeze-dry it. In addition to dogs and cats, Preserv-a-Pet has immortalized rabbits, turtles, snakes, gerbils — they've even freeze-dried a lion.

Pricey, though. A small chihuahua eternally hearkening to His Master's Voice is going to set His Master back about 450 bucks U.S. But if money is no object, then the sky is no limit.

Preserv-a-Pet can deliver a wingspread budgie or a pouncing Siamese or — get this — for a mere $2,000 U.S. — a full-grown German shepherd.

In the attack position.

Hmm. This opens up all new possibilities. I mean, a freeze-dried Doberman is just as scary as the real thing — plus, you don't have to feed or clean up after him, and his teeth don't fall out. And if you can freeze-dry attack dogs, why not . . . a night watchman? A bank security guard? A cop with a radar gun? Freeze-dried, they'd still be crime deterrents, but we wouldn't have to pay them and they'd never get old.

Americans are, of course, much more excited about this break-through than Canadians are. Heck, we mastered the technique of freeze-drying lap dogs years ago. We've even done an entire room of humans, all eternally frozen in their favourite poses . . . reading papers, staring out the window . . . chatting . . . mostly curled up and snoozing.

We call it the Senate Chamber.

PART 4
Terra Not-So-Firma

You're from WHERE?

WELL, I SEE Johnny Carson's in the soup again. "The Tonight Show" host may be the most popular TV comedian in most of North America, but in Nevada, he isn't. As a matter of fact, Richard Bryan, the governor of Nevada, has rented some television time himself to demand a public apology from Carson. Governor Bryan claims Carson "held the women of Nevada up to ridicule" in a recent monologue. How? By posing a riddle, that's how. Carson asked, "What's the difference between a parrot and a Nevada woman?" Answer: "You can teach a parrot to say no."

Sorry, Governor Bryan, but I'm with Carson on this one. Not that I have anything against Nevada or its womenfolk — I've never even been there. It's just that jokes made at the expense of places are one of the time-honoured mainstays of humour. And I'll take a waspish joke about a piece of real estate over a politician's outraged sense of dignity anytime.

Just think of the geographical rivalries that have enlivened daily life on this side of the border over the years. We've got Calgary versus Edmonton; Toronto versus Montreal; the rest of Canada versus Hogtown and — even though Ontario politicians would have us believe they don't exist anymore — Port Arthur versus Fort William.

One-liners sometimes snipe at greater entities than cities or states. Occasionally they take on whole countries. There's an old Czech raspberry about England that goes "Continental people have sex lives; the English have hot-water bottles."

Speaking of which, Marlene Dietrich once took a long, cool, Teutonic look at the U.S. and concluded, "In America, sex is an obsession. In other parts of the world, it is a fact."

Truman Capote described visiting Venice as "like eating an entire box of chocolate liqueurs at one go." John Gunther grumbled that Moscow was "the only city where if Marilyn Monroe walked down the street with nothing on but a pair of shoes, people would look at her feet."

You don't have to be an out-of-towner to run a place down. Writer Nelson Algren lived in Chicago, but that didn't stop him from calling it "a joint where the bulls and the foxes live well and the lambs wind up head down from the hook."

Many observers have swabbed selected chunks of Canada with similarly vinegarish prose. Wyndham Lewis wrote Toronto off as "a mournful Scottish version of America." Goldwyn Smith suggested the city of Winnipeg "wants lifting into the air ten or fifteen feet."

And Sir John A. Macdonald gently chided the early residents of Regina with "If you had a lit-tle more wood and a lit-tle more water, and here and there a hill . . . I think the prospect would be improved."

Here in Ontario the city of Sudbury has been the butt of jokes for so long that its detractors have failed to notice it is looking less like "the backside of the moon" with every passing year. Sudbury-bashing was even worse when I was growing up. Then, wiseguys would affect a W. C. Fields tone and say, "Ahhh, Sudburyyyyyy . . . where you find a pretty girl behind every treeeeeeee."

The real irony of the Carson-versus-Nevada kerfuffle is that Carson has been launching his barbs from Hollywood, and no place on the planet has been more thoroughly lampooned and savaged than "the home of the stars."

"Hollywood's a great place," said humourist Fred Allen, "if you're an orange." Critic Rex Reed defined it as the town where "if you don't have happiness, you send out for it." Someone else observed, "Hollywood is where people from Iowa mistake one another for stars."

One could just as easily substitute Nevada for Iowa.

You think Carson will eventually cave in to the political pressure and say something nice about Nevada? Actually he already has.

Sort of.

Recently he told his studio audience, "Nevada serves a useful purpose: it separates California from Colorado so John Denver doesn't keep Californians awake all night with weird songs about mountains."

Carson even had kind words to say about the wealth of Nevada. "It's a rich state," he pointed out, "with thirty-eight percent of the nation's gold."

Pause . . .

"Most of that in the teeth of six cocktail waitresses in Reno."

I figure Governor Bryan has two choices: he can dip into the state budget and hire a team of Hollywood gag writers, or he could just throw in the towel and join in the belly laughs.

Good sportsmanship is a lot cheaper in the long run. Healthier, too.

Your Fantasy Room Is Ready

THE NEWSPAPER ad read, "Fantasy Land Hotel . . . Now Open. Polynesian Room, Roman Room, Arabian Room, Victorian Room, Hollywood Night Club Room . . . Truck Room."

Truck Room??

"For reservations, call toll-free 1-800 . . . " Well, I did, and an enthusiastic honey-voiced operator in Alberta filled in the blanks. Fantasy Land Hotel, I learned, is the latest pearl in the ongoing retail reorganization of the Edmonton cityscape, courtesy of the Ghermezian Brothers. Fantasy Land is a $50 million addition to the already legendary West Ed Mall. It is a 360-room hotel, and 120 of those rooms are "themed," which is to say they are designed to make you think you have just been magic-carpeted to somewhere quite removed both in geography and time from late-twentieth-century central Alberta. The Hollywood Night Club Room, for instance, gives anyone who rents it for the night neon over-heads, a black-tiled Jacuzzi, a bubble machine, and a lush carpet studded with twinkling lights. It's the kind of hotel room you might end up with if your architect was, say, Sammy Davis, Jr. Same principle with the Polynesian Room. The bellboy parks your Samsonite behind the door, you pay him off, turn around, and *pow!* Suddenly you're Captain Cook discovering the Sandwich Islands. Your mattress is cunningly laid out in a beached catamaran. Over in the corner you've got a coral grotto hiding your walk-in Jacuzzi.

Why, there's even a mock erupting volcano in the Polynesian Room, just to give the place a little Krakatoan ambiance.

The other theme rooms strive for the same total effect — the Victorian Room, the Roman Room, the Arabian Room . . . and the

159

Truck Room . . .

Yeah . . . what about the Truck Room? Well, my telephonic tour guide tells me that the Truck Room has an "automotive theme." It features a queen-size bed located in the back of a '67 Chevy half-ton pickup. Taking the young sprat along with you on this fantasy weekend? No problem. The cab of your simulated half-ton has been customized into an extra berth that will comfortably accommodate half pints up to the age of . . . oh, about twelve, say?

Oh, yes, and to intensify that "Cruisin' Down the Trans Canada" atmosphere, the Truck Room features a life-size statue of a traffic cop frozen in the act of blowing his whistle.

A lot of people are going to laugh about Edmonton's Fantasy Land Hotel. They will tend to be folks from Victoria, Vancouver, or the Virgin Islands — folks from softer, more decadent, and forgiving climes . . . where people, if they think of winter at all, tend to think of it as a particularly sadistic Hollywood special effect. Anyone who has experienced the . . . *utterness* of a real Canadian winter is not going to snicker at the idea of a hotel where at the flip of a charge card you can be whisked away to a South Pacific atoll, a Roman piazza, or an oasis on the deserts of old Araby . . . or, sure — even the back of a climate-controlled '67 Chevy pickup. Why not?

I had a friend, a Nova Scotian, who had a good job in Edmonton once. I asked him why he left. He said he left because one winter morning he was walking to work when the sole of his shoe . . . *snapped*. God didn't intend us to walk around in places where it got so cold it broke your shoes, he said. He lives in Dartmouth now, but he would understand the Fantasy Land Hotel. He might never have left if the Ghermezian boys had been a little quicker off the mark.

Won't catch me sniggering at the Fantasy Land Hotel in West Ed Mall, either. I'm copying down that toll-free number is what I'm doing. And some frosty morning, not so very long from now . . . when the mercury dips into the nether reaches of the thermometer and the car's caked with clinkers and I'm fed up with galoshes and lost gloves and runny noses and slipping and sliding, I'm going to fish out that number and make that call and take that flight.

And if Polynesia's booked . . . well, what the heck. I'll take the Truck Room.

The Rock

IT'S Newfun*land*. It is not *Noo*funland . . . and it's certainly not New*found*land, despite what Miss Corbett told me in my public school geography class.

It's Newfun*land*. After I spent a week there, that may be the one thing I'm absolutely sure of. Newfun*land* is an island of contradictions, you see. You take the weather. There's a channel on Newfun*land*TV that gives you nothing but continuous weather reports for the entire province, section by section. "For Bonavista, Trinity, Conception Bay, and the St. John's area," your TV will prophesy, "fog, heavy at times with patchy drizzle, clearing tomorrow." You look out your hotel window and the entire town is bathed in golden sunshine. Mind you, in the time it takes you to shuck your jacket and find a short-sleeved shirt, it could well be wall-to-wall fog out there and the TV weather forecast could be talking about sunny skies. Contradictions.

You take Newfie jokes. Offensive under any circumstances, but triply so in the province they so cruelly spoof. As most Newfoundlanders will point out to you right away. Just before they tell you six in a row.

Or you take the phrase "The Rock." Two islanders told me that next to telling Newfie jokes, the most inappropriate thing I could do would be to refer to their homeland as The Rock. So I didn't. But everybody else did.

Including one city councillor, a Baptist minister, one television host, and a tableful of people in a St. John's bar. They were all Newfoundlanders. Curious, I checked my *Colombo's Canadian Quotations* to see what heathen mainlander had inflicted Newfoundland with the nickname The Rock. I found the blackguard. "This poor bald rock" is a phrase that first appeared in a speech made by one Joseph R. Smallwood. Contradictions.

You take the very symbol of the island, the Newfoundland dogs — you know the ones? Those great black beasts with the hearts of lions and the constitutions of Voyageur buses? The ones that look powerful enough to haul a trawler off a shoal single-pawed? Do Newfoundlanders treat those dogs with the awe and reverence they so obviously deserve? I got introduced to four Newfoundland dogs while I was there and heard the same opening remark each time. "Ah, pay him no mind, he's just a great big sook."

Let me tell you what it's like to fly into St. John's for the first time. The view out your airplane window is one that makes you want to suck in your breath and blink once or twice. That's the entrance to St. John's harbour down there, with Signal Hill looming up on one side of a little gap of water called the Narrows. With South Head, a rocky promontory on the other side, and those long, blue, bruising breakers of the North Atlantic crashing and moiling and creaming all over the rocks.

You can just imagine four centuries' worth of sloops and galleons and barques and yawls and freighters and ocean liners scooting through that little keyhole to the safe haven of St. John's harbour. It must be a blessed relief for the sailors and it's certainly a glorious sight from the air — which you might or might not see, depending on the disposition of the Grand Banks fog on your particular flight.

Ray Guy, one of Newfoundland's most famous literary products, comes as close as anyone I've ever read when it comes to explaining his fellow islanders. "We are like Texans," Guy has written, "but we do not boast so much. We are like Irishmen, but we don't cry in our beer so much about our poor country. We are like Cape Bretoners, except we have no connection with dead Prince Charlie."

Yup . . . and Newfoundland is not New Brunswick or Nova Scotia or P.E.I. And it certainly will never be confused with the Gaspé or the Golden Horseshoe or the Northwest Territories.

There's something very different about Newfoundland, and I don't know what to call it. I hate to go all Hobbitty on you, but there really is something quite magical about the place.

Confederation notwithstanding, that's another country out there on the doorstep.

And it's called Newfound*land*.

Understand?

Reincarnating a Town

ONE OF THE SADDEST ASPECTS of Canadian life is our ghost towns. You see them all over the country — in the Yukon, on the Prairies, in the Maritimes, and all across Northern Ontario. They all look like variations on the same blues theme — abandoned, swaybacked buildings with no glass in the windows and doors off their hinges. Grey wood and mouldering bricks. Weeds taking over everywhere.

Every ghost town I've ever seen suffered from a curse that killed it in the end. They were all one-industry towns. Some sprang up because of a gold field nearby; others were built around iron or asbestos or copper deposits. A lot of ghost towns owed their existence to a rich timber stand. But in every case, when the ore played out or the trees got too scrawny to cut, it was the kiss of death for the community. Soon some of the merchants would feature Going Out of Business Specials. Then, hand-lettered For Sale signs would sprout on a lot of front lawns.

One ghost town coming up.

Well, what's a town supposed to do when the Main Payroll breaks camp in search of greener pastures? It's pretty well got to die, hasn't it?

Not if Chemainus is any indication. Chemainus is a tiny logging town on the east coast of Vancouver Island. Correction: *was* a tiny logging town. The main reason four thousand people called Chemainus home was the MacMillan Bloedel sawmill that had operated there for the better part of the twentieth century. In the late 1970s, officials announced the plant would be closing. When the sawmill shut down, one out of every three workers in

Chemainus would be drawing pogey.

In any other town that would be about the right time to put your house on the market and start checking the Help Wanted columns in out-of-town newspapers, but they do things differently in Chemainus. The town took a vote and decided not to die. The council voted instead to spend a quarter of a million dollars on downtown revitalization. But how do you revitalize the core of a logging town that's just had its guts ripped out? With imagination. What they did was transform Chemainus into the largest outdoor art gallery in the country.

They commissioned artists from across the province to come to Chemainus and paint murals — huge ones — on the sides of buildings in the downtown area. Not just any murals. They had to be strictly historical, depicting scenes from the town's past. One that decorates the side of a coffee shop is called *Steam Donkey at Work*. It shows a logging operation as it was done a hundred years ago. Another mural depicts a Cowichan chief standing on a hill watching an eighteenth-century sailing ship drop anchor in Chemainus harbour.

Still another giant painting shows the interior of a long-vanished Chemainus general store. The artists worked from photographs to be sure they got the details right.

In all, sixteen murals now brighten the formerly drab downtown area of Chemainus. There are other changes too — new sidewalks and lots of flowerboxes and rustic, wood-carved signs abound.

Did it work? Did out-of-towners come to see the logging town that wouldn't lie down and die?

Only 175,000 of them over the past few years. The story of Chemainus caught the public's fancy. Tourists from as far away as California and New Mexico have flocked to the town, toting their cameras and, more significantly, their wallets. The cash infusion has spawned new businesses. Chemainus now has a Victorian mall, ice cream stands, a tea room, a pedicab service, and four art galleries.

The murals have put Chemainus on the map — and not just a map of British Columbia. At an international competition in New York a few years ago, Chemainus walked away with an award for Best Downtown Revitalization.

Chemainus isn't sitting on its laurels — or its murals. A few summers ago, town craftsmen built and launched a ninety-two-foot brigantine called *The Spirit of Chemainus*. She now plies a route between Chemainus and the Expo site in Vancouver, plugging tourism — and Chemainus.

MacMillan Bloedel contributed a final twist of ironic economics. Right in the middle of the town's tourist boom, the company reopened a scaled-down version of the Chemainus sawmill — the one that caused the town's transformation in the first place.

Chemainiacs could have sneered, but instead they showed class. And why not? It meant another hundred jobs, for one thing.

And besides, as they'd learned, it never hurts to have an extra industry in town.

Spud Island

Since I'm Island-born home's as precise
as if a mumbly old carpenter,
shoulder-straps crossed wrong,
laid it out,
refigured to the last three-eighths of shingle.
                                    — *Milton Acorn*

WELL, PRINCE EDWARD ISLAND'S tidy, for sure. P.E.I. poet Acorn got that right. All those emerald-green potato fields neatly divided by red clay roads. Tidy houses, tidy hamlets, tidy barns, and tidy mounds of lobster traps — heck, even the dairy herds look tidier than your average mainland Holsteins.

It really hits you hard when you hail from a big, brawny province like Ontario, sprawling as it does all across the middle of our country like some ungainly centrefold. Ontario's the antithesis of Prince Edward Island, which Milton Acorn described as "a red tongue in the fanged jaws of the Gulf."

Recently I got to spend an entire week in Prince Edward Island. That might not be long enough to do Europe or New York or Rio, but it's sufficient time to get a penetrating look at P.E.I. — after all, the place is only about 150 miles long and twenty miles wide on average. Number of nontidal lakes and rivers: one and one respectively. Number of cities with populations exceeding 100,000: zero.

The population of the entire province is only a little over 120,000, which is to say about the same as the city of Thunder Bay.

But I'm beginning to sound like a Texan here — YOU CALL THIS PIS-SANT CHUNK O' DIRT A *PROVINCE*, BOAH??? HAIL, BACK HOME WE GOT *RANCHES* BIGGER'N THIS!"

I come to praise Prince Edward Island, not to bury it under

167

layers of Upper Canadian snottiness. Besides, the place has one precious resource that I haven't mentioned yet.

Its people.

To take the ferry from the Canadian mainland to Prince Edward Island is to travel back in time. Remember when life was kind of slow and amiable and you could greet a stranger on the street with a smile and a wave and not worry about people wondering if you were weird? Well, in Prince Edward Island, it's still like that. I don't think I heard a snarky word or a raised voice in the entire seven days I spent on the island. I can't recall hearing the screech of brakes or the braying of a car horn, either. The Islanders I met — from the clerk in the liquor store to the premier of the province — were friendly, courteous . . . and so doggoned *innocent* that I had to keep pinching my arm to remind myself that I wasn't living through an episode of "Ozzie and Harriet" or "The Brady Bunch."

Don't get me wrong — the people of Prince Edward Island are not characters out of a Walt Disney movie. I spent the week in a cottage belonging to an ex-rumrunner. Clovie Perry is his name. He's eighty years old and packs a pacemaker beneath his bony chest, but his eyes are bright and his wit is quick and he loves to dig out his scrapbooks and jaw about the good old days of dodging Mountie patrol boats and American G-men.

There are other Islanders I'll never forget. Such as Anne Thurlow, a woman I'd known only over the phone. She showed up at the cottage one sunshiny day with a huge picnic hamper under her arm. We spent the afternoon watching the tide come into Bedeque Bay while we munched on marinated clams, smoked herring, barbecued chicken, and home-made bread.

There are lots of less pleasant ways to spend a sunny afternoon.

Speaking of unexpected treats, Clovie and his wife, Jean, popped in the evening before we had to leave for home. They had a young teenager with them, clutching a paper bag. As I chatted with Jean, Clovie disappeared into the toolshed behind the cottage, reemerging with a toothy grin and a bottle of his justly notorious home-brewed wine in hand. Then Jean asked, "Have you seen the step-dancing yet?"

Step dancing? I thought to myself, isn't that the stuff with kilts and sporrans and crossed cutlasses on the floor? "Why . . . no," I replied.

"Well," said Jean, "you're going to see it now." And responding to a curt nod from Jean, the younger girl (their granddaughter, as it turned out) stood up, pulled a pair of tap shoes out of the paper bag, and strapped them on. Jean sat down at the piano, Clovie dug a harmonica out of his shirt pocket, and for the next hour that wee cottage on Bedeque Bay rocked and rolled to the sound of Scottish reels and jigs that had been handed down from who knows how far back.

There was no shyness, no coyness, and certainly no suggestion of showing off. It was just two generations of Islanders trying to make sure that some "stranger from away" had a good time.

Did a fine job of it, too. I can't wait to go back.

Hogtown Real Estate

OKAY. Let's try to examine the thing logically. Why would anyone *want* to move to Toronto?

Sports? To watch the Argos? The Blizzard? The Blue Jays? To support an NHL franchise that finished eighteenth out of twenty-two and hasn't seen the Stanley Cup for the past five prime ministers?

No, you don't move to Toronto for spectator sports.

How about the active kind, then — skiing? Are you kidding? Twiggy's got more hills than Toronto. The slopes are ninety miles away — and sixty miles of that is the lineup for the ski tow.

Fishing, then? Hoo boy. You want to try fishing in the Humber or the Don River? You want to dip a line along Toronto's lakeshore? Good luck. Don't forget to wear asbestos gloves and a radiation suit. You can probably sell anything you catch to Stephen Spielberg. He can use them as extras in his next extraterrestrial horror flick.

What about scenery? Maybe people move to Toronto for the magnificent vistas and pastoral panoramas? *Sois sérieux, chéri.* On a clear day from the top of the CN Tower you can just make out the smokestacks of Hamilton.

That's if you can get to the tower through the herds of tour buses from Buffalo.

Hey, maybe *that's* why people go to Toronto — to gawk at all its architectural treasures and cultural meccas.

Well, there is the CN Tower, Casa Loma, art galleries, museums, the Metro Zoo, Honest Ed's . . .

The catch is getting to them. Toronto is networked by a system of superhighways, highways, biways, roads, and back alleys that may well be the envy of the Western world. *May*be— we'll never know because at any given time sixty percent of them are closed for sewer installation, resurfacing, widening, narrowing, or simple pothole repair. This leaves the other forty percent with the burden of carrying the thirteen trillion cars, trucks, and motorbikes that start their engines every morning. You don't drive in Toronto—, you just park and idle for hours at a time. Mind you, Toronto has discovered a brand-new transportation concept — Terminal Gridlock.

Well, that would seem to settle it. Nobody in his or her right mind would move to Toronto to watch sports, play sports, take in the sights, or bask in the cultural ambiance. It only leaves one tiny question . . .

Why is everybody moving to Toronto?

They are, you know. They must be. *Somebody's* buying all those houses.

The real estate market in downtown Hogtown is absolutely, totally take-all-your-clothes-off-and-hang-from-the-chandeliers nuts. Torontonians who put their houses on the market at ridiculously inflated prices get hysterical phone calls from people beseeching them to please take *more*. I know a guy who owns a house in the west end, five miles from downtown. It sits cheek by jowl with a dozen or so other houses just like it. Postage-stamp lawn, no driveway, two bedrooms. The house is . . . well, I have to say "modest" because the guy's a friend of mine, but between you and me, the place is a dump. Two weeks ago, my friend — happily married, good job — decided to list his house to see what it would bring. He asked for $350,000 — just to make sure he wouldn't be tempted.

He's retiring early and moving to Halifax next month. Right after the sale of his house goes through — for $410,000.

What's even more amazing is that my friend's story isn't even special. Tell it to a Toronto real estate agent and he or she will nod impatiently then relate a tale that makes it sound like small potatoes.

You want to know how crazy the Toronto real estate market is? House prices in Toronto have gone up by thirty-five percent in the past year alone. Thirty-five percent! The price of an average house — *average* house, mind, which takes in all the tumbledown shacks and sagging flophouses as well as normal domiciles you might actually consider trying to play house in — is in the quarter-of-a-million-dollar range.

And that's the price as we go to press. By the time you read this it'll probably be higher. By the time you turn to the next page it'll be higher still.

That means that real estate agents who usually collect a commission of six percent on a house sale are pulling in something like $15,000 for every "average" house they sell.

Hey.

I think I just solved the problem.

I know who's moving to Toronto. Real estate agents. Toronto's being taken over by an army of real estate agents.

Black's Hot Tip of the week: sell all your stocks. Put every cent you've got into plaid sports jackets.

Japan — Land of the Rising Yen

B OY, IT'S ODD how age sneaks up and bushwhacks you when you least expect it. The thought just occurred to me that there are adults walking around today to whom the phrase *Made in Japan* conjures up nothing but an image of high quality, reasonably priced merchandise.

Those of us who are a little longer of tooth remember a time when those three words carried quite a different connotation. Thirty or forty years ago Made in Japan was just about the nastiest epithet you could apply to a product.

Not that there were all that many products to apply it to. Our planet was just recovering from the Second World War and no nation had more rehabilitating to do than Japan. The Land of the Rising Sun had been thoroughly thumped by Allied Forces — land, sea, and air. Two of its most prosperous cities had been all but obliterated by atomic bombs. Japanese society was in total disarray; the economy was an utter shambles.

The country's first attempts to resurrect itself economically were pretty laughable, and as I recall, a lot of us Westerners had a pretty good time shaking our noggins at the ridiculously inept, hilariously shoddy manufactured goods that began to show up at our local five-and-dime stores — kids' toys that shattered if you dropped them, crummy electronic gizmos that failed to function, if they didn't outright fall apart in your hands.

Japanese folk tales began to spring up, too — like the one about the town of Usa, Japan. Legend had it that Emperor Hirohito and his advisers, in a frenzied effort to crack the lucrative North American commercial market, had actually renamed a small Japanese industrial town Usa. That way, so the story went, Japanese goods could legitimately bear the stamp Made in USA on the bottom, and thereby get around North American trade restrictions.

It was a good story. A complete crock, but a good story.

I also recall chortling over the tale of how a team of Japanese experts had travelled to Spain, sought out that country's finest guitar craftsmen, and spent hundreds of thousands of yen purchasing the best Spanish guitars they could find. Then they took the instruments back to Japan and literally tore them apart, trying to discover what made them so special.

"Can you imagine?" we Westerners chortled.

Well, no, as a matter of fact, we couldn't — and that was our mistake. Fact is, within a matter of a few years a whole series of very good Japanese guitars began flooding into North America — and they were selling for a fraction of the price of traditional European and North American guitars.

It wasn't just guitars, either. Japanese businessmen applied the same principles to a whole range of products, and suddenly there was a blizzard of cameras, stereos, TV sets, radios, motorcycles, fishing rods — all at least as good and usually better than anything manufactured domestically; all competitively priced if not a helluva lot cheaper.

And all marked Made in Japan.

I don't have to bring up automobiles, do I? We all know what the invasion of Hondas, Datsuns, and Toyotas did to the gas-guzzling chariots of Detroit. If memory serves, we chortled pretty heartily when those first Japanese cars came ashore.

All of which makes doubly embarrassing the scene that unfolded in a movie house in downtown Tokyo a while ago. The occasion was the official debut of a film put out by the Japanese department of International Trade. The film was aimed squarely at Japanese consumers and the idea behind it was — and hang on to your Naugahyde made-in-Osaka Barcalounger for this — to encourage Japanese consumers to buy more imported goods.

Why? Because every time the Japanese prime minister goes to negotiate an international trade agreement, Canadian, American, and European counterparts point out that while the West buys just about everything from Japan, Japan buys almost no manufactured goods back from the West — and Japan enjoys a whopping $50 billion trade surplus.

Unfortunately, the government promotional film backfired. It turned out to be curiously ham-handed. Among other things it tried to persuade Japanese to load up on American-made fondue sets.

The Japanese rarely entertain at home.

It touts oven thermometers, even though few Japanese kitchens have ovens; it flogs European fruit beverages, but in cartons too tall to fit in Japanese refrigerators. In a positive fit of inappropriateness the film even urges the audience to buy good old North American automobiles — you know . . . the big ones with a left-hand drive?

This in a country where tiny cars with right-hand drive are the norm.

How did Japanese consumers respond to the government film? Well, as you know, they are an exceedingly polite people. It was a good five minutes into the film before someone in the audience sniggered audibly. The movie was almost over before the entire theatre dissolved into helpless guffaws.

It must have been fairly demoralizing for the Western trade officials in the audience, but I hope they haven't totally lost heart.

After all, Japanese businessmen were primitive once, too.

My Maple: In Memoriam

I think that I shall never see
A poem lovely as a tree
— Joyce Kilmer

A MAZING. Kilmer wrote those lines without even laying eyes on the big old maple out my back door. Now *there* is a tree that's more beautiful than half a dozen poems, the entire Top Ten Hit Parade, and a couple of three-act plays put together.

Acer saccharum it's known as, among botanists. To us less learned folks, it's a plain old sugar maple and it is, as I say, a beauty. Thirty feet high. A good three feet around the trunk. Festooned with birdhouses in the summer (some man-made) and bedecked with bird feeders and suet bags in the winter, my old maple is a regular Salvation Army hostel for the swarms of jays, finches, chickadees, and grosbeaks that flap by here every year en route to their summer and winter hangouts.

Works for me, too, that maple. Holds up one end of my hammock for a couple of months each summer. I've spent more than one muggy afternoon under that tree, rocking gently and gazing at the hypnotically shifting patterns on the undersides of the maple leaves above, blocking out the sun. There may be more pleasant ways to while away a blistering hot July afternoon, but I don't know of them.

Yessir, it's a wonderful old tree, my maple.

A pity that it's dying.

Nothing to do with age or fungus diseases or hemorrhage from the dinky little hook that holds up my hammock. My maple is dying from the same thing that your maple's dying from. The same thing that's killing all our maples.

Acid rain.

Or so they tell me. To tell the truth, my maple looks pretty much the way it did last year and the year before. It turns colour a little earlier and sheds its leaves a little faster, but other than that it's pretty much the same.

But the experts tell me it's dying, and you know what — I believe them. Because I've never heard biologists talk the way they talk about the threat of acid rain. Usually scientists talk and write in academic-ese — language that is dispassionate, unemotional and, well, boring, actually. But the menace of acid rain is provoking some specialists to a vocabulary that's downright frightening.

"A catastrophe in the making," warns a McGill University professor.

"We're on our way to disaster," says an Ontario botanist.

How serious is acid rain? Tom Hutchinson of the Institute of Environmental Studies has a chillingly blunt answer to that: "It is," he says, "the AIDS of trees." It's not as if we haven't been warned. Acid rain has decimated the forests of several European countries, particularly West Germany's. Remember the Black Forest? Chances are, in a few more years that's what we'll all have to do — remember it. Its famous evergreens have been among the hardest hit.

In North America, though, it's maple trees — so far, anyway. Sugar maples have been particularly susceptible. Quebec's once-lucrative sugar maple industry is in a shambles. Why? Because according to a McGill University study, eighty percent — *eighty percent* — of the province's maple trees are dead or dying. Economic losses to Quebec so far: $110 million and climbing.

Can we turn it around? Hard to say. Trees don't respond to a couple of aspirin and a warm poultice. Foresters know that once you've interrupted a forest's cycle, the interruption can last for decades. There's talk of slow-release organic fertilizers and promising bone meal treatments, but everyone knows what really has to be done. We have to stop spewing our crap into the air.

And that's not likely to happen.

Not right after a former U.S. President could say, as Reagan did when he was governor of California, "Seen one redwood, you've seen 'em all."

Not when you have a provincial Ministry of Natural Resources that can publish a booklet listing all the possible causes of maple

tree "dieback" — everything from insects to fungus to viruses . . .
but never once mentioning the MNR *F* words.

Air pollution.

All I know is, somebody'd better act soon. Unless we want to
hear our kids standing up in school assembly singing revised lyrics
to our seminational anthem:

"The Maple Leaf . . . For a Little While."

Monuments to
Vanity

IT'S A SOBERING THOUGHT to ponder, but the fact is, of the Seven Wonders of the Ancient World, six have disappeared. The Hanging Gardens of Babylon — gone. The Statue of Zeus at Olympia — vanished. The Temple of Diana at Ephesus — destroyed by invading Goths. The Tomb of King Mausolus in Turkey — flattened by an earthquake. The Lighthouse at Alexandria — knocked to the ground by Moors who hoped to find gold hidden in the marble walls. The magnificent Colossus of Rhodes — that was toppled by another earthquake. The ruins of the Colossus lay on the ground for nine centuries before being broken up and sold for scrap — nine hundred camel loads, it came to. That's six wonders of the Ancient World. The only one that's still around is the Great Pyramid of Cheops — and it's seen better days.

It's humbling to realize that the grandest plans of the richest and mightiest monarchs are just so much grist for the mills of time. The Coliseum was once the most glorious building in the Roman Empire. Today it's infested with cats, encircled by noisy, smelly cars, and it looks like a gutted and abandoned warehouse. Stonehenge, a structure so massive, so elemental that one stone alone weighs thirty-five tons . . . surely that should survive the test of time? Well, barely. Authorities are thinking of closing Stonehenge. What's left of it is being ravaged by tourist traffic.

We're not very kind to our architectural wonders. And as time goes by, population pressures swell, industrial pollution gets more chronic, and we're even less kind than we used to be. The city of Venice is perhaps the most striking example. There, you can actually see how sulphur dioxide and other airborne poisons are

179

ravaging the statuary and the buildings. In other places the damage is less obvious, but ongoing nonetheless. A story in the newspaper recently lamented the fact that France's famous symbol the majestic Arc de Triomphe is suffering from fallen arches. Hundreds of pounds of masonry have tumbled from the edifice that towers over downtown Paris, and it's getting more dangerous all the time. A few years ago a British day-tripper was bopped on the head by a chunk of the arch. What's causing it? Traffic. Too much traffic buzzing around the base of the arch each day. The rumble of all those wheels creates vibrations that bit by bit are doing to the Arc de Triomphe what the Goths did to the Temple of Diana and the Moors did to the Lighthouse at Alexandria.

I wonder what will happen to Canadian monuments over vast periods of time. Of course, we don't have that many to worry about, Canadians not being a particularly vainglorious lot, but I suppose it's conceivable that a couple of millennia worth of acid rain could wear the huge Sudbury nickel down to the size of a bus token . . . and whittle the lofty CN Tower down to a pencil stub.

You know, the whole thing is probably a much needed lesson in humility for us. Gives us a little perspective. After all, what are statues and steeples and temples and mansions but thinly veiled exercises in human vanity? The only truly healthy attitude I ever heard on the subject came from Rossini, the marvelous Italian composer who gave us *William Tell* and *The Barber of Seville,* among other classics — not to mention a culinary delight called Tournedos Rossini, invented by the composer himself. For all his creativity, Rossini was not a rich man when he reached old age, but he was popular. So much so that a group of his admirers raised twenty thousand francs to erect a statue of Rossini.

When Rossini heard about it, he said, "Give me the twenty thousand, I'll stand on the pedestal myself."

The Not-So-Grand River

I WANT TO QUOTE something that, contrary to the way it sounds, is really quite sad. Ready?

"There are some fine falls upon the river, which is clear as crystal, flowing over a limestone bed, full of delicious trout . . ."

Those words were penned in a letter written 150 years ago by Adam Fergusson. He was describing the site of a town that he was about to found, which would bear his name — Fergus, Ontario — and he was talking about the Grand River, which flowed then, and flows now, right through the centre of that town.

The sad part comes when you compare the description of the Grand River before white men got hold of it with the Grand River as it is today.

It is not crystal clear. The limestone beds it flows over are caked and coated with that eerie green-brown slime that you see in just about every river and stream that has too many people around it. And trout? Any trout that had the misfortune to jump into the Grand River south of Fergus would be belly up before it made the next town.

To be fair, the Grand River is cleaner than a lot of rivers I know. There are fish in it — pike, suckers, catfish — and kids still can swim in the Grand without picking up diseases. But to think that only a comparatively short time ago those waters were crystal clear and full of trout — that's very sad indeed.

It's really quite obscene what we've allowed to happen to our rivers. And it doesn't seem to be a function of wealth or sophistication. Tiny northern mill towns kill their rivers; so do big cities. Toronto builds itself the largest tower in the world, a subway system that is the envy of other nations, a domed stadium. Right downtown is the Don River . . . so polluted it's almost a fire hazard. The Don River used to run through the Don Valley, which was once one of the most beautiful valleys in all of Southern Ontario. Now the Don Valley Parkway runs through the Don Valley and the Don River hardly runs at all.

I wonder why people let that sort of thing happen? We care about parks and green spaces and beaches and hiking trails. How come we don't care about our rivers? Is it because the job's too big? Is it because each of us thinks Aw, hell, sure it's a mess, but what can one person do? Is that it? Then we should pay attention to Marion Stoddart. Marion moved to Groton, Massachusetts, in 1962 and shortly after discovered the Nashua River. It wasn't hard to find. The Nashua had a paper company on its banks and it was so polluted that the water literally ran different colours, depending on what was being printed that day.

Marion Stoddart changed all that. She did it by arguing, wheedling, twisting arms . . . mostly by convincing everyone she met that it just made good sense not to have an open sewer running through the middle of town.

Mind you, she used a few tricks of the trade. She sent a bottle of filthy Nashua River water to the state governor and got him to pledge to keep that bottle on his desk until the river was cleaned up.

Well, the governor doesn't have the bottle on his desk anymore. That's because the river is cleaned up. Fishermen travel hundreds of miles to fish for perch, bass, and pickerel — this in a stream that was pronounced stone dead only twenty years ago. Blue herons and kingfishers feed where islands of toxic sludge used to wallow. The Nashua River is clean — and six brand-new waste-water treatment plants keep it that way. And it's all thanks to one determined woman, Marion Stoddart.

I don't know what it's like in your town, but my town could sure use a Marion Stoddart. Trouble is, there aren't many of them around. I figure I've got about maybe one-tenth the drive and gumption and brains of Marion Stoddart. One-tenth isn't enough.

Mind you, if I could find nine other people, we could maybe go some distance to getting our river cleaned up.

Be a grand thing to do for Adam Fergusson's memory.

Be a grand thing to do for the Grand.

Smells Fine to Me!

*Oh, give me land, lots of land under starry skies
above . . . don't fence me in.* — Popular song lyric

*Don't bury me in this prairie, take me where the
cement grows.* — Another popular song lyric

IN RESPONSE TO THE old question, which is better, urban or rural,
I'd say I live a terrifically democratic life. Four days of the week
I wake up in the country, with corn growers and dairy farmers for
neighbours, cardinals flickering across my verandah, and one
magical morning, a sloe-eyed, white-flecked fawn skittering awk-
wardly across my driveway like a little girl wearing her mother's
high-heeled shoes. For the other three days of the week, I gird my
loins, drive to the station and board a Via Rail train for the hour
and a half run to the Big Smoke, complete with superhighways,
skyscrapers, and an awful lot of people. It the city, I see more
human faces on one subway ride than I would meet in a month
in the country. In the country I can watch arrowheads of Canada
geese flapping phlegmatically across the sky under the watchful
gaze of a circling red-tailed hawk. In the city, I see great pregnant
747s waddling in from New York, Chicago, and the coast under
the watchful gaze of traffic helicopters.

I am not making a value judgement here. I enjoy both experi-
ences, the urban and the rural. It's just that sometimes the cross-
over can leave a person just a touch . . . well . . . schizophrenic.

Now, you take the question of smells. Each time I get to the city
and wind my way out of the labyrinthine tunnels of the train
station and onto the bustling, car-clogged streets, I get this very
strong burning sensation in my nostrils. You know how it is when

you drink a Coke too fast and it kind of backs up into your sinuses? It feels like that. There's a smell that goes with it, too — a sharp and acrid odour that I don't recognize.

But when I mention this phenomenon to city dwellers, they don't know what I'm talking about. They say their noses don't hurt and they don't smell a thing. The ominous aspect is that after I've been on a downtown city street for thirty seconds or so, the pain goes away and I can't smell anything odd either.

I guess this whole smell experience wouldn't be worth mentioning if it wasn't for what happened last weekend. I had a friend from the city visiting. Bright and early Saturday morning she came downstairs, went out on the verandah, took a deep breath . . . and collapsed in a coughing fit.

"What the hell is that?" she gasped.

"What's what?" I asked.

"That *smell!*"

I took a whiff. Oh, *that* smell. Why, it was just the farmer down on the next concession spreading manure on his fields. I took another judicious sniff, like a wine taster savouring the delicate bouquet of a fine Moselle. "Pig, I believe."

My green-faced guest looked at me with disbelieving eyes. "How can you stand it?" she muttered through clenched teeth.

Truth is, I never thought of it as an objectionable smell. The aroma of manure on the air has always been a welcome treat for me, signalling that winter is officially over, the cows are out of the barn, and the ground is being prepared for the crops I'll be sinking my teeth into in just a few weeks time.

Not that I couldn't sympathize with my house guest. I remember the first time I drove through the northwestern Ontario town of Kenora a few years back. I wheeled into a gas station, jumped out of my car, and all but doubled up by the gas pump. "What's that stink?" I croaked to the attendant. "Oh . . . you mean the mill?" he asked.

Pulp and paper mill. You haven't known stench until you've smelled one of those little rosebuds in full flower.

I think perhaps the British writer John Gloag said it best. In a book called Georgian Grace he wrote, "Our forerunners had faculties that we have lost . . . they ignored the natural smell of sweat and dung and dirt, as we ignore the artificial smells of petrol fumes and industrial effluents."

I guess that's true. And I guess if the old saying "beauty is in the eye of the beholder" holds any water, then it must also be true that stench is in the nostrils of the sniffer.

You smell something funny?

A Tree Grows in Haiti

Y OU KNOW WHAT I think we need a quick dose of? Good news. Especially good news about trees. There's precious little of it going around. Our global track record with trees is not good. Hardly a week goes by without some newspaper feature, radio report, or TV docudrama about how avaricious timber cutters are raping the equatorial rain forests of East Asia, Africa, and South America. And here in Canada we are relentlessly kept abreast of how ineptly we're looking after our own forest resources, thanks to our bizarre policy of overcutting and underplanting. Then, of course, there are the news updates about how acid rain is killing off our maples and spruce budworm is attacking our evergreens. We have stories about Dutch elm disease. Tales about tent caterpillars — oh, we're knee-deep in *bad* news. In fact, if bad news were trees, we'd have a jungle's worth.

One way of alleviating bad news is to look around and find someplace that has worse news — as in, "Hey, you think we've got bad news about trees, just thank your lucky stars that you don't live in . . ."

Well, Haiti, for example. The state of Haiti's forest industry, if it can be called that, makes a Canadian clear cut look like the Garden of Eden. Time was when Haiti was covered with thick, luxurious forests from the peaks of its mountains right down to the sandy beaches. Then in the 1800s the timber merchants came. They stripped Haiti so efficiently and so thoroughly that today ninety-one percent of a land mass that should be covered in tropical rain forest is as barren as a downtown Toronto parking lot. The few trees still left fall prey to hungry Haitians who want the wood for

186

fuel and use the land the trees occupy to plant subsistence crops.

It's a situation that does not correct itself. *No trees* means nothing to hold the tropical rainfalls, which means stupendous erosion, which means tons and tons of valuable Haitian topsoil sluicing down the rivers and into the Caribbean every year.

Nope, if you were looking for good news in the forestry line, Haiti would not be the place to start looking.

Unless you squinted very, very closely. Because as a matter of fact there is some good news about trees in Haiti — and Canada is responsible for it.

The Mennonite Central Committee of Waterloo, Ontario, is not a group known to blow its own horn. Mennonites are a quiet lot who prefer to *do* good things rather than talk about them — but recently the MCC permitted itself a tiny toot in the form of a press release — a press release announcing that Canadian Mennonites have just planted a tree in the Artibonite valley of Haiti.

It was a special tree — the one millionth to be planted by those Mennonite volunteers.

The Mennonite Central Committee has been quietly planting trees in Haiti for the past several years, with mixed results. Some years, because of drought and disease, only about half survived. In 1984, on the other hand, thanks to rainfall and the cooperation of local farmers, they had an eighty-five percent survival rate. But good years and bad years, feast and famine, there are now one million trees growing in Haiti that wouldn't be, if not for the Canadian Mennonites.

It's not the end of the story. One million trees will not transform Haiti into a verdant land. But it's a step. And even a journey of a thousand miles begins with a single step. I think Mao Tse-Tung said that.

You won't get a tree if you don't plant a seed.

I think Johnny Appleseed said that.

Let's Dispose of Disposables

I DON'T KNOW if you're a photography bug or not, but if you are, I'd imagine you're quite excited over the news of that new camera on the market. Oh, you haven't heard? Yeah. Brand-new model from the Fuji Film Company . . . 35 millimetre . . . 400 ASA . . . colour print capability . . . shoots from a preset f/11 aperture . . . takes twenty-four snaps. Oh, yes . . . and one more thing. When you've shot your full roll, you don't have to mess around trying to claw the camera open to get the film out. You just take the entire thing (which is only as big as a bar of soap) down to the photo shop and plop it on the counter for developing. The camera, you see, is disposable.

Throwaway cameras . . . it had to come, I suppose. The folks at Fuji call their number the Quick Snap. Eastman Kodak has jumped on the bandwagon with a similar model, aptly designated the Kodak Fling. Naturally you pay a little something extra for all that convenience. Both cameras sell for about three times the cost of the film they use . . . and they only work outdoors on subjects that are at least three feet away. Expert photographers may sneer at them, but Fuji and Kodak executives anticipate brisk sales among the amateur shutterbugs more interested in convenience than Yousuf Karsh quality.

Personally, I've always had trouble with the whole concept of disposable products. Why should I buy something that's designed not to last?

I still remember years ago beholding my very first disposable lighter. I must have looked like a Cro-Magnon squinting at a burning ember for the first time. I remember asking myself how can it possibly make economic sense to have people buying throwaway products as opposed to durable products? Oh, sure, I realize it means that lighter manufacturers make more money in the short run, but isn't that something like war? A terrific economic surge at the beginning followed by a dread reckoning somewhere down the line?

I dunno. I might feel a little easier if all those disposable items really *were*—disposable, I mean. They're not. Oh, we throw them out, all right. But the garbage goes into landfill sites. Which may one day do God knows what to our farmland and our water tables. Maybe *that's* the dread reckoning down the road. Our "disposables" don't all make it to the landfill sites, either. A lot of those Bics when they've flicked their last flick get thrown out car windows. I see them on my morning walk, lying in the ditch. Along with disposable cups, disposable cans, disposable bottles, even the odd disposable diaper. It's ironic — the Indians didn't have disposable diapers for their kids, so they used moss, which really is disposable. We use disposable diapers — which really aren't.

I've got a cigarette lighter at home. Solid brass. It was made out of a rifle cartridge by someone working in a British munitions factory, back during the First World War. Just a rifle shell, with a wick and a flint wheel all soldered together during some worker's coffee break.

It's not very elegant looking, but it'll work forever. It'll already worked for sixty-five or seventy years with no sign of wear. It was my grandfather's. Then it was my father's. Now it's mine.

I don't even smoke, but I keep it around to remind of how things used to be . . . back in the primitive days when people were so simple and unsophisticated that they went around making things that you didn't have to throw out.

Henry Merlau's Maple

WELL, SPRING IS HERE, give or take a freak flurry, and for me that means strategy time. Time to make like Montgomery of Alamein as I plan my assault on scraggly lawns, soon-to-be-weed-choked gardens, a hedge that currently sports a punk rocker hairstyle, and one incongruous mountain of rocks that some thoughtful long-forgotten settler left in my back field ninety or a hundred years ago.

Actually I'm getting way ahead of myself. Those are *final* assault plans. I've got a lot of minor spring offensives to mount before I'll be able to get to them. Important things like plopping the canoe in the river to see if it sprang any leaks over the winter. And I might as well take my fishing rod along, make sure it didn't rust up in those heavy rains last fall. Other jobs, too . . . I'll have to break out the hammock, I suppose, and ascertain that my lawn chairs, like the universe, are unfolding as they should. And there's one more spring job I plan to take care of before I get down to the realities of quack grass, cut worms, and caterpillar counterattacks.

I want to go and see Henry Merlau's tree.

I know where it is — on Henry Merlau's farm in Wellesley, which is just west of Kitchener-Waterloo, right in the heart of Southwestern Ontario farming country, which is to say, tame land . . . domesticated land.

Southwestern Ontario farmland looks like a patchwork quilt of neat square blocks of corn and wheat fields, grass and pasture land, with here and there small tufts of woodlots — second-, third-, even fourth-generation trees, not too tall and not too wild. Until you get to Henry Merlau's place. The trees in his bush are a lot taller than most. He's got beeches, cherry, and lots of maple that are better than one hundred feel tall — but that's not what really sets Henry's bush apart from the rest. What does, is the huge solitary sugar maple that towers over the other timber like a beach umbrella over a bed of petunias. If three large men join hands, they can just encircle the trunk of Henry Merlau's sugar maple at ground level. If you want to know what it would be like to sit on the crown of it, find yourself a high-rise, get on the elevator, and press 14. That's how tall Henry Merlau's maple is — 132 feet. Not huge for a skyscraper: mighty tall for a tree. Unheard of for a sugar maple. Henry Merlau owns far and away the tallest sugar maple in Canada, maybe in all of North America. Nobody's found a taller one anywhere so far.

Age? Four hundred years, give or take a decade. Which means it was a seedling when Drake destroyed the Spanish Armada; a sapling when Shakespeare's *Henry V* was seen for the first time at the Globe. The mind-boggling fact is that Henry Merlau's tree was getting on for a hundred years old *two centuries* before Canada was a country.

How Henry Merlau's maple escaped the pioneers axe and the lumberman's saw is a mystery. Henry recalls that the tree was actually sold to a lumber company by his father, back in the hard times of the Depression. But the lumber company went bankrupt before it could lay a saw blade on the big maple. Henry's father took that for a sign and vowed the tree would stand for as long as he did.

What about his son, Henry Merlau? There's an awful lot of good hardwood in a maple tree twelve feet around and 132 feet high. Worth a lot of money. The word has gone around to lumber companies that there's no point in even putting in an offer with Henry Merlau. He isn't selling. Henry has a simple outlook on the whole thing. He says the tree is one of the things God created and gave him the responsibility for looking after.

Which I guess gives me two prespring jobs I want to take care of soon.

First I want to see Henry Merlau's tree.

Then I want to shake Henry Merlau's hand.

Stop Me Before I Garden Again

YOU KNOW, there's something truly perverse about the human memory. Just a few weeks ago I would have given a pint of blood, a pound of flesh, *and* sworn off crunchy peanut butter for six months just for the sight of a spring crocus. That's because just a few short weeks ago the snow around these parts lay deep and crisp and even — as it had for several months previously. Back then, the maples were still bare and gaunt, the weatherman routinely rolled off phrases such as "chance of flurries," robins and orioles were still working on their tans somewhere south of Myrtle Beach, and it looked as if winter would go on forever.

Now, the snow's gone, songbirds are staking out their aerial turf, the trees are bursting into leaf, dandelions are plotting counterinsurgency measures on my front lawn . . . and still I'm gripped by that same terrible dread I feel when I wake up of a winter morning and realize I have to shovel my way out to the car.

I know *why* it is. It's because of that muddy brown fenced-off area in the backyard. You see it there? That swatch of scorched earth that looks as if something large, heavy, and rectangular sat on it for several years and then moved on?

I call that My Garden. Although when I think about it, I can't imagine why.

My dictionary defines a garden as "a plot of land used for the cultivation of flowers, vegetables, or fruit." That certainly doesn't describe the sinkhole in my backyard. Last year, after lovingly anointing my garden with enough loam, ash, peat, bone meal, and commercial fertilizer to form a minor Caribbean archipelago, I carefully planted corn, onions, cabbage, tomatoes, cauliflower, and if memory serves, even some eggplant. Last fall I harvested quackgrass, pigweed, burdock, bindweed, dandelion, and several green things I didn't recognize but that I knew were weeds. I knew because they were six feet tall and the tomato worms, cabbage butterflies, and garden slugs wouldn't touch them.

Actually, I'm exaggerating. I did harvest a crop last fall. You know those paper envelope packages you buy your seeds in? Well, I filled two of those to bursting. Planted thirty-seven packages, harvested two. We had my garden for dinner one night. As the hors d'oeuvre.

I particularly recall my cherry tomatoes. It said "beefsteak" on the seed package, but I'm sure that was a misprint. As I sat there, looking at my cherry tomatoes (all seven of them), it occurred to me that those seven . . . berries . . . had cost me roughly the price of a week's groceries. Not counting labour, of course. If you factor in the sweat of my brow — even at minimum wage — it became clear that those seven tomatoes huddled on a saucer should not have been eaten. They should have been bronzed.

Right now I'm at the denial stage of my annual garden ritual. I'm telling anyone who will listen that I'm through with gardening, that this year I plan to take the spiritual approach to agriculture. That's where you lie in your hammock from June till first frost with a succession of tall cold lemonades in your hand while you chant, "If God wants me to have avocados in my garden, he'll put avocados in my garden."

But I've been down this row before. It probably won't work. Come about the twenty-fourth of May the Gardening Bug will bite and I'll be back once again toiling like Sisyphus — and with about the same return.

In the meantime, I have nothing good to say about gardens. Well, I will say this. Joni Mitchell wrote a song called "Woodstock," in which she sings, "We are stardust, we are golden, and we've got to get ourselves back to the garden."

All I can say is, Joni, when you're finished with yours, you're welcome to start on mine.

The Misery Index

EDMONTON'S BAD, but not as bad as Regina. Newfoundland's capital, St. John's, is pretty crummy too, but Chicoutimi-Jonquière is crummier. Victoria and Vancouver? Leave those two wimps out of this. They don't even rate. We're talking *real* Canadian cities. Cities like, well, Winnipeg. Now *there's* a Canuck burg for ya! Winnipeg's the absolute top of the list.

Misery is what we're measuring here. As in urban winter misery, and it's official: when it comes to Canadian cities, Winnipeg is the worst one to spend the winter in.

The trouble with Canadian winters is that there really is no such animal. Winters here are very different, depending on where in the Great White North you choose to plant your mukluks. A Prairie winter is not like a Maritime winter, just as a winter in Prince Rupert would seem a little weird to a Mennonite farmer from Elmira, Ontario.

Except for one thing. There is one commodity that virtually all Canadian winters have in common.

Misery. It is safe to say that a Canadian winter is a miserable winter, one way or another.

Which is where David Phillips comes in. Mr. Phillips is a climatologist who toils for the Atmospheric Environment Service in Toronto. Looking out his office window one winter morning, across a scabby snowscape of dirty, salt-encrusted banks interspersed with ice patches, Mr. Phillips had a revelation. "What this country needs," he realized, "is a good Winter Misery Index."

So David Phillips designed one. He came up with a list of eleven pointed questions that he could ask about any city's winter experience, questions like: how much snow do you get, how many sunny days, how many times does the thermometer dip under 20 below, how much wind — questions like that. By assigning a numerical value to each answer, Phillips had a method of plotting any Canadian city's position on the Misery Map.

Winnipeg won, mittens down. On a scale of 100, Manitoba's capital copped a frosty 62. Regina wasn't far behind with a 61, and Chicoutimi-Jonquiere was nipping at both their heels with a rating of 60. That was Win, Place, and Show for David Phillips's Misery Sweepstakes. You'll be happy to learn that all other Canadian cities were way back in the pack.

Edmonton for instance, which I thought would rate pretty rotten, pulled a respectable 49. Toronto, which has never been my first choice for a January tryst, got a 34. A little farther south, Windsor scored a semitropical 29. As for equatorial hangouts like Vancouver and Victoria? Ten and 8 on the scale respectively. (I know, I know — I said I wouldn't talk about them, but I thought you should know just how bizarre things get in this country, winter-weather-wise.)

I'm glad we have David Phillips's Winter Misery Index. It's a stroke of genius that was long overdue. Especially when our only alternatives were the Druidic pronouncements emanating from Environment Canada — what in the name of heaven is an average mortal to make of a wind chill that is measured in *watts per square metre?*

And yet . . . the existence of the David Phillips's Misery Index begs one unignorable question: now that we know how miserable our winters are, what are we going to do about it?

Most of us would have trouble finding permanent work in the Greek islands, and retsina is an inferior substitute for Canadian lager.

Victoria's not big enough to take us all in. Besides, trading snowshoes for swim flippers is a dubious bargain at best.

Given the climate of economic restraint, I doubt that Ottawa will seriously consider financing a retractable dome stretching from the Queen Charlottes to Conception Bay.

And anyway, just think of the bill for windshield solvent.

Nope, let's face it. Dave Phillips's Misery Index only illustrates something that every Canadian knows in his permafrosted soul —

we have lousy winters.

The thing is not to whine about it. Just accept it. If it makes you feel better, you can go around reciting the words of the English poet Shelley: "If winter comes, can spring be far behind?"

Easy for Shelley to say, of course.

He'd never visited Winnipeg.

PART 5

Canada, Armageddon, and Kinky Sects

The Hal Who Came In from the Cold

THE OLD MAN glowered menacingly, like a CFL lineman, looming over the polished white pine expanse of his desktop. His craggy head with the bulldog jaws and the tank-turret eyes was backlit by a cone of light that splashed out from the lamp behind him, across the desk and into the pale, thin face of Agent 47, standing stiffly at attention. Agent 47 didn't look like the second most powerful man in all of Canadian Intelligence, but then nobody looked like *anything* when they were standing in front of the Old Man's desk.

"Well, Forty-seven," the Old Man rumbled, "out with it. Start with our American Operations."

Agent 47 cleared his throat, pinched the side seams of his trousers between clammy thumbs and forefingers, and began.

"Well, sir, as you know, the entire department is still reeling from the loss of Lorne Greene. He was one of our most highly placed operatives — a virtual father figure for Americans. We regard his demise as a real blow to the Operation."

The Old Man waved a huge ham hock of a hand impatiently. Forty-seven knew what that meant: get on with it.

"W-w-we also incurred a temporary setback with the Mansbridge offensive. Our CBS management mole went sour when we tried to pay him off in loon dollars, but on the whole, keeping Mansbridge in Canada may turn out to be a bonus. It frees up Nash for future operations.

"Then, of course, we still have the usual operatives in place — Keith Morrison, Peter Jennings, Peter Kent, Morley Safer on the hard-news front. In the Entertainment Department, Alex Trebek, Monty Hall, Art Linkletter, undercover Canucks all, all doing their job. When you factor in all the Canadians ensconced in Hollywood — the John Candys, the Dan Aykroyds, the Martin Shorts, and the Howie Mandels, not to mention the Arthur Haileys, the Joni Mitchells, the Neil Youngs, the Leonard Cohens, and Michael J. Foxes — it amounts to a virtual stranglehold on the American communications industry."

The Old Man sat immovable, his laser eyes glaring over the top of his reading glasses. Forty-seven could feel the heat of that gaze focused right on his Adam's apple. He cleared his throat, swallowed, and plunged on.

"Then there's our British field of operation — it still goes well. Not as well as in our heyday, of course, when we had old Max — Lord Beaverbrook — pulling the strings and calling the tune of Fleet Street. But the *Sunday Times* and the *Times* of London still belong to the estate of a poor lad from Sudbury, as do a raft of British dailies, not to mention TV and radio sta—"

The Old Man cut Agent 47 off with a wave and a growl. "Dammit, man, I know who our operatives in the field are and what we control. What I want to know is, how does the enemy feel about us? Is our cover holding?"

"Couldn't be better, sir," replied Agent 47 briskly. "Overall, the rest of the world continues to regard Canada as a nation of polite but boring drones, when they regard us at all.

"The Yanks have just published a book called *Chronicle of the 20th Century*. In the Canadian section, it spells our capital *Ottowa* and leaves Toronto and Montreal right off the map."

Agent 47 wasn't positive, but he thought he detected just the shimmer of a smirk flickering across the Old Man's face.

"Even better news from the British theatre, sir. The Economist magazine has declared Canada to be one of the world's most boring places — ranks us with Switzerland, New Zealand, and . . . East Germany.

There was no doubt of it now, the Old Man was grinning. Grinning! Wait'll they heard about this back at HQ!

The Old Man massaged his massive jaw. "Ott-o-wa, eh? God, that's good. And the Brits — that bangers-and-mash, Blackpool-by-the-sea, bowler-and-brolly, stiff-upper-lip island of dead fish has the nerve to call *us* boring? Haw!"

Agent 47 had never seen — never heard of — the Old Man being so animated. A feeling of irrepressible glee skittered up from the ice ball in 47's belly and nested in his throat.

The Old Man's mirth passed as suddenly as it had sprung up. He fixed the agent with a steely glare and rumbled, "Good work, Forty-seven, but the battle is far from over. I want to see more Indian maidens, lumberjacks, and singing Mounties at every border crossing. I want every film festival in the world to be flooded with NFB shorts about loons and Rocky Mountain sunsets and majestic moose."

"Remember the purpose of the operation, Forty-seven: to Keep Canada Secret. As long as the rest of the world thinks Canada is boring, we can keep Canada for Canadians. We all must do our part, Forty-seven. That includes you. And me. Dismissed!"

There was a low murmuring noise from behind the Old Man, and it was growing louder. Agent 47 could distinctly hear an organ, prolonged cheers, and a suggestion of the tune "O Canada." Forty-seven stood rigidly at attention as the Old Man pushed himself up from the desk, adjusted a hideous green-and-salmon striped tie, patted his orange hair into place and lumbered through the velvet curtain towards the noise inside.

Ah, thought Operative 47, not for the first time . . . if only Canadians could know the *real* Harold Ballard.

CanMed

*Canada is, alas, forgetting that it is its pioneers who
built this country and made it what it was; now it
wants to be like everyone else and have autocamps
instead of trees and Coca-Cola stands instead of
human beings.*

— Malcolm Lowry

L OWRY PENNED those thoughts way back in 1950. It is probably
just as well that he died a few years later. He'd have trouble
believing the unseemly haste with which Canadians are lining up
to leap into the giant American blender.

"Coca-Colonialism" someone once dubbed it — the process of
conditioning people to crave American goods and vibrate to
American sensibilities. Coca-Colonialism is a global phenomenon.
The Brits watch "Dallas" while Muscovites buy black market Levi's
and Chinese line up to buy bottles of, yes, Coca-Cola. The whole
world is being Americanized, but nowhere has the invasion been
more successful, nowhere is total victory nearer, than here in
Canada.

We buy our Cokes (or Pepsis) at McDonald's, then we drive our
Chevs and Fords and Chryslers to the movies to watch Sylvester
Stallone or Clint Eastwood fight for Truth, Justice, and the Ameri-
can Way.

And when Rambo or Dirty Harry has made the world safe for
democracy, we head home, crack a Coors or a Miller Lite, flip on
the tube, and catch a few minutes of Carson or Letterman. In
Toronto it's dead easy to rustle up a mob of thirty-five or forty
thousand people any summer afternoon, jam 'em into a leaky
domed stadium to watch a squad of twenty-odd Americans and
Dominicans perform in a game of America's Pastime — baseball.

Canadians eat, drink, talk, shop, drive, even dress like Americans, right down to our Fruit of the Looms.

Well, I don't know about you, but if I wanted to be American, I'd move to California. I don't and I haven't, which makes it doubly depressing to realize that my staying put is irrelevant — America's coming to me.

Still, it's nice to see that Canadians can still stiffen what's left of their backbones once in a while.

I'm referring to what I call the Club Med Kerfuffle.

You hadn't heard? Oh, it was a grand little dustup. Club Med is a multinational tourist resort operation that's heavy on the hedonism. Club Med tries to attract those jaded, lonely (but not indigent) North American citizens who are fed up with the humdrummity of a nine-to-five existence, not to mention the unpredictable vagaries of a weather system unduly influenced by Arctic highs and lows. Club Med is pleased, for a hefty financial consideration, to whisk such unfortunates off to one of their many Feel Good spas that dot the tropical climes. There, one encounters sun and sand and cheap wine and moonlight beach parties and ever-smiling Club Med flunkies in quantities sufficient to temporarily erase memories of the grimmest existence — say, life in Pittsburgh.

Recently, Club Med launched a campaign to attract more Canadians. They did this by running a newspaper ad that showed two pictures. One was of a tumbledown tarpaper shack. Next to it was a photo of a tropical island, palms swaying, surf crashing. The headline read, "There's up north . . . and there's down south." The copy in the ad went on to suggest that tourists could choose between the north with its "mosquitoes, hot and cold running mice, and rain . . ." or the carefree splendours of a Club Med vacation.

And that, as they say down at the McDonald's takeout window, is when the chips hit the fan.

Canadians were incensed. They blasted Club Med with letters, telegrams, and phone calls. The director of the North Bay Chamber of Commerce called it an offense to all Canadians. A B.C. Tourism official called it an insult. Ontario's then minister of Tourism and Recreation, John Eakins, branded it "a smear." Outraged customers began writing in to cancel bookings.

202

Club Med knows bad PR when it smells it. The ad was quickly yanked, and letters of apology from the Resort Giant began to cover the land like a fine blanket of . . . you know. Mr. Alex El-Kayem, Club Med's general manager for Canada, is still assuring anyone who will listen that his company will never, ever cast aspersions on Canada's "northness" again.

Only a minor skirmish in the ongoing Coca-Colonization of Canada, I suppose, but I find it cheering that despite having a leader who sings duets with Presidents and dances jigs for his supper, there are some Canadians who still refuse to roll over and cry "Uncle."

Annexation Will Be a Little Late This Year

I WANT TO TAKE YOU to an apartment in midtown Manhattan: 446 West Forty-sixth Street, to be exact. That's the address of an exceedingly odd couple named L. Craig Schoonmaker and his roommate, Fred. It's an unremarkable two-storey brownstone wedged into a kind of warehousey section of town, but L. Craig Schoonmaker and Fred are fairly unremarkable looking in their own right. Mr. Schoonmaker is pudgy and bald and bespectacled and middle-aged. Fred is his cat. Purpose in Life? Well, for Fred it seems to be to cop as many pats as possible and to sleep right through till the next dinner gong. L. Craig Schoonmaker is more ambitious: he would like to take over Canada.

And the Philippines. And England, Ireland, and Scotland, as well. No, I'm serious — or rather, L. Craig Schoonmaker is. He is founder and chairman of the Expansionist Party of the United States, the goal of which is to transform all the aforementioned nations into a sprinkle of brand-new stars and stripes on Old Glory.

Not . . . violently, you understand. Mr. Schoonmaker is not some firebrand Fenian bent on smashing our border in the dead of night and raising the Stars and Stripes over the battlements of Old Fort York. No, he believes the power of sweet reason and pure common sense will win over the Filipinos, the British, and Canadians, if only he can get his message to them.

As the Expansionist Party manifesto somewhat blithely puts it, "We believe that the United States is a microcosm of the entire

Earth. The prosperity we have achieved here can be achieved everywhere, through the same means."

Mr. Schoonmaker formed his party back in 1977 in response to a massive public demand perceptible only to Mr. Schoonmaker. Since then, he has spent all his spare time cranking out newsletters, press releases, and letters to editors of newspapers around the world. He has travelled to speak to any group that wanted to hear his views on annexation — he even crossed the border to speak at a couple of Southern Ontario universities, but he admits any groundswell of popular support on either side of the border has to this point not registered on the Richter scale.

It's difficult to convey how unnerving it is to sit in a cramped and cluttered living room, with a fat tabby named Fred curlicuing around your ankles, listening to a mild-mannered, middle-aged man explaining why it would be best for all concerned if he took over your country as soon as possible. It would have been easier if L. Craig Schoonmaker was a laser-eyed demagogue wearing a Nazi armband, army fatigues, and a Webley on his hip. L. Craig Schoonmaker wears a ratty sweater-vest with moth holes in it. He wears a New York Yankees baseball cap. Not exactly Alexander the Great.

The man is so remarkably placid. Even . . . well, dull, sort of. The only time he gets remotely belligerent is when I suggest that all he seems to offer Canada in this annexation deal is more acid rain, slacker handgun controls, terrible tea, weak beer, George Steinbrenner, and a complete lack of two-dollar bills. What about, I suggest, Canada annexing the United States instead? L. Craig Schoonmaker gets a little testy at that. It is a suggestion he has apparently heard before. It does not compute.

But he doesn't give up. L. Craig Schoonmaker goes on cranking out his newsletters, even though after nine years of effort his worldwide mailing list stands at only 250 and he counts it a good month when he gets ten inquiries.

Do you suppose it's an American trait, that blissful self-assurance that they live at the centre of the universe? Here's something another American wrote: "The annexation of Canada this year as far as . . . Quebec, will be a mere matter of marching and will give us experience for the attack of Halifax . . . " Ex-U.S.

President Thomas Jefferson wrote that in a letter dated August 4, 1812. Mr. Jefferson was a tad overconfident — as, I suspect, is L. Craig Schoonmaker. Either way, I'll sleep soundly tonight. I just can't get paranoid at the prospect of being taken over by anybody who shares an apartment with a cat named Fred.

Let's Make a Deal

I'VE BEEN THINKING about the differences between Canada and America ever since Victoria Day — which is one difference right there, right? Americans don't get a Victoria Day holiday. But then, I'm not sure why *we* do. It's not a great time for a long weekend — usually still too cold to lie around on a beach — and it's tough to work up feelings of profound loyalty and felicitations for a short plump British monarch who never even saw Canada and hasn't been around for the past eighty-eight Victoria Days. In any case, I found myself at loose ends one Victoria Day, flicked on the telly in the afternoon, and discovered . . . "Let's Make a Deal." I know it's been around for a million years. I'd just never actually sat down and watched the show.

It's amazing. It's the American Dream right there on Channel Six weekdays in living colour. First there is the host, affable Monty Hall, dressed in a plaid sports jacket so brutal to the optic nerve that you realize instantly why they're called blazers. There is luminescent Monty, adrift in a sea of grown people dressed as . . . well, there's a chap in mirror sunglasses over there dressed as an eggplant.

And here's a woman with dime-size dots painted on her cheeks, a pair of fake pigtails in back, and a thumb in her mouth who would be a perfect double for Raggedy Ann, if Raggedy Ann had ever tipped the scales at 220 pounds plus. And this lady over here in the chaps and leather vest, the string tie, and the ten-gallon Stetson that keeps slipping over her eyes . . . a John Waynette, or I miss my guess. This is the "Let's Make a Deal" Zoo. All these creatures sit before the cameras, oohing and aahing, squealing,

207

clapping their hands as Monty's minions work Doors Number One, Two, and Three. The zoo sort of percolates in place, as if a low-voltage current were surging through their chair bottoms every few seconds.

But it's not the costumes. It's not even the behaviour. It's what they *do* it for. This menagerie really craves and lusts after Speed Queen automatic washers, Turtle car wax systems, and a year's supply of Rice A Roni. Worse! It hits you that these few seconds with Monty represent their moment in the sun! That in years to come, in their dotage, they will be avidly telling and retelling their sagas in circles around some future flickering cathode tube. "So Monty said to Harry again, 'What'll it be, Harry — Door Number Three or whatever is in this plain brown paper bag?' And I whispered, 'Harry, you shmuck, if you don't take Door Number Three, don't come home tonight.'"

Amazing program. I think those Canadian editorialists who periodically twist themselves and our language out of shape trying to define the difference between Canada and the U.S. ought to be exposed to it, if only for a couple of shows. Here's a hypothesis: the difference between the U.S. and Canada is the difference between "Let's Make a Deal" and "Front Page Challenge."

On that side, you have people dressed as wastebaskets, layer cakes, and pizza toppings clamouring for the chance to win vacuum cleaners, microwaves, and thousand-dollar bills. On this side, you have Fred and Betty and Alan and Pierre chuntering amiably about headlines from Canadian history. "And twenty-five dollars is on its way to Mr. J. Doe of Mukluk, Northwest Territories, for that headline."

A Winnipeg notable by the name of M. Halparin once said, "You can learn more about America by watching one half-hour of 'Let's Make a Deal' than you can get from watching Walter Cronkite for a month."

M. Halparin ought to know. He himself left Winnipeg for Hollywood years ago . . . and changed his name to Hall. Monty Hall.

The Fine Art of Flannelmouthing

THIS MAY SOUND a tad presumptuous, but I'd like to issue a warning, if I may. It's about my Old Age. I'm not there yet. As a matter of fact, I face about two more decades in the harness before I become eligible for the gold-plated Timex, but I figure it doesn't hurt to let folks know where you stand — while you still *can* stand, I mean, without the aid of a Malacca cane or an aluminum walker. So here goes. For anybody listening who figures to be still around when I hit sixty-five . . . please remember not to call me a Golden Ager, a Senior Citizen, or a Person in His Sunset Years. Feel free to call me a codger, a fogey, or a crotchety old geezer — anything with a little fire or grit in it will be fine — but please, no Pablum talk. None of those namby-pamby euphemisms.

I've never liked euphemisms. Not since I was a little kid and a fellow down the street — old Mr. Ritchie, it was — died. Being a preschooler, I was not privy to the chit-chat and gossip of coffee klatches and party lines, so I didn't know Mr. Ritchie was dead. I just knew he hadn't been out fussing with his rosebushes the way he always did every morning. "Where's Mr. Ritchie?" I asked a neighbour.

"Passed over," she told me.

"He's sleeping," said another.

"Passed over where?" I asked. "Let's wake him up," I suggested. They told me to hush.

Euphemisms are by and large a cowardly device used by people more interested in withholding information than passing it around. Thus, car lots advertise "preowned sedans" — that's used cars to you and me. And brochures for a four-wheel-drive vehicle that refer to automotive options such as "impact attenuators." We used to call them bumpers.

For some reason, wild animals frequently bear the burden of euphemistic phraseology. Not long ago the U.S. Parks Department found there were too many wild donkeys in one of its Colorado parks. Officials decided that for the health of the herd, some of them would have to be killed. But they would never call it that, for heaven's sake! Too blunt! Hence, the press release explaining that the donkey herds were to be "harvested under a direct reduction program." Well, there's one word for that and the word is *shot*. Not that we speak of our own species much more clearly. Recently the *New York Times* gave its Grand Prize for Euphemism to the Central Intelligence Agency, for the code name it assigns to clandestine assassination teams. The agency refers to them as "Health Alteration Committees."

Ah, well, the world has never been short of bafflegabbers and flannelmouthers who would hesitate to call a spade a spade if they thought they could get away with calling it a "cordless, unibodied facilitator for the accessing and dispersal of soil . . . "

Reminds me of an anecdote featuring a man who never hesitated to call a spade a bleeping shovel — Sir Winston Spencer Churchill.

Seems that once the great man was a guest for dinner at a very tony Washington mansion. During the course of the meal Churchill asked for some breast of chicken. The Southern belle sitting next to him drew herself up and said, "Mistah Churchill . . . in this country we do not say . . . that word. We ask for white meat or dark meat." Churchill, ever the gentleman, apologized profusely.

The next morning, the woman received by special delivery a beautiful single orchid, along with a note penned in the unmistakable Churchillian script. It read:

"My dear lady . . . I should be greatly obliged if you would pin this on your white meat."

Slow Down, Fast Food!

YOU LIKE FAST-FOOD restaurants — I mean, the McDonald's, the Pizza Huts, the Wendy's and the Burger Kings? I don't like them much, and I've always felt kind of guilty about it, because obviously what I don't like, tens — make that *hundreds* — of thousands adore. Besides, what's not to like? Those places are bright, they're efficient, they're clean, and the staff is cheerful (often relentlessly cheerful). The food? Well, it's not five-star restaurant fare, but neither are the prices. And when you cook the way I do, you should be grateful for anything that's warm and doesn't walk off the plate.

For a long time I couldn't put my finger on just what it was that bugged me about the fast-food restaurants. Then I came across a little newspaper story out of Salem, Oregon. It's about Cloe Curry. Cloe is a seventy-eight-year-old pensioner whose idea of a good time was to toddle down to the local Burger King with some knitting under her arm and pass the time of day chatting with the staff over a cup of coffee. She did it every morning. For years. "It got me out of that old dumb apartment," Cloe recalls.

I would guess Cloe, being a pensioner with not much money and not many other friends, could nurse a cup of coffee for a good while. That must have been the case, because along towards the end of last month, Cloe looked up from her knitting and her lukewarm java to see the Burger King manager looking down at her, arms crossed, tapping his foot.

The manager, one Robert Boss, told Cloe politely but firmly that he would like her not to come to his Burger King anymore. She was loitering, he said. And his restaurant didn't have time for loiterers.

When I read those words in the newspaper story it was like a big penny dropping in the back of my brain pan. *That's* why I don't like fast-food restaurants, I realized in a flash — because they don't like loiterers. Because for all their bright colours and friendly, smiling happy faces, fast-food restaurants are designed on the same principle as the laundry chute — maximum flow-through, minimum drag. They suck the customers in at one end, take their orders and their money, sit 'em down, fill 'em up, and move 'em out just as fast as they decently can.

I, on the other hand, am a born loiterer. I like old restaurants with high-backed wooden booths, with coffee that comes in chipped, green-and-white china mugs served by a slow-moving counterman in a white apron with an eternal Export "A" smouldering on his lip, a man who doesn't care if you stay all night, as long as you lift your feet when he makes a pass with the floor mop. Used to be quite a few restaurants like that. Lots of folks used them to warm up and to chat. To read books, write poems, spend some innocent time with their sweeties. Those restaurants were only incidentally in the food-selling business. What they mostly were were havens. Sanctuaries. Not-very-private clubs open to any-body who could rustle up the price of a cup of coffee. .

Speaking of which, the Cloe Curry story has a happy ending. Word got around about Cloe's being kicked out of the Burger King. The townfolk rallied, and pretty soon Cloe Curry had more invites to drop in for a morning coffee than she could shake a spoon at. One of those invites came, along with a bouquet of flowers, from Robert Boss, the Burger King manager. "I told her I'm only human and I made a mistake," he said. So Cloe Curry is back at her accustomed stool in the Salem, Oregon, Burger King and if the other fast food chains have any business sense they'll snap up her services — get her to bring her knitting and drop by for a cup of coffee at their outlets. Cloe will bring the one ingredient those places lack most. Heart.

Kinky Sects

Epiphany (i-pif'-e-né) 2a: a usu. sudden manifestation or perception of the essential nature of something; an intuitive grasp of reality through something usu. simple and striking.
— Webster's Third International Dictionary

SURE — AN EPIPHANY. Back in the sixties, druggies used to call it a "flash," as in, "Oh, wow, man! Like I was just — you know, grooving on Hendrix and I suddenly flashed, like, what if . . . the meaning of life was . . . *a guitar chord!"*

I had an epiphany once — way back before I could even pronounce the word, much less have a clue what it meant. It happened in my uncle's study. He was a United Church minister and the only person I knew who owned an entire roomful of leather-bound volumes. I loved his study and he encouraged me to use it. I think he thought I had scholarly, if not ecclesiastical, potential. In truth, I just liked sniffing his books. And daydreaming over his globe of the world.

Sitting on my uncle's desk was one of those burnished antique globes with a brass chain leading to a light bulb inside. The globe identified the oceans by their Latin names. It showed the mountain ranges of the world as so many swatches of what looked like raised scar tissue. It rendered all the British Empire, real and imagined, in steadfast royal pink. And it made a wonderful throaty rumbling sound as you twirled it on its axis.

In any case, there I was one sleepy summer day in my uncle's study, savouring his library through my nostrils while one hand idly spun the globe. Absent-mindedly I watched the blur of terrestrial real estate roll past. Canada up here . . . China way down there . . . Canada up here . . . China way down there . . .

Suddenly I skidded the globe to a halt with the heel of my hand. Canada up there . . . China down there! Canada facing the ceiling . . . China facing my uncle's somewhat worn broadloom! If this little Caucasian kid was sitting up here in his United Church minister-uncle's study, it follows that some little Chinese kid could be sitting in his Confucian priest-uncle's study . . .

Upside down.

In the spirit of scientific inquiry I even conducted a rigid control experiment to verify my conclusion. Lacking the necessary funds to fly to China and feel first-hand the blood rushing to my head, I gathered two toy soldiers and approached the globe. I planted one tin soldier firmly on Lake Ontario. I placed the second, identical soldier so that his tiny leaden feet obscured Peking and several hundred square miles of surrounding suburbs. Just as I feared. My metallic warriors were upside down to each other.

Bingo. My epiphany. I understood in one fell flash that the world is — *must be* — flat.

Well, there it is, out in the open at last. I am a Flat Earther — and a silent one no more. You can't imagine the relief I feel, coming out of the closet like this. No more hypocritical nods from me when people start prattling of Great Circle Routes, North and South Poles, and the sun going down "over the horizon." Hah.

You there, sir. Is that a smirk I see playing about the corners of your mouth? Then answer this: What proof do you have that the earth is not flat? Please don't quote books or point to films or recite laws of physics at me. Those are all outside resources. I want to know how *you know* the world is round.

See what I mean? You're probably a Flat Earther, too.

Don't take it too hard. There are a lot of really screwy cults out there that we could be mixed up with instead. True, the Bhagwan's not operating from his old Oregon address anymore, but there are plenty of perfectly exotic, not to say eccentric, creeds and persuasions left to choose from. If you're the sporting type, you might want to look over the Perfect Liberty Kyodan prospectus. Perfect Liberty — PL to its adherents — has its headquarters at Tondabayashi, Japan, in a compound that makes Oral Roberts University look like a Cub Scout campsite. The PL complex boasts a hospital, several schools, mausoleums, a temple, and a 550-foot Peace Tower.

Oh, yes . . . it also features a clutch of baseball diamonds and one enormous golf course. The golf course is especially important — so much so that many PL churches are instantly recognizable wherever you run across them because they have driving ranges built right on top of their roofs. Hence PL's nickname in Japan: "the golf religion." PL-ers will tell you that golf is not sacred per se — only as a means of self-expression, which the Perfect Liberty kyodan is very keen on.

If you're seriously interested in the Perfect Liberty Religious Sect, here is a word you'll need to know:

"Oshie-oya."

It means *patriarch*. He is the head man of the PL movement and the chap to whom you address the church envelopes.

If you're really, *really* interested in the Perfect Liberty religious sect, here is another word you will need to know:

"Fore!"

BUT PERHAPS, like mine, your most remarkable physical feature is an unreplaced divot on the top of your noggin. In that case you might give some thought to signing up with Baldheaded Men of America. A call to the North Carolina headquarters (no pun intended) confirms that Canadian skinheads are welcome, and all you have to bring with you is a five-dollar bill and a sense of humour. BHM of A's motto: "The Lord made millions and millions of heads and those He didn't like He covered up."

Why, there's even a cult for those afflicted with the Passion That Dares Not Speak Its Name — namely, garlic addiction. Lovers of the Stinking Rose is an organization formed in Berkeley, California, "to bring to garlic lovers . . . and cultured people everywhere up-to-date information on the miracle bulb, garlic."

STILL NOT QUITE what you were looking for, Nirvana-wise? I'm not surprised. As I said before, you have all the makings of a closet Flat Earther. Well, not to worry. From Berkeley, a short drive south and east will bring you to the farm of Charles Johnson, which squats on the edge of the Mojave Desert.

We're home, pal. This is Mecca. Charles Johnson is founder, president, and all-round custodian of the International Flat Earth Research society. This is the man who will tell you with perfect equanimity that the moon and the sun, both mere asteroids thirty-two miles in width, hover only three thousand miles above the earth's surface — which, needless to say, is as flat as a pizza, all dressed to go. Men on the moon? A NASA hoax, says Johnson. Photos of the Earth taken from space flights? "Grade-Z movies," he scoffs. President Johnson can wax positively lyrical when it comes to creative explanations for popular misconceptions. Remember the Space Shuttle? You probably thought that was some kind of scientific research project, right?

Oh, you guileless naif. Charles Johnson can tell you that the whole "space shuttle caper" was nothing more than a clever way of transporting cocaine in the John De Lorean affair.

Which is about where it begins to unravel for me, I'm afraid. I lied about being a Flat Earther. The truth is, Charles Johnson and his theories are just too wacky to swallow — even for a gullible cuss like me.

So how do I answer my own question? How do I know that the Earth is not flat? I don't. Instead, I take refuge in an old saw that says, "If you come across something that waddles like a duck, swims like a duck and quacks like a duck . . . it probably is a duck."

That's the way the world is for me. I've never been able to see with my own eyes that it's a sphere, but everything makes sense if I think of it as a sphere.

Well, almost everything.

I still don't understand how one billion Chinese manage to get along, living upside down like that.

Silver Threads Beneath the Headband

There's nothing sadder than an aging hipster.
— *Lenny Bruce*

WELL, IT FINALLY HAPPENED — the day I've been waiting for and dreading ever since my teenage hormones settled down long enough for my acne to clear up. It was my personal moment of truth: the day I began to feel old.

It was a newspaper ad that did it to me. I opened up a Toronto paper and there, staring out at me in a quarter-page ad, was the face of a very elegant woman, greying hair cut fashionably short, eyes tastefully mascaraed and linered and whatever other alchemy women perform to make their eyes look gorgeous.

There was something very familiar about those eyes . . .

The headline said, "Eaton's Invites You to Meet Joan Baez."

Joan Baez?

Eaton's??

Sure enough, the silver-voiced troubadour of the sixties was in the middle of an international book tour, flogging copies of her new autobiography. I suppose I shouldn't be surprised . . . it's just that I remember a time when Joan Baez wouldn't have crossed the threshold of a crass capitalist institution like Eaton's, much less hustled books for them.

That would have seen back in the volatile sixties when Joan Baez, blue jeaned and long haired, climbed up on coffee house stages with a scruffy kid named Dylan and belted out songs like "The Masters of War" and "The Times They Are A-Changin'." She's still a peace activist, I guess . . . it's just that protestors lose a certain

217

cachet when they trade in their love beads and bedrolls for an American Express Gold Card and chauffeured limos.

It's probably foolish, but seeing the sixties songstress decked out like a Tupperware executive and plugging her own hardcovers made me suddenly feel old. It also made me cast my mind back a quarter century or so to when I was long haired and blue jeaned and hitchhiking through North Africa. It took me all the way back to a café table in, corny as it sounds, the Casbah in Tangier. As I sat there sipping sweet tea, a pint-size and slightly sinister figure in a hooded djellaba materialized at my elbow and hissed, "Hey, mannn, want to go to a party? We have hashish . . . great records . . . Joan Baez . . ."

I have no idea what he was trying to sell to — or steal from — me. I just remember sitting there thinking:

Joan Baez?

Morocco??

She affected a lot of people, Joan Baez — from Moroccan street urchins to U.S. Presidents (she made Nixon's Enemies List) — not to mention countless millions of folks who fell somewhere between the two extremes. I guess I shouldn't find it surprising that a couple of decades after helping galvanize an entire generation to think thoughts of revolution and world change, Joan Baez is now to be found signing flyleaves in the book department of Eaton's. That probably shouldn't seem odd to me, but it does.

But, hey, why pick on her? Who hasn't changed since the early days? Remember black revolutionary Eldridge Cleaver? Last I heard he was scuttling around trying to find backers for his own line of men's wear fashions. Jerry Rubin? The guy who used to drive American superpatriots into a frenzy by draping himself in an American flag now sports conservative three-piece suits as he plays the stock market and hopes his brand-new Manhattan restaurant is a hit with the yuppies. Even Baez' old boyfriend Bob Dylan has a-changed with the times. Several times. What is he these days — Jewish zealot? Christian fanatic? Existentialist? Nihilist? Whatever he is you can be sure it's different from what he was last month — and not even close to what he was when he and Baez combined his anthems, her voice, and their guitars and almost changed the way we Earthlings think about things.

Seems so long ago. Seems even longer when I switch on my TV and catch Ringo trying to sell me a case of wine cooler.

But I don't really have to turn on my TV or read the People section of *Maclean's* or check up on Baez or Dylan or Jerry or Eldridge to be reminded of just how much things have changed since the sixties. I have a graphic updating device much closer to home.

The bathroom mirror.

Take a few words of advice from Carly Simon, another aging hipster, who sings, "These *are* the good old days."

Navel-gazing
with Cher

DOES ANYBODY OUT THERE remember Cher when Cher was just . . . Cher? I do. This would be pre-*Moonstruck,* pre-*Witches of Eastwick* Cher, way back in the early seventies when the slim raven-haired vampette parlayed a minimal vocal agility and a penchant for dressing à la bizarre into modified global celebrity.

We're talking Sonny and Cher days — Sonny being the sawed-off, nebbishy first in a relatively long line of romantic liaisons for the lady in question. After Sonny (and in no particular order) came one of the Allman brothers rock stars, then a dancer, then a writer, then a couple of Hollywood hunks who flexed a mean biceps but never got to leave their palm prints in wet cement outside Grauman's Chinese Theater.

I've never been what you'd call a major fan of Cher's, but like millions of other nonentities, I watched her and her antics. I heard about her get-togethers and breakups; her feuds and her fiestas. I caught the *People* magazine spreads of Cher arriving at the Academy Awards; Cher mugging for the cameras at some Beverly Hills nightspot or other; Cher in smoked glasses and a slit-to-the-hip black dress being whisked away in a limo.

I never learned a lot of substance about the woman, but one thing I just kind of assumed was that if there was any subject Cher could claim a Ph.D. in, it was men. She may not be the best singer ever to huff into a mike, she may be no better than a competent actress and a so-so clotheshorse, but I took it for granted that she knew men and all their frailties the way Gretzky knows goalposts.

Not so.

Thumbing through a recent edition of *Ladies Home Journal* (hey, it was a rainy day), I came across an interview with the lady, in which she said, among other things, that she knows sweet boo-all about men. She says that Sonny Bono bowled her over when she was only sixteen years old. "I don't know why, I didn't even like him that much, but there was this attraction. There was always something strange about our relationship that defies categorizing, even for me."

As for the other men in her life, Cher says, "You could fit everything I've learned about men on the head of a pin and still have room for the Lord's Prayer."

To which all I can add is . . . amen, Cher. I hear you.

From a man's point of view, I mean. Thanks to Cher's candour, I can now stand up and say without fear of ridicule that after the better part of a lifetime dealing (and duelling) with the opposite sex, I too have distressingly little in the way of conclusive data. I haven't actually etched it out, but I reckon you could lay down all I know about women on the head of a pin and still have room for the Lord's Prayer and possibly Michael Wilson's last budget address, to boot.

Why is it so hard? You would think, given the interest men have in women and vice versa, that we would have progressed a little further down the path of mutual enlightenment than we have. How could people as smart as we are end up with pathetic devices like computer dating, Companions Wanted newspaper columns, and singles nights at the local supermarket?

Intelligence is no magic ticket. Near the end of his career, Sigmund Freud wrote somewhat plaintively, "Despite my thirty years of research into the feminine soul, I have not yet been able to answer . . . the great question that has never been answered: 'What does a woman want?'"

The humourist Ogden Nash might not boast the cerebral baggage of Freud but he was at least as close to the mark with this bit of doggerel:

There is one phase of life that I have never heard
Discussed in any seminar
And that is that all women think men are funny and
All men think that weminar.

I don't know if Cher would get any solace from those thoughts or not. Perhaps she'd derive more comfort from something a rather famous husband once said about his rather famous wife.

"She is an extremely beautiful woman, lavishly endowed by nature with but a few flaws in the masterpiece: she has an insipid double chin, her legs are too short, and she has a slight pot-belly. She has a wonderful bosom, though."

Indeed. The observer was Richard Burton speaking about his wife Elizabeth Taylor.

I'll bet he slept on the living room couch the night after he made that assessment.

Is There Life After Sex?

Welcome, ladies and gentlemen, to the tail end of the twentieth century. The subject is sex and you can leave your clothes on . . . the times they are a-changin', and so apparently is humankind's attitude towards its favourite pastime — after bingo, I mean. Remember the repressed fifties? The let-it-all-hang-out sixties? The little-bit-of-everything seventies? The my-God-this-is-work eighties? Well, we are stripping the veil on a brand-new frontier. Make that "redonning the veil." John and Liz Hodgkinson, a pair of British authors, are out there somewhere on the talk-show circuit flogging a book that advocates . . . celibacy. The Hodgkinsons are married. To each other. But they don't indulge. Haven't for the past five years. When the urge is upon them they . . . take out the garbage . . . feed the goldfish . . . read the obits in the *Times* . . . write another book, maybe . . . whatever they do they *don't* scratch that itch. And they claim they're better people for it.

Wasn't easy, mind you. Mr. Hodgkinson says he had to go on a strict vegetarian diet to subdue his carnal cravings. Says it took nearly three years to get his mind off it. Sex, the Hodgkinsons argue, is bad for blood pressure, plays havoc with one's mental health, and causes everything from sprung sacroiliacs to wrinkled bedsheets. It spreads diseases, fans the flames of unworthy emotions such as jealousy, lust and regret — and, as the root cause of all those how-to manuals, threatens the very future of our forests.

The quiet British couple and their not-tonight-dear-I-have-a-deadline approach to wedded bliss are just one more sign of a movement that's been growing for some time now. Some have

223

been calling it the New Celibacy, but I think that's a little far-fetched. Celibacy is just the extreme wing of the movement.

What we are really talking about is moderation . . . control . . . Actually, what we're talking about is endurance.

It takes strong legs, a young heart, and a pair of lungs like a smithy's bellows to play the game of love at fever pitch. The simple truth is, the Erica Jongs, the Doctors Ruth and Reuben and others of that ilk who make a living telling us what we think about sex are getting a little long of tooth and short of wind ever to be confused with frisky thoroughbreds at the starting gate. They can't, to be blunt, keep up the pace. And neither can their audience. We are all of us getting, shall we say, more mature.

The swing of the sexual pendulum doesn't necessarily mean a return to Muslim veils, scarlet letters, or a rebirth of the Victorian pastime of crocheting skirts to cover up those naughty naked piano legs. It may just be that we're headed for someplace a lot . . . funnier. An end to earnest sex. No more dreadful sex. Maybe . . . funny sex?

And it is really pretty funny when you think of it.

Comedians are already staking out the terra incognita of sex as absurdity. Joan Rivers: "After we made love he took a piece of chalk and made an outline of my body."

Woody Allen: "I sold my memoirs of my love life to Parker Brothers and they're going to make a game out of it."

Rodney Dangerfield: "My wife has cut our lovemaking down to two times a month. But I know two guys she's cut out entirely."

And not just the field of comedy. Here's actress Glenda Jackson on her craft: "The important thing in acting is to be able to laugh and cry. If I want to cry, I think of my love life . . . If I want to laugh I think of my love life."

And after we learn to laugh — or at least smile — at sex . . . what then? What comes next? Relax. We're in good hands right to the end — and even beyond. According to Lily Tomlin, there will even be sex after death.

We just won't be able to feel it.

For a Good Time, Call MCX VLIV

IT WAS A FAMILIAR if somewhat pathetic little drama: lonely businessman — in this case, a West German — in a strange city — in this case, Beijing — finds himself with time on his hands and a couple of drinks under his belt, staring into a barroom mirror. He locks eyes with a winsome and unattached woman three bar stools down. Small talk leads to a candlelight-and-wine dinner, which leads to a tour of the nightspots, which leads to some close dancing and the inevitable question — would she come back with him to his hotel room? She would.

It's a drearily commonplace scene that's replayed a thousand times a day in hotel rooms from Toronto to Timbuktu and from London, Ont., to London, Eng.

But not in China, as our West German Lothario found out. His cozy little Oriental dalliance instantly became a *ménage à troop* as a squad of Chinese policemen burst through the hotel room door and arrested the couple on the spot.

In China, you see, sex between unmarried people is illegal. Not "frowned upon," not "discouraged" — illegal. The Chinese woman was shipped off to a rural work camp for "reeducation." The West German businessman was plunked on the next available Lufthansa flight bound for *Der Vaterland.*

Wondering, no doubt, exactly how he was going to explain all this in his sales report.

So much for illicit sex in China, circa 1989. The irony is, the same newspaper that carried that story recently also had a story about sex in the Middle East, circa 400 A.D.

Seems a team of archeologists from fifteen Canadian and American universities has been poking around in the rubble of a city called Ashkelon, in Israel. Now, people have lived on the site of Ashkelon for at least the past nine thousand years, and the archeologists knew that even in the time of the Caesars, Ashkelon enjoyed a reputation as a kind of early Las Vegas. For centuries, generation after generation of Egyptians, Assyrians, Persians, and Greeks had flocked to its sandy beaches for their annual R and R. But even armed with that knowledge, the archeologists were not prepared for what they unearthed earlier this month.

What they found was . . . well, a hot tub, really. A sunken marble bath about the size and shape of a modern Jacuzzi, with enough room to accommodate perhaps a half-dozen Roman Empire yuppies. It even featured heart-shaped pillars that formed a kind of canopy over the tub.

The archeologists speculate that the pillars served to contain the heat, creating the "hot tub" effect. They also speculate that the heart motif was no accident. What they have uncovered, say the archeologists, is the remains of a 1,500-year-old brothel.

What makes them think so? Well, the artwork, for one thing. Some of the oil lamps used to light the place show decidedly erotic vignettes (depictions of positions one through twenty-nine). "This kind of art isn't unusual for the time period," says Douglass Esse, associate director of the excavation, "but the quantity of it certainly is."

Can you imagine standing over the remains of a Byzantine brothel in the middle of a town that operated under the motto Anything Goes for a couple of millennia? It must feel especially weird to stand there knowing that just a couple of countries away maniacal disciples of a mad Ayatollah preside over a country in which women can be thrown into jail for not wearing veils over their faces — or even stoned to death.

Sexual mores shift with the times and the circumstances. Back at the turn of the century, when Toronto the Good was a deadly dull graveyard of purse-lipped Puritanism, the tiny town of Dawson in the Yukon was awash with hookers and houses of ill repute. (Hogtown had them, too, of course — it was just more hypocritical about it.)

Pre-Castro Havana was the Sodom and Gomorrah of the Western hemisphere. Today it's more like . . . well, Toronto circa 1900.

The archeologists have one puzzle piece they haven't been able to figure out at the Ashkelon dig. It's the remains of a sign that welcomed visitors to the brothel. It reads, in ancient Greek, "Enter In, Enjoy and . . . "

And *what*, we'll probably never know. The rest of the sign is unreadable, having fallen victim to fifteen centuries of decay and decomposition.

It's fun to speculate, though. And what? And Wipe Your Feet? And Just Say Charge It? And Leave the Driving to Us?

It's not hard to figure out how the sign would read if it hung over a hotel in modern day Beijing, however.

Enter In, Enjoy and . . .

Spread 'em, Sucker — You're Under Arrest.

We've Got Our Laughs to Keep Us Warm

M Y MOTHER will be mortified to read this, but the earliest voice I can remember, going way, way back to my mewling, puking days in the crib in the bedroom corner, was not hers, not Dad's . . . but the voice of Senator Claghorn.

The Senator, for those of you too short in the tooth to remember, was a pork-barrelling, gravel-voiced politico from the Deep South who appeared as a regular on a radio program called "Allen's Alley," which, in turn, was one of the funniest shows ever to hit the airwaves. It infiltrated North American living rooms beginning in 1943, introducing an unsuspecting public to characters such as the kvetchy Mrs. Pansy Nussbaum, the flinty Titus Moody, and a whole menagerie of bizarre figures, from Falstaff Openshaw to Socrates Mulligan — all of them foils for the acid wit of Fred Allen.

But it was Senator Claghorn — Beauregard to his friends — with his honey-dipped basso profundo unctuousness that sticks in my mind. Particularly his tag line, which followed his corny, ham-handed jokes as surely as julep follows mint.

"They-uh goin' tuh bring — ah say, they-uh goin' to bring Senator Aiken back . . . achin' back — haw!" (Then the trademark pause.)

"That's a joke, son!"

Ah, sweet laughter. My dictionary defines it as "a convulsive activity of the muscles of respiration, producing spasmodic exhalations and inhalations and characteristic sounds together with the facial movements exaggerating those of the smile." The definition

228

is so wordy and windy and whimsyless that it's a bit of a joke in itself.

I wonder when the world's first laugh happened — and what caused it? The sounds of a domestic dispute two caves down? The sign of a Neanderthal colleague stepping in some mastodon's meadow muffin and doing a loop-the-loop followed by a two-point pratfall? Odd that we'll speculate endlessly about the discovery of fire, the invention of the wheel, the creation of weapons, but nary a word about the world's first belly laugh.

And it's important. Listen, give me one more mug of that Châteauneuf du Niagara and I'd be willing to argue that it is the sense of humour, not the opposable thumb, that separates us folks from the rest of the fauna. Leopards don't laugh. Fish and fowl are notoriously sobersided. A humour inspector could check out the entire assemblage of Canadian wildlife, from field mouse to bull moose, and not turn up so much as an enigmatic smile.

In fact, of all our fellow creatures, only the hyena has a comparable reputation for chuckleheadedness, and he's not even a serious laugher — more a dropout from a Barking Academy.

And how we do laugh! We chuckle and chortle, cackle and crow. We snigger and simper, snicker and snort. We guffaw and we giggle, we hoot and we howl. We titter and tee-hee and whinny and yuk.

We do a lot of laughing in a lot of different ways, and thank the gods for that. It may be that laughing is the only thing that keeps us sane.

Strange thing, humour. The word, which we lifted from the Latin, means *moisture* or *fluid*. And humour is indeed the viscous liquor that keeps life from seizing up and screeching to a halt. Humour's slippery, too — sort of like a banana peel. The perfect consistency for slipping under the strutting heel of Life when it gets too pretentious.

Because it's liquid, humour can accommodate and engulf just about any human endeavour, no matter what the dimensions. Humour cocks a snook at anybody — and the mightier the better.

"When former U.S. President Reagan blundered into that utterly loony Iran/Israeli/Nicaraguan/White House Basement shamozzle, politicians and serious pundits were shocked almost to speechlessness by the enormity of the foul-up. Not humourists. They rolled up their sleeves and had a field day. They worked as hard strip-mining the fiasco as the White House did trying to sweep it under the rug. Even the headlines were a delight. "Contradiction!" "Gipperloo!" "Iranamok!" "Saudi Night Fever!"

The scandal was so outrageous that the headline writers almost forgot to "gate" it — as in Watergate, Koreagate, and Tunagate.

But then of course, Jim and Tammy Bakker had first dibs on that designation. What else to call their comedy of errors but Pearlygate?

Not that the U.S. has a hammerlock on continental humour. We folks north of the forty-ninth are holding our own in the one-liner department. Canadians specialize in regional humour. Newfie jokes, of course, but also Toronto jokes, Ottawa jokes, and Maple Leaf hockey team jokes. What do the Pope, Margaret Thatcher, the Sultan of Brunei, and Stevie Wonder have in common? They all own teams that have won the same number of Stanley Cups over the past twenty years as Harold Ballard's.

We also have Canadian variations on old themes. Why did the chicken cross the road? To get to the other side. Why did Brian Mulroney cross the road? He didn't. He just said he did.

We have interregional jokes, too. Torontonians make jokes about Hamiltonians and Steeltowners return the volley. Out west the skies over Edmonton and Calgary are thick with salvos flying back and forth.

What's the difference between Edmonton and a bowl of yoghurt? There's more culture in the yoghurt.

What's the difference between a pigeon and a Calgary oil man? The pigeon can still make a deposit on a Mercedes.

There are jokes that do not make the headlines, of course. They are called sick jokes and they deal with every subject imaginable. There are AIDS jokes and Chernobyl jokes, Ethiopian jokes and Challenger spacecraft jokes. Many people find such material utterly repugnant and beyond the bounds of humour.

Repugnant, perhaps, but not, I think, out of order. It is the very nature of humour to poke and prod all boundaries to the point of hemorrhage and to slide its jester's slipper across the DMZ called "good taste" whenever it can.

Besides . . . listen to the next sick joke you hear. Really listen.

230

Can't you hear the plaintive whimper of dread? Sick humour is just humanity's way of belling the cat. Scaping the goat. Whistling past the graveyard.

Fortunately a taste for sick jokes is not a prerequisite for having a sense of humour. There are lots of alternatives in the comedy closet. You can choose from shaggy dog stories, practical jokes, ethnic jokes, hoaxes, satires, limericks, riddles, puns, Spoonerisms, clerihews, and sarcasm, just for starters. Comedy caters to an amazing variety of tastes, served up by sales reps who run the gamut from Borscht Belt comedians to laid-back Letterman clones. There's similar abundance for those who feel humour should be seen rather than heard, and again it's a matter of taste. Some folks celebrate the balletic elegance of Charlie Chaplin while others will settle for nothing less than the primal buffoonery of the Three Stooges. When it comes to visual rib tickling, comedy is in the eye (aqueous humour?) of the beholder.

So what are we to make of it, then . . . this strange affliction that seems to affect only us two-legged and hairless bipeds? Is it an essential to our well-being or a decadent frivolity? There are more opinions about that than there are mother-in-law jokes. Stephen Leacock put it right at the top of his priority list. "The world's humour, in its best and greatest sense," wrote the bard of Marisposa, "is perhaps the highest product of our civilization." Another man, engaged in the same line of work, demurred. "There's something secondary about comedy," wrote Woody Allen. "Comedy teases a problem, it pokes fun at it, it never really confronts it."

For American essayist E. B. White, the whole question was academic — boringly so. "Humour can be dissected, as a frog can," he growled, "but the thing dies in the process and the innards are discouraging to any but the pure scientific mind."

I suppose it's only fitting that something that takes its name from a word meaning *liquid* should be so elusive and difficult to pigeonhole. Whatever its quicksilver vital statistics, humour has seldom been healthier. Television sitcoms rule the living room ether. A large chunk of Hollywood's money-makers are comedies, and cabarets are reincarnating all over the place. On this side of the border even the old chestnuts are thriving. Wayne and Shuster are towelling off from yet another TV special. CBC Radio's most popular variety program is a hoary kit bag full of made-in-Canada skits and satirical tomfoolery called "The Royal Canadian Air Farce" — nearly two decades old and never stronger.

It's gone even further than that — big business has discovered humour, and vice versa. Many firms that find themselves with a few extra shekels in the Guest Speaker Fund are eschewing the efficiency experts and the time-management specialists in favour of a bizarre sermonizer named Dr. Marcellino Gonzalez. The doctor is one of the hottest acts on the international seminar circuit — partly because there aren't many subjects on which he is not prepared to lecture. In fact, there probably aren't any.

He has appeared as a guest expert before executives at Polaroid and General Electric, Ford and Howard Johnson's. He has cast his pearls of knowledge at the Daks-shod feet of high administrators from Merrill Lynch, Gulf + Western, and Eaton's.

And they get their money's worth. Any lecture by Dr. Gonzalez is an Event. The slightly mad-looking doctor (ill-fitting suit, hair like a rogue Brillo pad) prefers to give his address at the tail end of a full day of brain-staggeringly ponderous presentations. It's important that his audience be data glutted, slightly cranky if possible, and utterly convinced that Dr. Gonzales represents more of the same.

And so he does — for the first ten minutes. You have not truly plumbed the nether reaches of terminal boredom until you've numbed your bum through the first couple of light-years of a Dr. Marcellino Gonzalez lecture.

For one thing, the man barely speaks English. In a guttural, singsong, Jose Jimenez-accented voice, the doctor drones on about impossibly technical aspects of whatever commodity his audience deals in. Automobile executives? Dr. Gonzalez might choose to regale them with reams of statistics about salt-resistant finishes for hubcaps. Marketing men out there on the floor? Perhaps the doctor will recite page after page of raw data from the Tokyo Stock Exchange, circa 1954.

And just when his audience, by now a veritable Milky Way of glazed eyes is winking out, two by two, someone in the front row will jerk upright in his seat . . . squint in disbelief . . . cup a hand behind his ear . . . murmur something like, "Say, did he just say — naw, he couldn't have . . ."

But by this point, people throughout the audience are stirring, looking incredulous, whispering to their neighbours. Good God! Did you hear that? He just called our treasurer an embezzler! And now he's dumping a vase of chrysanthemums over the chairman's head! The man is going crazy up there!

Crazy like a fox who pulls down $5,000 per speaking engagement. The wacky Dr. Marcellino Gonzalez is really Mr. Rey Baumel, a corporate jester who has been hoaxing some of North America's most powerful businessmen for the past twenty years.

The zany doctor is not the only evidence that business is rediscovering its sense of humour. Companies that specialize in tickling the corporate funnybone are springing up — companies like Comedy Consultants of Toronto, for instance. For a fee that runs anywhere from $500 to $2,000, Comedy Consultants will put on a presentation that should have the staff rolling in the aisles. But it's not just a vaudeville routine they offer. Comedy Consultants tries to provide a permanent boost to office morale by teaching employees how to break out of the ruts and to mine their own neglected humour reserves.

And why shouldn't industry and humour learn to tango? There's no law that says life on Bay Street has to be grim and cheerless — just a tired old stereotype that should have been scrapped long ago. Some of the funniest people I've known have been folks who toil in the bowels of Big Business, and it's high time they saw their names up there in the credits.

It works both ways. Perhaps as business learns to lighten up, stand-up comics and sitcom writers will learn to stop taking cheap shots at the people who keep the country on the rails economically.

As that old gag writer Anon once observed, "When I hear artists making fun of businessmen, I think of a regiment in which the band makes fun of the cooks."

As Senator Claghorn might say, "That's a j — I say, that's a joke, son."

We Live in Testing Times

I WOKE UP this morning in a total cold sweat. I was panting, my stomach was churning, my teeth were clenched, and my mind was vice gripped in a pervasive sense of total dread as if a Steinway was poised over my head, hanging by one frayed cord.

"What," I asked myself, "is this?" Flu? Hangover? The old war wound? Nah. None of the above. It took me a while but I finally recognized what I was suffering from.

Senior Matriculationitis. Grade Thirteenophobia. Final Exam Flashback.

Exam Anxiety.

It's amazing. It's been more than a quarter of a century since I actually lived through the horror of High School Finals, and I can still have nightmares about them.

And I'm not alone. Medical researchers at the Mayo Clinic have discovered that Examination Trauma is one of the most common anxiety dreams North Americans suffer from. There are variations on the theme. Some folks dream they're late for their exam. Others dream that they haven't studied enough. The worst of all is the dream that you've shown up all prepared for the final in French composition, only to discover that today is the trigonometry final.

For me and people of my generation, exam anxiety is merely an unpleasant memory, but right this moment it's a malaise that's gnawing at the guts of high school kids right across the country. They're behind in their work. They haven't understood a word the teacher's said since Christmas. They're positive they're not going to make their year.

They're not going to sleep very well tonight.

234

Well, as lame and fuddy duddyish as it sounds, kids, I have to tell you that it could be worse.

You could be Japanese.

Care to hear what Japanese kids are going through right now? Well, one of them — Shinichiro Kitada of Tokyo — is probably straightening his carefully laundered and crisply pressed military-style school uniform in front of the bathroom mirror, just before he sets off for school. Classes start at 7:00 a.m. for Shinichiro, and they carry on for seven hours, five days a week. He also puts in two and a half hours doing homework each night and shows up Saturday mornings at school for another half-day's whack at the books. Oh, yes, and Shinichiro goes to cram school, as well — two or three evenings a week for another two and a half to three hours a pop.

What's a little alarming to a Western observer is the fact that Shinichiro Kitada's grinding academic commitment is not unusual in Japan. The hours he puts in are about the accepted average for a student of his level. A full sixty percent of his classmates attend weekly cram school classes, just as Shinichiro does.

Is it worth it? Well, it depends on your values, of course, but for most middle-class Japanese the returns more than justify the output. Academic excellence means access to positions in senior government departments, or better still, a job with a top-of-the-line Japanese corporation such as Mitsubishi or Suntory.

Mind you, the price is high. A workday that includes seven hours in the classroom plus two and a half hours in cram school plus two and a half hours of homework doesn't leave a lot of time for sipping sodas down at the corner store or shooting baskets with the boys at the schoolyard. For Japanese students like Shinichiro Kitada, the school year is just one eye-blurring stretch of study-eat-sleep-study-eat-sleep endlessly repeated.

Which is all the more impressive when you learn what niche Shinichiro Kitada occupies in the Japanese academic hierarchy.

Shinichiro Kitada is enrolled in the Japanese equivalent of what we would call junior high school. The boy is only fifteen years old.

If he does well in his exams this year — which is to say, ninety percent or better — he goes on to high school.

Then things really get tough.

The Lawsuit Blues Got That Ol' Swimmin' Hole of Mine

T HERE'S AN OLD RHYME running through my head today. It goes:

Mother, may I go out to swim?
Yes, my darling daughter:
Hang your clothes on a hickory limb
But don't go near the water.

Sound advice for anyone who lives in my neck of the woods, because it's just been announced that the local swimming hole is closed indefinitely.

You and I can't swim there anymore. Against the law.

Is it because the swimming hole's polluted and we must be protected from infection and disease? Nah. This is an old limestone quarry I'm talking about. The water's deep and green and full of perch and rock bass. I might not care to take the water with my Scotch, but it's fine for swimming — as clean as it's ever been.

Are they closing it because they can't find lifeguards to patrol the place? Not at all. The quarry is part of a park controlled by the local conservation authority and it's run tighter than a Russian mine sweeper. There are gates, parking lots, a ticket office, and enough lifeguards and supervisory personnel to launch a Gilbert and Sullivan operetta.

The reason we can't swim there anymore is that last year a tourist wrecked his back jumping into the swimming hole. He sued for two million bucks. The conservation authority does not have a spare two million lying around in the bottom drawer — particularly when it doesn't take a mental giant to figure out that, if this guy wins, there will be no shortage of people lining up to jump into the swimming hole and claim their payoff.

All of which has made the insurance companies go "Eeep!" and tuck their corporate heads way down inside their pin-striped vests. They've jacked the insurance rate so high that the conservation authority can't get public liability insurance. That's why you and I can't go for a dip down at the swimming hole.

This is where the Canadian legal system gets a little wacko for me. Nobody held a gun to that tourist's head and ordered him to jump. He did it all by himself — as hundreds of kids have done every sunny day for as many summers as the swimming hole's been there. Now, the walls of the quarry are high — I wouldn't jump off. But if I did and hurt myself in the process, I wouldn't have to look too far to find the person to blame.

It's not the first piece of public liability absurdity we've seen around here. Up until last year there was an exceedingly pleasant way to spend a Sunday afternoon in these parts. You could go into town, rent a canoe, and pass a bucolic hour or two drifting down the Grand River past spectacular limestone cliffs, under bridges, watching blue herons and mallards and kingfishers all the way to the next town, a distance of perhaps four or five meandering miles downstream. There, you could leave your rented canoe at the dock, stroll uptown for a cool drink, do a little shopping and sightseeing, then catch a free bus ride back to where you started.

That's gone now. Someone figured out what might happen if some tourist in a rented canoe scraped his knee or caught a chill or pinched his pinky and decided to sue. The insurance rate for the canoe rental company went right through the roof. The business folded.

Where will it end? Who knows? Maybe someday our lawyers and judges will get reacquainted with common sense and accept the rather simple concept that we humans do, occasionally, have to accept some responsibility for our actions.

In the meantime, sky's the limit, chum. We've got folks suing tobacco companies because those same folks were stupid enough to suck several thousand cigarettes and get cancer from it. We've got folks who, after sitting in a bar and getting plastered, go out and kill someone in their car — then turn around and sue the bartender who served them. Recently in Montreal a barber was sued by a customer for *cutting his hair too short*. The customer caught a cold. His lawyer feels a $25,000 settlement would warm his client right up.

Still, things could be worse, I suppose. We could be living south of the border, where they really know how to gang-rape the concept of public liability.

A few years ago, a despondent Manhattanite decided to end it all by throwing himself in front of a speeding New York subway train. The train ran over him, but he didn't die. He was left a paraplegic, but a paraplegic with chutzpah. The guy sued the New York Public Transit System for several million dollars. His lawyer argued that the transit system had been negligent in . . . not preventing his attempted suicide.

That's the bizarre news.

The incredible news is, he won.

Advice to Amateur Editors: Go Directly to Hell

Y OU KNOW what I wish? I wish people would leave our books alone. I'm not even talking about the flat-out censors and book burners. I'm talking about the tinkerers, the tidy-uppers, the prissy little self-appointed arbiters who take it upon themselves to "improve" our reading fare.

Dr. Thomas Bowdler started it all. In the early 1800s, the doctor took it upon himself to geld the works of the most famous writer of English the world has ever known. Dr. Bowdler published what he called *A Family Shakespeare,* in which "all passages of irreligious or immoral tendency have been removed."

This meant, of course, that some characters like Macbeth, Hamlet and King Lear were virtually unrecognizable. Wantons such as Falstaff and Doll Tearsheet disappeared completely.

The doctor unleased a fad that persists to this day. There is right now a chap in England by the name of Geoffrey Hall who has decided that Mother Goose nursery rhymes are too "imperialistic." What those fables need, decided Hall, was a little touch of the pink paintbrush to make them more socially responsible. "Old Mother Hubbard," for example. Mr. Hall has refashioned that fable so that it more correctly mirrors Society As It Ought to Be. Remember how old Mom Hubbard went to check her supplies and got a nasty shock — "when she got there, the cupboard was bare"? Not in Geoffrey Hall's new improved edition. It reads, "When she got there, she found plenty to spare."

Tremendous dramatic impact, eh wot?

Geoffrey Hall has also taken it on himself to expunge the

gratuitous violence and animal abuse from "Three Blind Mice." No longer do the three visually disadvantaged rodents have to suffer the indignity of a triple tail docking. He has the farmer's wife "cut off some cheese with a carving knife."

Can't you just envisage kids clambering all over you, begging you to repeat the thrilling saga about the farmer's wife who cut the cheese?

The literary revisionists are at work on other fronts too — Beatrix Potter's *Tale of Peter Rabbit* has just been reissued in a "simplified and updated" edition.

Peter Rabbit? Simplified?

Yep. Gone are the author's exquisitely wispy watercolours depicting Peter and his pals in the garden. In their place are stodgy photographs of . . . puppets. Gone, too, are any references in the text that might possibly offend children and cause them to . . . well, think. The fact that Peter's father wound up as the main ingredient in a rabbit pie is no longer mentioned. Even the way Peter moves has been "dumbed down." His paws no longer go *lippety lip*. In the new edition he just *hops*.

Why would any publisher knowingly gut a classic tale? "This is an attempt to appeal to the non-book-buying public," says the publisher.

Oh, good idea. Get those nonreaders interested in the nonstory of Peter Rabbit. If this works, next time we could take out *all* the original material and insert something really attractive.

Like, say, the TV listings.

It would be bad enough if these unnatural descendants of Dr. Bowdler confined their prudish predations to children's literature. They don't. They are also chipping away at a literary work from which even Dr. Bowdler shied away.

The Bible.

Now available at better religious bookstores everywhere is a handy tome called the *Inclusive Language Lectionary*. It's put out by the U.S. National Council of Churches. Purpose: to strip selected Bible passages of all vestiges of male chauvinism.

Thus the *Lectionary* recommends that the famous prayer be altered to being: "Our Father *and Mother* who art in Heaven, hallowed be thy names . . ."

"Father, son, and Holy Ghost" becomes "Father and Mother,

Child, and Holy Ghost" (which sound like the Holy Trinity has been boosted to an Unholy Quartet). In Matthew, the revisionists grudgingly allow the Three Wise Men to keep their gender, but proclaim that it was the *ruler*, not the King of the Jews, they were searching for.

Just in case Jesus turned out to be a closet queen, I guess.

All of this would be a lot funnier if it turned out to be a skit in "Saturday Night Live" or a satire from the CBC drama department. It isn't. Geoffrey Hall is alive and blue-pencilling in Britain, as are the hacks rewriting Beatrix Potter. The U.S. National Council of Churches is alive, if not well, and seeking to direct and channel the thought patterns of the Christian faithful.

Depressing.

I can't say I wish all of the aforementioned would go to hell. That would be uncharitable, not to mention un-Christian. But it wouldn't bother me if they spent a few months in purgatory.

I visualize purgatory as a dentist's waiting room, where the only reading material is a dog-eared copy of *All's Well That Ends Well*, in which all words that can be construed as sexist, racist, ageist, elitist, violent, suggestive, or anything other than pure beige neutral, have been blacked out.

Happy reading, turkeys.

Meet You at the Corner of Klondike and Yukon

T HERE'S AN OLD SAYING that if you go stand on the corner of
Broadway and Forty-second, I think it is, in New York, eventually you'll run into all the friends you ever made. Can't prove it
statistically or justify it logically, but I think I'd be more inclined
to go and stand at the junction of the Klondike and the Yukon
Rivers. That's downtown Dawson City, Yukon. Sure, it's tucked
away up in the northwest pocket of the great Canadian pool table,
and sure it's only got a population equal to about the first three
rows of a not-very-important Rangers game in Madison Square
Garden, but you'd be amazed at how many friends a person can
meet there.

I spent four days at the Dawson Music Festival some time ago.
First guy I met knew my next-door neighbour back in rural
Ontario. Then a lady introduced herself by saying she'd been
talking to my daughter on the phone a few days earlier. This is
taking place, you understand, twenty degrees north and three time
zones west of where I normally hang out. All kinds of folks turned
out to be friends of friends in Toronto and Nolalu and Elora and
Halifax and Montreal. And then there was Laurie Conger. Laurie's
an old pal, ex of Thunder Bay, ex of the Parachute Club, now
playing keyboard for anybody with the good sense to hire her. We
ran into each other again up in Dawson, where the Klondike
meets the Yukon.

Laurie Conger is about as close as a human body gets to being pure music. She doesn't love it, she *is* it. One of my favourite pleasures in life is watching Laurie, listening to music. A close second is staying up all night to watch the sun not set in Dawson. It really is the land of the midnight sun, you know. Sun doesn't go down . . . it just kind of does a low carom behind a mountain and swings around again.

For anyone who's never been to the Yukon, I'm not even going to try to describe the scenery. Suffice to say that the Yukon, near as I can make out, is 207,000 square miles of suck-your-breath-out photo opportunity. That's mostly because of the stunning land-scape, but partly because there are very few people to get in your snapshot. Fewer than 25,000 in the whole territory and three-fifths of those live in Whitehorse. The drive from Whitehorse to Dawson takes over six hours. But it's worth it, because then you're in Robert Service country. There really is a Dawson Trail to mush over and a Lake Laberge with a marge. And it's not hard to imagine a Dan McGrew and a Malamute Saloon — not in a town that boasts establishments such as Diamond Toothed Gertie's Gambling Em-porium, the Midnight Sun Restaurant and the El Dorado Hotel, Gold Dust Accepted.

Checking into the El Dorado (which also takes Visa), one is accosted by a ruddy-faced man well lubricated with High Test, which is what Yukoners call O'Keefe Extra Old Stock Ale, a fortified brew not available in more effete duchies of Canada. "My partners and I took out a ten-ounce nugget," he says by way of introduction. Ten ounces, huh? Even a callow, puffy-handed greenhorn from the East realizes that we are talking of a chunk of gravel worth something in the range of $4,000. The gold rush goes on.

Four days is not a long time to spend in a place. But it's more than long enough to get yourself thoroughly smitten. They have a saying in the Yukon. If you go there twice, you'll be hooked for life. Well, I've been there once. And ever since I got back, the words from an old Robert Service poem have been ricocheting through my head:

There's a land where the mountains are nameless .
And the rivers all run God knows where;
There are lives that are erring and aimless,

And death that just hangs by a hair;
There are hardships that nobody reckons;
There are valleys unpeopled and still;
There's a land— oh, it beckons and beckons,
And I want to go back and I will.

And When We Call It a Tanktop, We Mean a TANKtop!

THERE'S A BRAND-NEW FASHION FAD out there — so new it doesn't even have a name yet. What to call it? Sneakchic, maybe? Furtive Fashion? Covert Couture?

What it is, is a whole new line of clothes and clothing accessories that allow you to be stylish *and* to foil would-be kidnappers and assassins at the same time.

Antiterrorist outfitters are springing up everywhere and they owe their very existence (not to mention their juicy profit margins) to two K factors: Kevlar and Khaddafi. Khaddafi and what he represents is the problem. Kevlar is the solution — well, a partial one, anyway. Kevlar is to the threat of terrorist violence what a defenceman's jockstrap is to a Messier slapshot from the point — not perfect, but much better than nothing at all.

Kevlar is a kind of miracle fabric that is much stronger than steel and pliable, to boot. This means Kevlar can be turned into a variety of snazzy duds ranging from safari jackets at $652 U.S. a pop, all the way down to a Kevlar-lined baseball cap that not only keeps the sun out of your eyes, but deflects anything up to a 9 millimetre slug.

This is not merely a market for the Macho. Defensive dressing for *women* rates equal if not extra time. Safariland Ballistics, for instance, puts out a line of bulletproof bra and panty sets that run up to $450 U.S.

Match that, Frederick's of Hollywood.

Of course, there's no point in being suited up like a Jedi Knight and then jumping on a CCM one-speed, is there? You're gonna need some wheels to go with your anti-terror togs. How about a nice refitted jalopy from Fontauto, Italy's top-line armored vehicle outfitter?

They've got a demonstrator model on the lot right now that features an armour-plated body, bulletproof windows, fire extinguishers all-round, and tires that keep on rolling even after Druse or Shi'ite Muslims have emptied their Kalashnikovs into them. Fontauto offers a really unusual dashboard option, as well — an environmental control system that lets you breathe easy even while driving through regions rendered uninhabitable by pesky nuisances like nuclear fallout. A steal at $335,000.

Lots of other "must have" fashion accessories for the paranoid at heart — such as the Trionic 008. It's a briefcase that comes fully loaded with a lie detector, a tape recorder, a tap recorder *detector,* a tracking beacon, a bomb sniffer, and a high-intensity flashlight to blind a kidnapper or a would-be briefcase thief — that's if he hasn't been deafened by the megadecibel banshee wail that goes off the minute the briefcase leaves your hands.

Other bargains? Well, a Miami fear boutique called Spy Shops International (really) offers on-the-spot tailoring to sew a tiny transmitter into your coat collar so that in case of kidnapping you (or your coat collar) can be quickly traced. While you're there, why not pick up a pair of night-vision glasses or even a James Bondian spike scatterer that fits right into the trunk of your car?

You think this is just for the idle rich and loony? Spy Shops International of Miami is expanding. This year Washington . . . next year . . . Toronto.

Well, sure, it's nuts, but you know what's really weird? Guess who we have to thank for this Garment Armament paranoia? Queen Victoria, believe it or not. Back in 1842, some nut tried to assassinate her and failed. The Queen responded by having chain mail discreetly sewn into her parasols.

Still, its a long long way from chain-mailed umbrellas to bulletproof bras. I'm certain if Her Majesty had been presented with the latter, she'd have been the first to sniff, "We are not amused."

Deciphering Postal Codes

Now, DON'T MISUNDERSTAND ME — I am not a wimp. I'm not the kind of guy that caves in just because some new concept is a little hard to grasp. I'm willing to give any innovation a decent trial run, but this has been with us for nearly fifteen years now, and I'm just as buffaloed as I was the first day the post office dropped it on us. I give up. I know when I'm whipped.

Is there anybody out there who truly understands postal codes?

We all have one — a meaningless agglomeration of letters and numbers that is supposed to speed delivery of our mail. Does your mail come more swiftly than it did fifteen years ago? Mine doesn't. Back in P.P.C. (that's Pre Postal Code) days, you could drop a card in the mailbox addressed "Joe Blow, Punkydoodles Corners" and it would find him. Today if you don't know the magic six-figure mumbo jumbo, Joe will never even know you're alive.

N0B 1S0 — that's my personal postal code. What the hell, you well may ask, is an N0B 1S0? It's a question I've asked myself more than once. There is no answer. An N0B 1S0 just . . . *is* . . . like athlete's foot or the budget deficit

Actually, N0B 1S0 isn't all that bad, as postal codes go. I used to be saddled with P7A 4C6 until I moved. Before that I was known as P0T 2E0.

You try holding your head up in society when you're lumbered with a postal code like P0T 2E0.

Naw, N0B 1S0 is . . . almost memorable, really — although sometimes if I'm rushed I'll blank out and scrawl NABISCO or NOVELLA or NOXEMA.

The people in charge of public relations at Canada Post suggest that I invent my very own mnemonic rhyme to help me remember my postal code — you know, like — oh, let's see . . . NOB 1S0 might become Nerdy Old Bureaucrats I'll Snuff Out. I could do that, I suppose, except that I don't really have time to go around coining rhymes and assigning them to the postal codes of everyone I know and all the business addresses I have to write to. If I invented rhymes, then I'd have to remember them, and I have enough things to remember already.

Such as my anniversary, where I parked the car, and the rest of my address.

Ever given any thought to just how absurd our postal code system is? At least the Americans had sense enough to stick to straight numbers. Not us. We've got letters *and* numbers. Didn't anyone at the post office twig to the fact that 1's would look like I's? Or that 6's would get confused with G's and B's mistaken for 8's?

The worst of it is, you now get penalized if you don't use the postal code. Recently I sent a package to a friend who lives in a rural community in Northwestern Ontario. I spelled his name perfectly. I had the correct province printed in capital letters. I even had his street and his rural route number, plus the name of the community, which is Kaministiquia.

Wanna guess how many communities there are called Kaministiquia in the Dominion of Canada?

The package took six weeks to arrive. When my friend finally got it, there was a big black stamp across the front, bearing a snotty stencilled message that read, "For quick, efficient service, be sure to use the Postal Code."

Needless to say, I hadn't.

Which brings up another fascinating aspect of the whole fiasco — how do you find out somebody's postal code if you don't happen to know it? Well, you can drop into your local branch of the post office — it keeps a directory of postal codes for every community in every province. So do the public libraries. What's that you say? You don't happen to live between a post office and a public library? No problem — just call up the party you're trying to write to and ask them for their postal code.

And while you're at it, tell them what you were going to write to them about and save yourself the price of a stamp.

Welcome to Postal Paranoia — the growing belief that postal codes are really a nefarious telephone company plot to increase long-distance business.

A couple of months ago, I decided to investigate the efficacy of postal codes in a logical manner. I sent off three letters to an out-of-town friend. Each letter was in a standard envelope and consisted of a single sheet of paper. One letter had the correct address with postal code; one had the correct address with no postal code. The third letter had a totally fictitious series of six letters and numbers that wasn't even close to the correct code.

The results were as I feared. The presence, absence, or accuracy of the postal code made no appreciable differences.

All three letters arrived late.

But hey, what would life be if everything worked all the time? My advice to people who rant and rail against our postal code and other perceived postal inequities: Forget it! Laugh it off. Lighten up, pal.

And for crying out loud, stop whining about the cost of mailing a letter while you're at it. Thirty-eight cents ain't so much to pay for first-class delivery.

Especially when you consider that at least twenty-five cents of that goes for storage.

Racism — It's Really Black and White

YOU KNOW what's wrong with life today, eh? It's too damned grey. Nothing's this or that, cut and dried, right or wrong, black or white. It's all . . . grey.

Take Free Trade. Is that the chance of a lifetime or the end of Canada as we know it? Search me. I watched people on "The Journal" passionately arguing pro and con. They all seemed decent, they all dressed well, they all sounded bright. Half of them say Free Trade will destroy the nation, the other half say it's the turnstile to the Garden of Eden. And these are experts! How are *we* supposed to know? Meech Lake Accord, same thing. Crow's Nest Freight Rates, same thing. One side screams yin, the other side yells yang. Go figure.

And what about South Africa? Apartheid? I mean there's Maggie Thatcher, tut-tutting and pish-pishing and scolding the rest of the Commonwealth for behaving as it does towards South Africa. Would anybody who wears her hair like that try to con us? And there's my morning paper every week or so sporting a glossy full-page ad telling me that I'm getting bad info about life in South Africa, that blacks are coming along just fine, that it's Communists and terrorists and kinky left-wing journalists who are stirring up the pot.

And then there's Glen Babb. Did you ever catch Glen Babb? He was South Africa's official representative to Canada not too long ago. Hey, Glen Babb could sell ice cubes to the Inuit. Suave, smooth, urbane . . . I heard him on "As It Happens" debating Desmond Tutu, and *Tutu* came off sounding shrill and intemperate. Now when you can outsilk a Nobel Peace Prize-winning archbishop, I'd have to say you've either got God in your corner, or you are one very . . . smooth . . . operator.

But then I've always had a weakness for smooth operators. I'm the kind of mark that encyclopedia salesmen tell jokes about around the water cooler. A patsy. A fall guy for any smooth line of patter. I'd have bought Glen Babb's blandishments and the South African government's ad campaign and Maggie Thatcher's unctuous virtue if it wasn't . . . for a couple of things.

John Kani, for one thing.

Mr. Kani is an actor who appeared in a Shakespearean production in Johannesburg. The production was *Othello*. Mr. Kani played the lead. He drove theatregoers right out of the house. He caused the theatre company staging the play to be inundated with hate mail. That bad an actor, is he? Naw. It's because he kissed Desdemona. Desdemona, like the Johannesburger audience, is white . . . John Kani is black, which is the way Shakespeare wrote the play nearly four hundred years ago. Still too racy for white South Africans to handle, apparently.

There's another factor that kind of crystallizes Pretoria and apartheid for me. It's a riddle that I heard from Pieter Dirk Ace, a South African satirist who toured Canada a while back. The riddle goes something like this: What's the difference between a fifty-six-year-old Nobel Peace Prize-winning South African archbishop and a twenty-one-year-old beer-swilling South African redneck goon?

The answer is . . . a vote. Providing there's a white face above that red neck, the white thug can vote. The black archbishop cannot.

That's the reality of South Africa . . . of apartheid. And that's what separates it from things like Free Trade and Meech Lake and the Crow rate. South Africa isn't grey. It is brutally black and white.

The End Is Nigh: Details at Eleven

I'VE GOT a confession to make — I don't watch Peter on "The National" anymore. I don't wait up for Barbara on "The Journal," either. Truth to tell, I very seldom get past the third of fourth beat of the CBC National News theme these days. I know what the news is going to be. It is going to be shootings and stabbings and bombings and bodies in the street. Call me lily-livered, but I don't wish to have such grisly vignettes etched on my eyeballs just before I blow out the candles for the night. Used to be the lead-off item would be about a snowstorm in Manitoba or a bankruptcy in Montreal or more prattle from the pols on Parliament Hill — not anymore. Now it's all grenades and car bombs and ambushes and kidnappings. And the datelines are Belfast and Beirut, Palestine and Paris. The nightly news has been hijacked by terrorists and nobody seems to have noticed. And it's not just terrorist scoresheets and updates. The nightly news won't rest until we've stumbled down those smoking alleys and seen the fresh blood on the stones and stood over the crumpled heaps of battle fatigues and rags that used to be people.

I don't wish to be a wimp about this. I'm not saying, "Just bring us the pleasant news about strawberry socials and Lawrence Welk reruns," but I am saying, from now on include me out of this nightly parade of pornography.

Because I'm getting worried. It's no longer clear to me who wins the Immorality Sweepstakes going on here. Is it the terrorist, willing to kill innocent people if that's what it takes to get interviewed by Dan Rather? Is it the media, which wouldn't give this guy a glance until he pulled out a gun . . . and now offers him everything from prime time to book contracts?

Or is it us? The millions of passive viewing schlemiels who tune in each night to ooh and ahh in the appropriate places and to respond with outrage and revulsion practically on cue?

Reason I bring it up is I noticed a curious thing happening between me and the nightly news hijack-and-kidnap roundup. I was getting used to it. The sight of a body in the dirt or wailing widows or bewildered orphans didn't make me catch my breath anymore. The junkie analogy suggests itself. I needed a bigger fix. More gore.

It's an infectious condition, I'm sure. It won't be long before terrorists read their Nielsens and realize that to maintain "audience share," they'll have to up the carnage. God knows, when they do, TV will gladly up the coverage. *I'm* the only factor in the equation that I have any control over.

That's why I don't watch the nightly news anymore.

There's another reason. A letter to the editor in the *Globe and Mail* recently. I don't get paid to print other people's words, but sometimes somebody gets it so right that there's no point in competing. This letter came from Albertan Bruce Holt.

Far away from Paris, on a fall day in the Rockies, it does not appear that the world will end because madmen threw a bomb into a department store in Montparnasse, killing and injuring many. The world will end when no one goes outdoors to watch the larch trees turn orange and when there are no fish in the Bow River and Policeman's Creek turns to asphalt. The world will end when little children don't collect pine cones and no one turns up for the Anglican Church Women's annual turkey dinner — not even the cooks.

Finally, the world will end when the old collie is dozing in the sun on the porch of the white house down the street, where he was the day before at the same time . . . and it doesn't make someone smile.

But the world is a chillier and sadder place because madmen throw bombs in Paris. No one can kill the Paris I remember. But how much of this stuff can people stand?

It really doesn't leave much else to say, does it?

Advertising Condoms: Is It Safe?

SHHHH! You hear that r-r-ripping sound? Ten to one it's another perfectly good, impeccably tailored three-piece pin-stripe getting shredded right up the back. There's been an awful lot of rending of garments and gnashing of capped teeth going on in the big television network boardrooms this past little while — CBC included. The boob tube barons are locked in a soul-searing debate over whether or not it's okay to flog condoms on the air.

Personally, I find it tough to even address the question . . . because I'm pretty sure they are talking about the same condom displays that I trip over down at the drugstore when I'm lining up to buy my toothpaste or cough drops. Which aren't so very different from the ones the ancient Romans fashioned out of sheeps' intestines two or three thousand years ago . . . which closely resemble the ones the English have been calling French Letters and the French have been calling *capotes anglais* for a couple of centuries . . . which, to bring it all back home, are just like the ones involved in that tiresome but unavoidable Canadian male adolescent rite of passage in which said vessels are filled with tap water, slung off roofs or out windows, and then giggled over until you wet your pants.

No, I'm pretty sure the average television viewer is mentally equipped to cope and grapple with the concept, at least, of the condom. It's the television executives that can't get a handle on it, so to speak.

They're afraid that condom ads might violate their tenets of good taste. That the networks might be seen as promoting casual or illicit sex.

These are the same folks who brought us "Charlie's Angels," "Three's Company," "The Dating Game," "Love Boat," and all those steamy soft porn evening soaps like "Dynasty," "Dallas," "Falcon Crest." Did we mention commercials yet? Commercials for cars that show leonine women draped over hoods, or slinking across the upholstery . . . commercials for airlines — "Hi . . . I'm American . . . Fly me." And commercials for beer, which show more hopping breasts than brewing hops. What, these guys? Promoting casual sex? Heaven forfend.

As for the non-TV folks who are flat-out opposed to TV advertising of condoms because they think it will open the floodgates of licentiousness and libertinism, I think their fears are unfounded. Condoms may be effective in preventing the spread of disease; they will never expand anybody's sensual horizons.

Aside from rubber plantation stockholders, I don't know anybody who likes condoms. Whoops — I take that back. The Australian army likes them. They must. A couple of years ago they bought 541,000 of the things. Not for R and R-bound Aussie G.I.'s — for their rifles. Put 'em over the muzzles. To keep 'em waterproof.

Now *there's* a concept — effective prophylactics for rifles. And pistols. And rockets and torpedos and missiles.

Talk about prevention of disease.